The Soviets, Germany, and the New Europe

The Soviets, Germany, and the New Europe

Robbin F. Laird

Routledge
Taylor & Francis Group
LONDON AND NEW YORK

First published 1991 by Westview Press, Inc.

Published 2019 by Routledge
52 Vanderbilt Avenue, New York, NY 10017
2 Park Square, Milton Park, Abingdon, Oxon OX14 4RN

Routledge is an imprint of the Taylor & Francis Group, an informa business

Library of Congress Cataloging-in-Publication Data
Laird, Robbin F. (Robbin Frederick), 1946–
The Soviets, Germany, and the New Europe / Robbin F. Laird.
p. cm.
ISBN 0-8133-8048-0
1. Soviet Union—Foreign relations—Germany. 2. Germany—Foreign relations—Soviet Union. 3. Soviet Union—Foreign relations—1985– 4. Soviet Union—Foreign relations—Europe. 5. Europe—Foreign relations—Soviet Union. I. Title.
DK67.5.G3L25 1991
327.47043—dc20 91-24783
CIP

ISBN 13: 978-0-367-29620-9 (hbk)

ISBN 13: 978-0-367-31166-7 (pbk)

To my brother and sister
Harriet and Bruce Laird,
who have had a much better
relationship than the
Soviets and the Germans

Contents

Acknowledgments

This book has taken several years to complete, and my intellectual debts are considerable. I would like to thank Susan Clark for her contribution throughout and especially for providing the material for the monthly summaries. Armin Leon of the University of Bonn has provided me with travel and conceptual support in Germany for a number of years and was especially helpful in assessing Soviet public diplomacy in West Germany. Daniel Peris of the University of Illinois worked with me as a research assistant for a number of years and was a major force in shaping the chapter on the Soviet assessments of the West European security cooperation process. Theo Gemelas provided help throughout, especially with the index.

The United States Institute of Peace provided a grant that allowed the book to be written. The American Institute for Contemporary German Studies provided a congenial environment where the manuscript was brought to completion. Thanks go to my friends on the staff, Gerry Livingston, Jack Janes, and Lynn van Norstrand.

Finally, I would like to thank my intellectual *kollektiv* over the years—Ken Maxwell, Erik Hoffmann, Chris Jones, Fred Fleron, Blair Ruble, Heinrich Vogel, Marie Mendras, Murielle Delaporte, Marc Perrin de Brichambaut, Phil Williams, Ron Asmus, Bob Nurick, Dale Herspring, and Harry Klein.

Special thanks should go to my colleagues who have analyzed Soviet-German issues over the years, notably Hannes Adomeit, Michael Sodaro, and Angela Stent. My work should be seen as contemporary supplement to their historical assessments of the Soviet-German dynamic.

Robbin F. Laird

Overview

This book assesses the evolution of the Soviet approach toward European security policy since the mid-1980s, as seen from the prism of assessments of and policy toward the Federal Republic of Germany. The first part of the book addresses the general context within which the Soviets have framed their policy toward the Federal Republic of Germany, while the remaining parts focus specifically upon Soviet assessments of the Federal Republic from 1985-1990. The book concludes with a prospective on the Soviet approach toward the new Federal Republic of Germany as a component of the domestic debate about how to deal with the new Europe.

The Soviets and European Security Policy: The General Context

The first part of the book analyzes the general context within which the Soviets have addressed the question of how to deal with the Federal Republic of Germany. Each chapter in this part deals with an aspect of the general Soviet approach. The first chapter addresses the evolution of Soviet foreign policy and the role of the West in that evolution. The second chapter identifies the classic Soviet anti-coalition strategy toward the West. And the third chapter outlines in detail how Soviet analysts approached the problem of Europeanization or European construction in the Gorbachev period. Increasingly, the problem of Europeanization came to overshadow the classic Soviet foreign policy paradigm and anti-coalition approach. The German problem would emerge as an important manifestation of the Europeanization challenge.

The Soviets and the West in Historical Perspective

Chapter one addresses the question of the general approach the Soviets have taken toward the West since the founding of the USSR. Eight phases in the development of Soviet foreign policy are reviewed and a cluster of ten key elements making up the Soviet foreign policy paradigm is defined.

In the classic approach of Soviet policy, Soviet leaders tried to balance carefully competitiveness and cooperation with the West. The West provided a model of progress in the economic sphere, but not in the cultural, political and military spheres. The Soviets strove to keep the West at bay as they developed their own unique model of historical progress.

The Soviet foreign policy paradigm and the classic Soviet approach toward the West are under challenge today. Gradually, the belief in a unique Soviet socialist model gave way to a search for a new model. The West remains an important challenge to the Soviets as they seek to find a new developmental model, but how to relate Soviet foreign to domestic policy in the new global setting is not at all clear. Even though interaction with the outside world has been vastly expanded in the Gorbachev period, the power instruments available to the Soviet elites to develop their own country remain unidimensional. Military power remains important. But how will the Soviet elites develop the economic power to participate in their own reconstruction within a global economic setting? How will the Soviets develop a culture compatible with twenty-first century modernization?

The Soviets are an increasingly significant negative factor overhanging European development. The Soviet Union no longer threatens the West by means of a cohesive national elite with awesome military might at its disposal and with the intention of crushing Western growth and development. Instead, it represents a challenge primarily in terms of whether it can overcome its past and join the modernization process. If the Soviets fail to find a peaceful transition to the future, the weight of the past will challenge the West once again. The dreams of building a new Europe and a new world order will be dashed by the inability of the Russians to leave their autocratic and autarchic past.

The classic Soviet approach toward the West rested upon a process of controlled interaction. Military power was the means whereby the Soviet Union protected itself from Western contamination and untoward influence. In dealing with the Western Alliance, the Soviet leadership developed an anti-coalition strategy to contain the West and its negative influences.

The Anti-Coalition Strategy Toward the Western Alliance

Chapter two outlines the main characteristics of the anti-coalition strategy. Soviet analysts were well aware of the voluntary quality of membership in the Western alliance as well as the increased national assertiveness among alliance members. They also recognized the collective strength of the alliance when cohesion prevails. Hence, the maximization of Soviet power required the reduction of alliance cohesion and the pursuit of an anti-coalition strategy to drive wedges and expand fissures within the alliance.

Policy toward West Germany has been a critical component of the anti-coalition approach. The basic Soviet effort to influence the evolution of West German policy wavered between military pressure and diplomatic persuasion, the former playing an increasingly important role beginning in the second half of the 1970s. The three Soviet leaderships prior to Gorbachev apparently thought that forcing the pace of military competition in Europe and improving the Soviet preponderance in conventional and intermediate-range nuclear forces would make it possible to translate military power into political influence. The role of "nuclear hostage" was to be impressed on the West German mind as a way of lessening the West German attachment to the United States.

The classic anti-coalition strategy was designed simultaneously to provide protection for the Soviet Union against undue Western influence and to expand Soviet influence over Western policies toward the USSR. This strategy was designed to promote transatlantic and intra-West European fissures. For the classic Soviet approach, Atlanticism and Europeanism were alternative outcomes. If Europeanism was promoted, the trans-Atlantic bond would weaken and Soviet influence would expand.

Nonetheless, as Western defense and security policies developed during the 1980s, the Soviet Union was facing the possibilities that Atlanticism and Europeanism might become merged into a new phase of alliance development. The European component of the alliance might be augmented, but not at the expense of the transatlantic or Western system. Indeed, Europeanization might be a form of revitalizing the Western alliance.

The Soviets and West European Security Cooperation

The third chapter examines Soviet treatments in the Gorbachev period of the Europeanization challenge. Soviet analysts increasingly underscored the significance of the European construction effort for the future of Western defense and foreign policies. By remaining outside of these processes, the Soviets were only stimulating the emergence of worst case scenarios for themselves--the emergence of a United States of Europe that was closely connected with the original United States.

In other words, the classic Soviet foreign policy paradigm and the anti-coalition strategy were generating a negative result for the Soviet Union. The Soviet Union was isolating itself from the mainstream of global historical development rather than merely protecting itself from Western contamination of the socialist model.

For some Soviet analysts, the Soviet Union was considered to have failed to notice the rising power and strategic implications of an increasingly strong and united Western Europe. The French, the British and the West Germans were perceived, each in their own way, to be promoting the notion of a greater European role within the alliance. The integration process was perceived to be proceeding with broad European public support and Soviet leaders realized that they could not expect it to cease with the election of an opposition party in any European capital. It was further argued that continued blindness on the part of Soviet leaders in dealing with West European integration would simply play into the hands of continuing American leadership within Western Europe.

The growing concern of at least some Soviet analysts with the secular trend toward greater European integration in economic, political and security matters predated the Revolution of 1989 and the year of unification. Prior to the groundswell of revolution in Eastern Europe, Soviet analysts posed a simple alternative to deal with the European integration challenge--eliminate the blocs and create a common European space. One variant proposed was to remove all American and Soviet troops from other countries in the two blocs and to create a "Findlandization" of Eastern Europe and a "Swedenization" of Western Europe.

The key assumption of the Gorbachev leadership up to the Revolution of 1989 was that the two military blocs would exist indefinitely. The task would be to promote Europeanization which would overcome the blocs and lead to a process of mutual disarmament.

But the German unification process reversed the order of overcoming the blocs -- it came through Westernization, not Soviet style Europeanization. It was through coping with the German question that the new European security situation emerged, not vice versa.

Soviet Assessments of West Germany, 1985-1989

This part of the book examines basic Soviet analyses of West Germany in the period prior to unification. Also, the basic public diplomacy strategy followed by the Gorbachev administration is identified and assessed.

This part of the book consists of three chapters. Chapter four presents Soviet assessments of West Germany in the early Gorbachev period (1985-1987). Chapter five examines Soviet perspectives on West Germany from 1987 to 1989. Chapter six then identifies the main elements of the Gorbachev Administration's public diplomacy toward the Federal Republic from 1985-1989.

Soviet Assessments of West Germany, 1985-1987

The main emphasis during this period was an expressed concern over German "revanchism." Soviet analysts defined this implicitly as pursuing assertive national behavior by the West Germans which threatened the hitherto accepted division of Europe into capitalist and socialist components.

The INF issue was seen to be reflective of the German "revanchist" position. Notably, Soviet analysts focused upon the growth in German aspirations to control nuclear weapons evidenced by FRG behavior in the INF crisis. This would occur, Soviet analysts asserted, either through production of their own weapons or through some kind of joint agreement, most likely with France or the United States. The French were treated as especially serious stimulants to West German nuclear aspirations.

Soviet Perspectives on West Germany, 1987-1989

Chapter five examines changing Soviet perspectives toward West Germany in the period up to the Revolution of 1989. During the 1987-1989 period, the tone and approach toward the West Germans began to change. Whereas the West Germans were characterized by most Soviet analysts as forces for revanchism and obstructionism in the earlier period, in the new phase the West Germans were treated as possible partners in building a new Europe. Notably, the task of building a "common European home" was linked explicitly with the effort to change the Soviet-West German relationship. But this change was still conceived within the framework of a divided Europe with the Soviet-West German relationship being critical to building a new Europe overarching the old.

Soviet assessments in the 1987-1989 period focused upon West Germany as a country in transition from traditional thinking (whether conservative cold war or left-wing detente thinking) to a more dynamic reassessment of what was possible in European and East-West affairs. Increasingly, the West Germans were portrayed as eager to see a new order in Europe in which they would play a leading role in carrying out Western reconciliation with the "legitimate aspirations" of the Soviet Union.

The central role of West Germany within the European construction process was especially significant to Russian analysts. That is, some analysts perceived that there was a reciprocal process under way whereby the enhanced significance of the European construction process to the USSR for its own development in turn elevated the importance of West Germany to Soviet foreign policy as the key nation shaping the European construction process.

Associated with the expanded "objective" role of the FRG within the Western and East-West systems was change in the "subjective" perceptions of the West Germans of their role. West Germans were becoming increasingly resistive against the limitations placed by other Western countries on Germany.

In other words, Soviet analysts in the 1987-1989 period were coming to the conclusion that West Germans were seeking to expand their role within the Western world. As the West Germans tried to do this, they would be seeking to expand their leadership role as well within the East-West system. Therefore, Soviets needed to sort out how to redefine the Soviet-West German relationship as the Germans sought to reshape their role in the East-West system.

But for Moscow to be able to play a German card, they would have to change their approach to Bonn and to forge a new Soviet-German relationship. Such an effort would have required real change in how the Soviets had historically treated Bonn and the recognition of the threat which Moscow posed to Bonn by following classic Soviet anti-coalitional politics. In other words, the Soviets would have to develop a policy toward Bonn as part of a reconstruction of Soviet European policy and not simply try to use Bonn as a tool to implement Soviet influence within the Western community.

The nuclear issue, notably the follow-on-to-Lance (FOTL) debate, became central to Soviet analyses during the development of West German foreign and security policy in this transitional period. The Soviets increasingly believed that the Germans would resist Lance modernization and would thereby lay down the groundwork for the reworking of NATO's approach to nuclear issues.

Just as INF was a dominant theme in earlier Soviet treatments of West Germany, so now it was the Lance modernization issue and the question of eliminating tactical nuclear weapons in Europe that took center stage in Soviet analyses. Soviet analysts focused on the direct confrontation between the United States and West Germany over the follow-on to Lance issue. After the INF issue had bonded the American and German governments on the nuclear deterrence issue, the FOTL issue promised to place serious strain on their bilateral relationship. Clearly, Soviet analysts saw this as an opportunity to reinforce the Soviet-German dynamic at the expense of the American one in a zero-sum relationship. For the Soviets at this time, the common European home held the promise of becoming a nuclear free one, at least with regard to the American guests in that home.

Soviet analysts also highlighted a number of key elements in West German military strategy in the 1987-1989 period. First, the West Germans remained committed to the concept of forward defense regardless of the allied military framework which might evolve. Second, the desire by West Germany to shift away from excessive reliance on nuclear weapons called for the enhancement of the role of conventional forces in Western strategy. In such an shift, Bonn would have played a critical role. Third, West Germany would have to expand its technological capabilities in the conventional area, for example in air defense. Finally, the West German military was seen as shifting its strategy in a more offensive direction. As the West German military worked toward improving its capability to fight maneuver warfare, the line between defense and offense had become blurred and the challenge to the Soviet military was increased.

For Soviet analysts in this period, Bonn was pursuing a contradictory policy of Atlanticism and Europeanization. Soviet analysts implied that only a turn away from classic Atlanticism and a partnership arrangement with the Soviet Union could provide for genuine Europeanization. The negative side of this was most often noted by Soviet military analysts.

The more positive side of Europeanization was the focus of attention by diplomats, politicians and political analysts. Usually framed as the quest for the common European home, the goal was to promote "genuine" European cooperation, not West European integration which revolved around military and security issues.

Soviet policy in this regard was best symbolized by Gorbachev's speech to the Council of Europe in Strasbourg in July 1989. This speech called for overcoming the division of Europe by a new detente process. It did not suggest the end of socialism in the East and certainly did not support the Westernization of Eastern Europe and the Soviet Union. The Soviets were soon confronted with this challenge in the context of the Revolution of 1989.

There were six major elements of the "Strasbourg synthesis" expressed by Gorbachev in his speech. First, there was the assertion that capitalist and socialist Europe would continue to exist and that it would be illegitimate for the West to put the socialist system into question.

The second element was an emphasis upon a process of gradually overcoming the differences between the two social systems, perhaps by creating a new synthesis or a new European civilization. Not in the cards was an expectation that Westernization would spread East and rapidly engulf "socialism."

Third, the European states had the right to determine for themselves the nature of their social systems. Asserting this right was correlated with Gorbachev's belief that "socialism" in the East had taken root and would continue to exist after the Brezhnev doctrine was allowed to lapse.

Fourth, the military factor will become less and less determining in relations among the European states. The military factor's reduced significance was especially significant in determining the Soviet Union's place within the European system. Fifth, along with the decreased salience of the military factor there would be an increased importance of economic, cultural and political interdependence among the European states.

Finally, the common European home was defined as the residuum of all of the above -- an interdependent, less militaristic, freer and dynamic world whereby East-West differences would gradually be overcome.

But, notwithstanding Soviet aspirations, history was to take a sharp turn. Instead of gradualism, there would be a series of explosions. Instead of an evolutionary path, there would be a revolutionary one. Instead of the gradual forging of a new East-West synthesis, Westernization would explode Eastward. The Soviets would need to confront a serious crisis of analysis, policy and redefinition of themselves.

Soviet Public Diplomacy Toward West Germany, 1985-1989

Gorbachev's approach toward the Federal Republic was designed to deal with the most troubling trends in West German security policy. "Revanchism" was to be deflected by encouraging the West Germans to return to their detente policy of the 1970s, a policy which accepted the territorial and political status quo in Europe. To deflect "revanchism," Gorbachev emphasized a new detente with the Alliance in which the Soviets accepted the "realities" of the foundations of Western security policy in exchange for a recognition of the "realities" of Eastern security policy.

To reduce "militarism" in West German policy, the Soviet leadership emphasized the possibilities of serious reductions in the Soviet military threat. In fact, the Soviet goal was to minimize the ability of the West German conservatives to use the "excuse" of the Soviet military threat to justify West German military expenditures. Furthermore, the Soviets emphasized the possibilities of shifting East-West military policy to a "defensive" basis, a policy which would allow the Social Democratic Party (SPD) to move back toward the center of the political spectrum on security issues.

To reduce Atlanticism and Europeanism, the Soviets emphasized the primacy of the common European home but without European military integration. The emphasis on the common European home suggested a distancing from the Americans, although the new "realism" in Soviet policy led to a recognition of the durability of NATO and the legitimacy of some form of American military presence in Europe. The goal was simply to reduce the cohesion of the Alliance and the nature of the American military presence. But the Soviets did not want to see a reduction in the American role lead to an enhancement of the European role in the Alliance, a process which could occur only with vigorous West German involvement. While the Soviets emphasized the legitimacy of developing West European economic and even political integration (some even said they could accept a West European role in Eastern Europe), they clearly denied the legitimacy of West European military integration. The common European home would be possible only if there were no military integration of Western Europe, according to the Soviets.

Unquestionably the state visit of Soviet President Mikhail Gorbachev was the most important event in Soviet-German relations during the 1988-1989 period. What mattered most was not the treaties and agreements that were signed during the visit; rather it was the way Gorbachev presented himself to the West Germans and their response to that image.

The Gorbachev visit to Bonn was an important milestone in the Soviet approach to West Germany. Above all, the visit symbolized the desire of the Soviet leadership to end the cold war and to strengthen ties with Western Europe.

The visit represented the culmination of a number of public diplomacy efforts from 1985 through the middle of 1989. Above all, the Soviet leaders promoted the idea that there was a "new" look in Soviet policy. Soviet officials were more realistic and willing to accept the "realities" of modern society as they understood it. The Soviets claimed to accept the legitimacy of a number of Western institutions which used to be anathema to them, such as NATO and the EEC.

While the Soviets might not like any of these institutions, they do exist, and they finally recognized that these institutions had to be dealt with. For example, with respect to NATO, high-ranking Soviet officials, including Gorbachev himself, frequently stated in this period that they were not trying to drive wedges in the Alliance and that they accepted the legitimacy of some form of American presence in Europe.

Furthermore, the Soviets emphasized to West Germans that the nature of Soviet society was changing. The image became one of a society which had been stultified by the old but which had been unleashed by new thinking. Over the past thirty years the West German elite had perceived the vitality of Soviet society to be in steady decline. The Soviets were explicitly trying to reverse this trend by using the "new thinking" and glasnost campaigns to highlight innovation in Soviet society.

Above all, Soviet spokesmen underscored that there was a growing and more realistic possibility of East-West reconciliation if Soviet initiatives were met with correspondingly serious proposals by the West. Simply put, the message was as follows: "We are now reasonable; work with us and we can put the old confrontations behind us and live in a more peaceful and interdependent world."

In short, Soviet public diplomacy was significantly aided by the new dynamism of Soviet domestic and foreign policy, as well as by the new realism in Soviet assessments of developments in the West. The Soviet Union also promoted its image as a society in crisis, which therefore could no longer pose a serious threat to West Germany.

The Soviets and the Unification Process, 1989-1990

The book concludes with an identification of the Soviet assessment of the German unification process and proper Soviet policy toward it. Chapter seven addresses how Soviet analysts debated the issue in the year of unification. The parameters of the debate are identified at the outset and then detailed treatments for each month are provided through December 1990. The debate was so fluid and dynamic that a monthly coverage is necessary to follow the terms of the debate.

In the final chapter--chapter eight--the general cleavages of opinion within the Soviet elite over the German unification issue are identified. The chapter concludes with an assessment of the emerging Soviet debate about the new Federal Republic and how to deal with the new Europe.

The Fall of the GDR

Earlier Soviet public diplomacy under Gorbachev concentrated on how West Germany would react to change in the Soviet Union, but in late 1989 and 1990 the diplomatic focus shifted instead to how the Soviet leadership would deal with change in Germany--especially the future of East Germany. When Gorbachev attended the celebration in East Berlin in October 1989, it was clear that while he advocated certain reforms for the GDR, he still envisaged a socialist East German state. But to East German citizens Gorbachev symbolized a broad hope for reforms; they greeted him with chants of "Gorby, Gorby" when he joined Erich Honecker to attend the public ceremonies. After Egon Krenz had replaced Honecker, Gorbachev reportedly told him that he had felt uncomfortable at Honecker's side during the ceremonies once he perceived how the public mood had shifted. Gorbachev is said to have told Krenz that in recent years Honecker had failed to realize what was really going on in the GDR. Gorbachev also reportedly expressed regret that Honecker had not enacted necessary reforms two or three years earlier, and that he had seemed unwilling to listen to Gorbachev's arguments for reform.

Despite these calls for reform, however, it is clear that initially the Soviet leadership never questioned the continued existence of two German states. Soviet officials even warned that discussion of reunification of the two German states could have disastrous consequences for European stability. After meeting with other European leaders Gorbachev reportedly concluded that the post-war balance of power in Europe had to be maintained; a position he believed was shared by American elites.

This early rejection of any discussion of reunification became clear when the Soviet Union rejected the 10-point plan presented to the Bundestag by Helmut Kohl on November 28, 1989. This step-by-step plan called first for a German confederacy and eventually reunification. While Kohl did not mention a time frame, he later said that 10 or more years would be likely. However, the Soviets rejected the Kohl initiative, with Foreign Minister Eduard Shevardnadze terming it a "direct diktat" from Bonn. During a meeting with his counterpart, Hans Dietrich Genscher in December, Shevardnadze said the confederacy idea would lead to "confusion." Gorbachev also reportedly warned Genscher against aggressively taking advantage of the difficulties caused by perestroika. Instead, he advised West Germany to support reform within the Warsaw Pact countries. He also expressed concern that if change in the GDR got out of hand it could threaten the security of the Soviet forces stationed in the GDR.

During a December 19 speech to the Political Committee of the European Parliament in Brussels, Shevardnadze absolutely rejected calls for a speedy German reunification. He made clear that peaceful cooperation between the GDR and FRG should be based on the acceptance of equality and sovereignty of the two German states. Future developments would have to be left to the course of history, within the framework of an all-European process.

For Shevardnadze, there was no guarantee that German unity would not threaten other nations and the stability of Europe as a whole. He was especially concerned about possible territorial claims that might be pursued by a united Germany. He also stressed that Soviet citizens had the right to know how changes in central Europe could affect their future security. Shevardnadze made a point of reminding his audience that the Soviet Union had paid with 20 million lives for Europe's current stability. He conceded that once Europe had passed beyond its period of confrontation, then there would be opportunities to overcome the division of the continent, based on the values of all Europeans.

Shevardnadze took a similar line in an article published in the January 19, 1990 issue of *Izvestiya.* He wrote that the German question was an integral part of the overall question of European unity. While the relationship between the GDR and FRG could be an important factor in the process of European integration and consolidation, if that relationship moved too far or contradicted the existing international order then disastrous consequences could result. There could be no doubt that an artificial acceleration of the "inter-German" process would lead to its separation from the realities in Europe, with disastrous consequences for all. More specifically, Shevardnadze rejected calls from West Germans that a united Germany could remain in NATO.

In an interview with the West German Communist Party newspaper *Unsere Zeit* on February 2, 1990, the Soviet Ambassador to the FRG, Yury Kvitsinsky made clear that both German states were part of the existing European structure of states, and that the all-European process could only develop undisturbed on that basis. Kvitsinsky described the GDR as an ally that the Soviet Union should not abandon. He expressed Soviet concern over West German influence on the issue of free elections in the GDR. Kvitsinsky acknowledged the right of self-determination for all peoples in Europe, but added that no principle of international law could be viewed in isolation.

Accepting the Inevitable

During the first months of 1990, it became increasingly obvious that East German citizens desired unification with West Germany. While nationalism certainly was a major factor, the principal motivation was unquestionably the GDR's economic crisis, which worsened daily. More and more West Germans also began to view reunification as inevitable, and that it would not have to wait a decade or more. This growing perception contrasted sharply with the decade-plus timetable implied in the Kohl plan.

In addition to this rapid change in West German perceptions of what was possible, in early 1990 the Soviet leadership also seemed to have accepted that the German question was on the agenda. Recognizing the pressure for unification because of the GDR's economic chaos, on February 1 East German Prime Minister Hans Modrow presented a plan for self-determination and confederation that he first discussed with Gorbachev during a visit to Moscow on January 30. Modrow's plan endorsed "free self-determination of the Germans in both states" and a gradual move from confederacy to unification, as joint institutions assumed more and more responsibility. For this confederacy to be transformed ultimately into a federal state, Modrow laid out a key pre-condition: in a step-by-step process, each of the two states would loosen ties to their respective military alliances and move to a neutral status. At his January 30 meeting with Modrow, Gorbachev told journalists in Moscow that in principle no one should question the right of the Germans to unify, as long as all involved acted responsibly. Then, during Kohl's visit to Moscow in February, Gorbachev accepted that the Germans themselves could decide the timing and manner of their unification. Three days later, the USSR, the US, the UK, France, and the two German states agreed to begin the so-called "Two Plus Four" negotiations.

On March 18, 1990, the German Democratic Republic held its first free election, with results surprising almost all observers. The three parties comprising the Allianz fur Deutschland (Alliance for Germany) unexpectedly won a plurality with 48.15 percent of the vote. The coalition's dominant party, the GDR-CDU, alone won 40.91 percent. Prior to the election, it was widely expected that the Alliance would finish second to the SPD, although by the end of the campaign it seemed that the gap had perhaps closed. Still, no one expected--least of all the Soviets--that the SPD would only end up with 21.84 percent. Probably the biggest surprise was that the Party of Democratic Socialism (the revamped communist party) managed only 16.33 percent.

As a result of the election, the CDU's Lothar de Maiziere took office as the GDR's first freely elected prime minister. Ironically, since his party was committed to unification as rapidly as possible it was clear that de Maiziere also intended to be the GDR's last freely elected prime minister. The CDU's success in East Germany undoubtedly eased coordination between the two German states in the subsequent unification process, especially in the Two Plus Four talks.

The election also made clear that at least since mid-1989, the Soviet leadership had backed the wrong horses: first Erich Honecker, then Egon Krenz, new PDS chairman Gregor Gysi, and Hans Modrow. In the last few weeks before the election, as Moscow realized that the PDS would surely lose, the Soviets even made clear their official support for the Social Democratic candidate Ibrahim Bohme, but to no avail. Despite all these problems in figuring out who could be the right man for the future of the GDR and Germany as a whole, the Kremlin actually proved relatively willing to finally accept the new reality. After Gorbachev reached the conclusion that unification would be inevitable, he focused on the question of alliance ties and economic relations, especially Soviet-GDR trade.

Before moving to those two issues, it should be noted that once Moscow had accepted the inevitability of unification, the Soviets still believed initially that this did not mean that the GDR would simply join the Federal Republic under Article 23 of the West German Grundgesetz. Instead the Soviets apparently expected a new state to be established. Moscow also criticized the speed with which Bonn and East Berlin agreed on economic and monetary union.

From Neutrality to NATO Membership

Moscow's acceptance of one German state still left unsettled the security aspects of unification, particularly concerning borders, alliances, and Four Power rights. The Soviets made clear that the future of peace and security in Europe depended on the resolution of these issues.

After some initial hesitation by the Kohl government, the border question was solved fairly easily by parliamentary decisions endorsing the existing borders and pledging to negotiate a separate treaty with Poland following unification. The political-military status of the unified Germany proved more contentious, especially concerning alliance membership. Initially the Soviets strongly criticized -- and resolutely rejected -- the prospect of a unified Germany as a NATO member. In his February 2 interview with the West German communist newspaper *Unsere Zeit*, Ambassador Kvitsinksy said it would be an illusion to believe the Federal Republic could avoid changing its membership in NATO. Without change, the balance of power and security structure in Europe would be destroyed. On the same day, the Soviet Foreign Ministry's deputy spokesman said during a visit to East Berlin that it would be unrealistic and unacceptable to think that a united Germany could be a member of either NATO or the Warsaw Pact. Instead the solution would be somewhere in between. He recommended that the two German states leave their alliances, adding that the Soviet Union supported either disintegration of both alliances or their transformation into a more political context.

Valentin Falin, a Gorbachev advisor and a leading German expert, gave an important interview on this subject in the February 19 issue of *Der Spiegel.* Falin completely rejected the view that Soviet security interests might actually be served by Germany remaining within NATO, bluntly terming such an argument as "absurd." He repeated the Soviet argument about preserving the balance of power in Europe. However, he also said that in the past the concept of "neutrality" had been defined too narrowly. The Soviets viewed neutrality as meaning that no new military threat could emanate from German soil, but that Germany could still maintain a military capability to provide a reasonable defense. He added that Germany should not be discriminated against, since that could lead to an explosive situation. Falin also disagreed with a suggestion attributed to Nikolai Portugalov that the Soviets might accept a "French status" for Germany--politically an alliance member but militarily independent. In general, Falin warned that if NATO would not give up its demand for German membership then there would be no unification. He also said that the Soviet Union would still have "latent rights" concerning East Germany, and that even after the March elections, the GDR would have to fulfill all its commitments to the Warsaw Pact.

Ultimately these issues all fell under the auspices of the Two Plus Four negotiations, which were viewed by all sides as an integral link to the broader Conference on Security and Cooperation in Europe (CSCE) process. As these talks began, the Soviets initially maintained their position that the united Germany should be neutral. Then Shevardnadze, Falin, and other Soviet representatives proposed that Germany could simultaneously remain in both alliances, which Shevardnadze described as a compromise between the Western demand for NATO membership and the Soviet demand for neutrality. After such a transitional phase, Germany would simply become part of an all-European security system that would emerge from the two alliances.

At the May 1990 Two Plus Four conference in Bonn, Moscow revised its earlier stance that unification could not proceed without resolution of all foreign as well as domestic issues. Instead, Shevardnadze said, it would be possible to resolve the domestic and foreign elements separately. In other words, the Soviets recommended that the Germans proceed establishing domestic unification, while certain external questions might have to wait for the future. To the Germans, this clearly meant future restrictions on sovereignty, which was unacceptable to

Bonn, especially the Foreign Ministry. Chancellor Kohl had already made clear that there would be no all-German election without prior agreement on the foreign aspects of unification as well. Still, the Germans were optimistic that the six foreign ministers could complete their work by the CSCE summit scheduled for November 1990. In various statements, the Soviets indicated that they did not intend to delay the unification process, and that the Soviet Union could not afford to continue simply following events after the fact.

The solution to the united Germany's military status came with the July 6 declaration from the NATO summit in London. In late April, Gorbachev had opened a window of opportunity by informing GDR Prime Minister de Maiziere that NATO membership would only be possible if NATO made significant changes in structure and strategy, especially concerning forward defense and flexible response. Thus NATO responded in July by announcing doctrinal shifts intended to emphasize the Alliance's defensive orientation, including a description of nuclear weapons as only a "last resort." NATO also called for a non-aggression pact with the Warsaw Pact and invited the Warsaw Pact nations to send official observers to Brussels. In a surprise development coinciding with the summit, Kohl announced that West Germany would unilaterally agree to a ceiling on its military manpower as an attachment to the CFE-I treaty, providing similar limits were quickly negotiated for other countries under CFE-II. In addition to the London summit, the G-7 summit in Houston later that month also expressed Western willingness to support the Soviet reform process.

The climax of these developments was Helmut Kohl's meetings with Gorbachev July 15-16. At Zheleznovodsk, Gorbachev ended up conceding on virtually all remaining points, giving Kohl a coup that seemed to ensure his victory in the first all-German elections in December. In explaining the Soviet willingness to accept Western demands, Gorbachev emphasized the positive outcome of NATO's London summit. Some observers suggested a more complex logic: that the Soviets were hoping that an improved relationship with Germany might give them a kind of advocate to represent their interests within NATO. The Kohl-Gorbachev agreement included the following points:

1. Unification of Germany was defined as unification of the territory of the FRG, GDR, and Berlin.

2. On the day of unification, Four Power rights would end, with Germany regaining full sovereignty.

3. The united Germany would be free to make any decisions concerning alliance membership and participation. Kohl informed Gorbachev that Germany would be a member of NATO, which Gorbachev accepted.

4. Germany and the Soviet Union would negotiate a treaty for withdrawal of all Soviet troops from German territory by the end of 1994.

5. As long as Soviet forces are still deployed on German territory, no NATO forces will be extended to what was East German territory. However, German territorial units not allocated to NATO could be stationed on this territory immediately after unification.

6. Pending the complete Soviet troop withdrawal, the US, UK, and France may continue to deploy forces in West Berlin.

7. By 1994, the combined manpower of the German armed forces would be reduced to 370,000, as part of the CFE-I agreement.

8. The united Germany would not produce or possess weapons of mass destruction.

The Price of Unification

Despite all the attention devoted to the political-military status of the united Germany, many Germans had assumed from the start that the most important questions to be resolved would actually be economic, particularly trade commitments and financial aid. The Soviets also stressed that they could not afford to lose their traditional trade privileges with the GDR.

During Gorbachev's February 1990 meetings with Kohl and Genscher in Moscow, the Soviets made clear that their acceptance of unification depended on two guarantees: German acceptance of Poland's western border and continued fulfillment of the GDR's current export obligations to the Soviet Union. Kohl and Genscher assured Gorbachev that the united Germany would indeed take over those trade obligations. Then in April and May, it became more obvious that the Soviets hoped to link acceptance of unification to further German provision of financial support for the bankrupt Soviet economy. Genscher described the Soviets as seeking a "gigantic investment for the future." More specifically, in May Soviet Prime Minister Nikolai Ryzhkov told West German Minister for Economic Affairs Helmut Haussman that the Federal Republic should pledge to repay all financial losses incurred by the Soviet Union from East Germany's movement from the socialist bloc to the capitalist bloc. The Soviets also wanted to ensure a continuous economic relationship rather than a one-time compensation payment, which they feared would isolate them further from the economic development of the European Community.

Gorbachev also raised this economic argument at the end of his July meeting with Kohl at Zheleznovodsk. He emphasized that the Soviet Union's role in ensuring global security required that its "powerful economy" be integrated smoothly with the world's economic relations. For the Soviet Union to make fundamental changes it would be desirable and necessary to make use of the international division of labor and "certain financial resources." But Gorbachev insisted this would not mean gifts or charity; he proposed negotiated agreements which would be mutually advantageous. More specifically Gorbachev urged a rescheduling of Soviet foreign debt.

Moscow also argued that the Soviet troop withdrawal would represent an economic burden. Providing housing for the withdrawn Soviet troops and their families posed a particularly serious challenge. It would also be difficult to ensure a job for every soldier returning from East Germany. Thus the Soviets sought German support for housing construction and job creation.

Over time it also became clear that the Soviets wanted financial compensation for the troops remaining in East Germany until 1994. Ostensibly the Soviets justified this demand on the grounds that the currency union between the two German states would pose a great hardship on the Soviet troops. As a result, in June 1990 the West German Finance Ministry announced that it would pay the Soviets DM 1.25 billion for the 380,000 Soviet troops in the GDR; this payment apparently only covered the second half of 1990. Both sides made a point of explaining this payment in the context of the currency union's impact, rather than a straight payment by Bonn for the cost of maintaining the Soviet deployment.

In August 1990 the Soviets presented a draft treaty containing the points negotiated during the Kohl-Gorbachev meeting. The draft contained 14 points, including a DM 2.5 billion payment in 1991 for the maintenance and initial withdrawal of the Soviet troops in East Germany. Ostensibly the Soviets would repay half that amount by selling off infrastructure in East Germany, but actually most of the land and housing used by the Soviets had been provided free of charge by the GDR. Bonn would also pay the cost of transporting the troops to the Soviet border. The Soviets also wanted Germany to fund 500,000 square meters of new housing in the Soviet Union for each year from 1991 to 1994. The draft treaty also scrapped a 3.6 billion ruble Soviet debt for goods imported from East Germany.

Finally, on September 13, Shevardnadze and Genscher signed a 20-year bilateral treaty containing among other items a German pledge to pay the Soviets DM 13 billion through 1994. West German Finance Minister Theo Waigel justified this payment as simply the cost for regaining German sovereignty; Genscher frequently used the phrase "the price of unification."

The Future

In general terms, since the early 1970s Soviet foreign policy toward Western Europe has gone through three phases of development. The first phase continued into the beginning of the Gorbachev administration; it inherited the classic approach refined by the Brezhnev administration. In this approach, the Soviets gambled on winning a bet: to expand their influence within Western Europe while undercutting Western Alliance institutions in exchange for the risk of greater West European influence over Eastern Europe. This bet rested on the ability to contain change in the East while promoting the disintegration of the Western bloc. But for this bet to be won, the Soviet Union would need to contain a dynamic course of development.

By the time the Gorbachev administration came to power, it was clear that the Soviets were losing this bet. Notably, the Soviet model was disintegrating due to domestic pressures which were reinforced by an inability to crack the Western coalition. The Brezhnevites had succeeded in combining two failures: Soviet economic and political decline with encirclement by the foreign enemies of the Soviet Union.

Gorbachev acted to try to reverse the negative course of history in the second phase of Soviet policy. He placed his own bet for historical development. No longer did the Soviet leadership try to work simply within the confines of the mediated relationship of Eastern and Western Europe. Europeanization and Westernization were moving too briskly for conservative management of a mediated intra-European relationship. It was necessary to announce a new synthesis of East and West within which "socialism" in the East would be informed by and influence the development of "capitalism" in the West.

The fall of the Berlin Wall made it clear that the Soviet leadership lost this bet as well, at least for the time being. Perhaps over the long haul Westernization and capitalism will fail in Eastern Europe and may never take root in the USSR and the pressures for a new synthesis will return. But the dramatic events of the fall of 1989 meant the end of the viability of the Strasbourg synthesis. Ergo, the need to develop a third phase in their approach, but this new phase would prove difficult.

Throughout 1990, not only did the Gorbachev administration have to deal with the German unification process and the explosion of political change in Eastern Europe, but it had to deal with the explosions of tensions within the USSR as well. Suddenly the Russian leadership was faced with the pressure of Westernization moving East (to the GDR and to Eastern Europe) as well as the pressure to create a new Russian and/or Soviet development model. This book closes with the signing of the Soviet-German treaty of December 1990, but this treaty and the process which led to its conclusion are clearly not the beginning of the end, but the end of the beginning.

1

The Soviets and the West in Historical Perspective: The Emergent European Security Challenge

With the dramatic changes in Europe and the Soviet Union at the end of the 1980s and in the early 1990s, both the nature of Soviet policy toward the West and the analytical questions necessary to understand that policy have changed. This chapter will examine the basic dynamics of change in Soviet foreign policy toward the West and will assess the implications of those dynamics for Soviet foreign policy.

Phases of Soviet Foreign Policy

Soviet foreign policy has gone through a number of significant phases of development, and each phase has left its imprint on the evolving debate about the nature of that policy.[1] First, there was the period of the Russian revolution and the civil war in which the basic ideological nature of Soviet foreign policy was established. The regime sought to protect the revolution from penetration by "counter-revolutionary" forces abroad and inundation by the "backward" Russian masses at home.[2]

The most notable feature to outside analysts in this period was the ideological cast of Soviet foreign policy. The goal of the Soviet Union was to build a revolutionary order and traditional European geopolitics was to take a back seat to the new class-character of Soviet foreign policy.[3]

The Soviets sought to accelerate the revolution at home by promoting revolution abroad. This phase of Soviet foreign policy left in its wake the issue of the role of ideology in the making of foreign policy. Was Soviet foreign policy different from other Euro-Asian states on ideological grounds? If so, how important was the ideological variable in the conduct of Soviet foreign policy?

The ascendancy of Stalin as General Secretary of the Communist Party of the Soviet Union in the 1920s led to a new phase of Soviet foreign policy which lasted until World War II. During this period, the party purges and the great terror closed off the Soviet Union from the outside world. The Russians became a "riddle wrapped in a mystery inside an enigma," as Winston Churchill so aptly characterized them. A "fortress USSR" was built to protect the communist revolution of 1917, the state building and forced-draft industrialization and collectivization of the late 1920s and 1930s, and the personal rule by the General Secretary of the CPSU. A new "tsar" and a new autocracy began to emerge triumphant in this period.

The Stalinist model of economic and political development altered Soviet foreign policy as well.[4] A new model of domestic development required the subordination of foreign policy to this model. Autarchy or the closing off of the USSR from outside influences became the order of the day. International revolution no longer was an operational goal, which required a revolutionary interaction with the outside world.[5] Instead "socialism in one country" required the protection of the dynamic new model from outside disturbances.

This period of Russian foreign policy underscored the tension between autarky and global influences. Did the Russians now possess a unique model of development? Could the Russians develop an autarchic model of development which would allow them to shape a new force in the global arena? (When I use the term "Russians" I am referring to the Russian leadership of the Soviet Union).

The third major period of Soviet foreign policy was that of the years of the "Great Patriotic War." The German invasion of the Soviet Union ended the debate about the preservation of "socialism in one country." Instead, the question became the preservation of the Russian nation. Stalin suddenly embraced pre-Communist symbols of Russian nationalism and he shifted dramatically from the foreign policy premises of the 1930s. Also, defense of the homeland required an alliance with the Western democracies. In short, Stalin shifted from autarchic modernization to a more classic authoritarian model, one which combined traditional nationalism and cooperation with major capitalist nation states.

This period introduced new questions, most of them associated with the failure of the wartime coalition to continue to cooperate in the post-war period. Had the Russians shifted from ideological goals to national ones? Could the Russians cooperate with capitalist countries in pursuing a classic Russian geopolitical strategy? As the Stalin leadership appeared to revive the national style of the tsars from the 16th to the 19th centuries did nationalism matter more than communism? Had the operational ideology of the Soviet leadership undergone a dramatic transformation?

The fourth major period in the evolution of Soviet foreign policy was the formation of the cold war bi-polar international system.[6] Stalin rapidly shifted from the interdependent authoritarianism embraced during the war to the autarchic totalitarianism of the pre-World War II period, especially after the purges of the mid-1930s. But now this system was to be imposed on the new "allies" of the Soviet Union, namely the people's democracies of Eastern Europe.

In retrospect, it is clear that the downfall of the classic Stalinist model began with the attempt to engulf Eastern Europe and to promote a "socialist model of development."[7] The Stalinist system rested upon isolating Russia from the outside world, but the building of even a system of socialist "interdependence" undercut the classic autarchic model.

The great tragedy for the Soviet Union was the reimposition of the system of the 1930s upon the Soviet Union during the late 1940s and early 1950s. Now the challenge was to preserve a socialist model built on Russian nationalism by imposing that model upon Eastern Europe. Foreign policy shifted from defending "socialism in one country" to building socialism in Eastern Europe and forging a new "socialist community" in the East as a basis of competition with the West.

In the early 1950s, the ideological confrontation assumed new dimensions. Now the Soviets had a bridgehead in the West and military forces within that bridgehead to challenge the West. The "old" values of the bourgeois West were now challenged by the "new" values of the Soviet socialist order.

But the ingestion of Eastern Europe from the beginning was based on a contradiction. How could an autarchic model of development incorporate national entities with traditions and ties to an outside world that rejected isolation? How could one destroy the influence of hundreds of years of "alien" influence in Eastern Europe simply by Soviet occupation and by establishing surrogate "communist" regimes?

This period introduced a new set of questions for analysis. Was the Soviet Union inherently expansionist? Would "socialism in one country" become the model for "international socialism"? Was war with the West inevitable? Did the Russians believe that military victory over the West was the way to advance socialism, even in the nuclear age?[8]

The fifth period was associated with Khrushchev and the reexamination of the Stalinist legacy. Khrushchev's secret speech in 1956 denouncing Stalin and Stalinism began a debate that continues today. To what extent is Stalinism the same as Communism? Is there a genuine socialist alternative for the Soviet Union devoid of Stalinism? Did Stalin represent the Russian national character, or were non-authoritarian alternatives possible in a continent with no democratic experience?[9]

But the times of Khrushchev were optimistic ones. The Soviet economy was growing; the Soviets were consolidating their control over Eastern Europe; and the Soviet leaders believed in their spiritual superiority over the West. In 1956, Soviet tanks repulsed the Hungarian revolution. In 1961, Khrushchev promised to "bury capitalism" by peaceful means, and the party program boasted that the USSR would surpass American economic growth before the end of the century.

The sixth period of Soviet foreign policy was initiated by the overthrow of Khrushchev and the installation of the collective leadership. The Brezhnev-Kosygin leadership of the mid-1960s promised to combine the "advantages of socialism with rapid scientific and technological advancement.[10] These less impulsive new leaders claimed to be more "rational" and more responsive to the "objective laws" of historic development.

The foreign policy of collective leadership was to be less ideological and more pragmatic. While continuing to view the West as a competitor, these Soviet leaders hoped to let the West participate in its own demise. Western cooperation with the USSR in economic and arms control accords was possible as long as the West's cultural influence was held at arms length.

But this hopeful beginning was dashed by the seventh period of Soviet foreign policy. This period was begun with the repression of the Czechoslovakian revolution in 1968 and ended with the ascendancy of Yurii Andropov as General Secretary in early 1982. In retrospect, the Czech reform movement in the mid-1960s was the last chance for Soviet socialism to become a force of global significance.[11] The Russians, along with their Warsaw Pact allies, crushed a peaceful revolution within the confines of the Czech communist party. Unlike the action against the Hungarians in 1956, the 1968 repression was against a ruling communist party.

The so-called Brezhnev doctrine was articulated by the collective leadership in the wake of the events in Czechoslovakia. This doctrine allowed Russian intervention within Eastern Europe to eliminate anti-socialist elements. Needless to say, the Russian leadership would identify these elements itself. Never had a regime more boldly stated a naked power principle than did Brezhnev and his cohorts. It was also a clear statement of an empire in decline. It could tolerate only those changes it sanctioned itself.

The dynamic thrust of domestic change associated with the Bolshevik revolution and with Stalinism was waning.[12] Economic problems became more noticeable, and political sources of legitimacy began to be challenged. Attachment to the party became less significant than personal aggrandizement. The moral crisis which would ultimately bring down the regime actually began in earnest during the 1970s.

Soviet foreign policy became ever more traditionalist in this period, and became increasingly geopolitical and global. In order to defend the Soviet empire in Eastern Europe and within the USSR, the Soviet leaders sought to promote socialism abroad. The Soviet leadership sought to preserve the legitimacy of their empire by showing its continued relevance to a dynamic global development. The way they were able to accomplish this was less by setting an example or by dynamic economic growth than by military aid and intervention.

As the Soviet leadership under Brezhnev aged, it followed an ever more myopic policy. Top politicians began to believe their own rhetoric about the collapse of capitalism and the salience of the Soviet Union to global development. They saw their economic and social problems as solvable by only modest changes within the existing order. They sought to enhance the "scientific management" of society and nurture "developed socialism," which was to evolve into a more advanced variant of the old system.

The foreign policy necessary for this leadership was that which would protect the Soviet Union from outside influence but promote pragmatic links with the West.[13] Given Soviet leaders' confidence in their ability to compete globally, the USSR's competition with the West was pursued in areas of perceived Soviet advantage. But there could be no linkage between Soviet compromises with the West in arms control "and other technical issues" and the continued "political competition" with the West in Europe and beyond.

The postwar economic success of the West underscored for the Soviets the need in Soviet eyes to create a more innovative economy.[14] Especially in the Brezhnev period, the Soviets no longer perceived their economy to be the most innovative; rather, they regarded those sectors in the U.S., West European, and Japanese economies capable of rapid technological innovation as the harbingers of the future. They therefore sought to study and copy these sectors in order to bring similar Soviet economic sectors into the advanced industrial age. Clearly, the Soviet economy was in need of innovation, change, and reform to bring the Soviet Union into the advanced industrial age.

The scientific, technological, and commercial success of certain key sectors of Western economies, with the concomitant lack of success in the Soviet system, led to ideological change. There was a fundamental change in the Soviet outlook since the days of Khrushchev. Marxism-Leninism evolved from a rather dogmatic ideology which saw class conflict as the motor force of historical change to a more pragmatic point of view which stressed instead the importance of science and technology as the basis for modern economic growth and social change. Soviet dogmatists assumed that the Soviet Union was an advanced society because the means of production had been socialized. Soviet pragmatists recognized, however, that in the application of modern knowledge to development, their country was not only not catching up, but was steadily falling behind the United States, Western Europe, and Japan.

The Soviet pragmatic outlook emphasized that the USSR needed to make effective use of science and technology. The pragmatists remained within the framework of Marxism-Leninism by maintaining that "socialist" societies are better able than "capitalist" ones to take advantage of the opportunities for human betterment offered by the revolution in science and technology. Although in due course all societies will progress from "capitalism" to "socialism," in the Soviet view at the time, the ultimate victory of socialism was not seen in terms of class conflict or military victory. Rather the superior ability of socialism to develop and apply advanced science and technology was required.

The implementation of this pragmatic perspective led to efforts to improve production and management as well as to expand foreign trade as a means both of importing advanced technology and of providing a competitive challenge to the Soviet products that must be sold to pay for imports. But in spite of a number of changes in the organization and operation of the Soviet economy over the many years, the Soviet Union has not been able to close the technology gap with the West. The inability to close this gap underscored the seriousness of the Western challenge to the Soviet economy.

The Soviets perceived a serious Western challenge in the economic and military spheres generated by Western superiority in the area of scientific and technological innovation. But developments in the West associated with scientific, technological, and economic competitiveness among the Western powers permitted the Soviet Union to develop and expand East-West ties as a means of enhancing their scientific, technological, and economic capabilities.

Critical issues for analysis which emerged in this period were how to understand the pragmatic aspects of Soviet foreign policy and their interconnections with broader Soviet foreign policy objectives. Did Soviet pragmatism mean an end to the classic Soviet definitions of East-West competition? Or did the policy of peaceful coexistence merely mean that the Soviets were continuing the international class struggle on another basis?

The impact of the West on the USSR in the 1970s and 1980s was to stimulate modernization without fostering liberalization. Historical patterns whereby the Tsarist autocracy sought to use an opening to the West to bolster key elements of the system it ruled were repeated. But in contrast to the past, the Soviet leadership under Brezhnev, or at least influential segments of that leadership, recognized the need to maintain an opening to the West in order to foster an on-going process of modernization.

The need for on-going ties of various kinds as part of the modernization of the Soviet system meant that a number of problems nurtured in part by Western contact (such as ideological subversion) were prices to be paid over the long term. The Soviet leadership recognized that the control of "negative effects" was a key policy problem which must be dealt with on an on-going basis. Thus, managing the ambiguity surrounding the West's influence on the Soviet system was a significant policy problem for the Soviet leadership as it sought to accelerate the modernization of the Soviet system in the 1970s and 1980s.

The Gorbachev Period

The eighth period of Soviet foreign policy began with the emergence of Andropov, continued during the rise of Gorbachev and ended with the Revolution of 1989. The disintegration of the Soviet empire in Eastern Europe and the unification of Germany constituted a genuine revolution in European affairs, the consequences of which have not yet been fully worked out.

The new Soviet leadership recognized that the system was in crisis.[15] The Soviet Union was suffering a moral, cultural and economic crisis. The main difference between Andropov and Gorbachev was that the latter promoted genuine political change in addition to dealing with the other crises confronting the USSR.

The new Soviet leaders became increasingly preoccupied with the process of change, or perestroika as it became known. The vigorous domestic debate and struggle over the future of the Soviet domestic model became closely tied to a new political style and approach in the USSR. Rather than emphasizing the most dangerous aspects of competition, the Soviet leaders began to embrace the possibilities of cooperation. But this cooperation was to occur between a reformed socialist Europe and USSR, on the one hand, and the United States on the other. A new synthesis of East and West would somehow aid the perestroika process.

Gorbachev's initial policy toward the West in general and Europe in particular represented a mutation in the basic Soviet approach.[16] But major innovations occurred primarily in coping with the Revolution of 1989 and its aftermath. What were the fundamental elements of Gorbachev's policies toward the West?

Unlike previous Soviet leaders, Gorbachev and his advisors explicitly recognized the existence of a Soviet threat to Western Europe. In the past, Soviet analysts referred to the significant role the "myth" of the Soviet threat played in justifying Western defense efforts. Under Gorbachev a more open discussion of the threatening aspects of Soviet conventional forces was generated. And while the Soviets limited this discussion, a fundamental understanding of the threat which a surprise attack scenario poses for the West underlay Gorbachev's unilateral arms reductions initiatives.

Gorbachev adopted the "common European home" theme to underscore the notion of a common European civilization cutting across the ideological divide of East and West. To Americans, the Soviets underscored that the common European home theme did not exclude Americans. But in private discussions with West Europeans, the Gorbachev leadership underscored the common interests between Europe and the Soviet Union at the expense of the United States.

Gorbachev's speech in 1989 in Strasbourg, France before the Council of Europe provided the most explicit and wide-ranging presentation of the common European home theme. The basic notion was that the Europe of the blocs should be replaced by a cooperative security environment with no military alliances within Europe. What was new was the explicit recognition of the dynamics and legitimacy of Western European economic and political cooperation. In the past, Soviet analysts as well as policy makers were skeptical of the value and validity of the European integration process. Increasingly, Soviet analysts and leaders recognized the reality of these processes and the need to come to terms with West European political, economic and security cooperation.

To deal with the Europeanization process, the Soviets argued that there was a good and bad form of Europeanization. The good form of Europeanization occurred in the economic domain. Thus, economic integration and economic cooperation across the ideological divide were supported. The bad form of Europeanization was West European military integration. Soviet analysts were especially concerned that European military integration would allow the United States to remain in Europe, but at a much lower cost. The military "confrontation" would continue, but with the dynamic of a European integrative process as its stimulant.

To deflect such Europeanization pressures, a softer touch was required. It was reasoned that the policy of threat reduction would undercut European military integration efforts. The notion was that Western European elites and publics would be much more interested in military integration if there were a perception of a serious Soviet threat. If the Soviets altered threat perceptions, the Western European military integration process would necessarily be deflected.

The Soviet campaign against nuclear weapons is as old as nuclear weapons themselves. Under Gorbachev, the Soviet leadership pursued this campaign with new vigor and energy.[17] This is quite clear by the fact that Gorbachev unveiled his multi-phased proposal for a nuclear-free world, quite early in his tenure, in January 1986. The Soviet leader has since also introduced significant conventional reductions as a means to achieve the elimination of nuclear weapons from Europe.

Soviet leaders and security analysts also introduced discussions of alternatives to the extant structures of defense. They drew on the assessments of the European left in developing such alternative defense concepts and even the Soviet General Staff was drawn into discussions about these concepts with Europeans as well as Americans. Admittedly, the General Staff's concepts focused more on restructuring for manoeuvre warfare than on restructuring to eliminate an ability to attack.

Also critical to dealing with the Europeanization process was the continued pursuit of a policy of differentiated bilateralism. For example, the Soviet approach toward France played on French concerns vis-a-vis other West Europeans, notably the reunification challenge posed by Germany. The Soviets emphasized privately to French officials the idea of reviving the "old" alliance between them to deal with a resurgent Germany.

The Revolution of 1989 challenged the Gorbachev mutation and, indeed, the Gorbachev revolution in the Soviet Union was an important precondition for that Revolution. Throughout his General Secretaryship of the Communist Party of the Soviet Union, Gorbachev has nurtured "new thinking" in Soviet foreign policy. Most fundamentally, the theme of the Gorbachev administration has been the goal of overcoming the East-West divide. Gorbachev's book on perestroika (which sold millions of copies in the Western world) was simplistic and awkwardly written. Nonetheless, it contained one powerful and overriding theme-- the Soviet Union was in the process of change and this process would lead to the end of the East-West confrontation in Europe. The Soviets were no longer the enemies of the West and the West should be partners in the reconstruction of the Soviet Union.

The reform process in the Soviet Union is obviously complicated and difficult. This process has been widely perceived in Western Europe as eliminating the Soviets as an immediate threat to the West. Already before Gorbachev, West European publics perceived the Soviets to be a much less immediate threat than did the American public. After Gorbachev, this gap deepened and a new element was added. Increasingly, West European publics began to perceive the Soviets as a declining threat in the middle and long terms as well. In short, the reform process has been perceived to be part of a long-term trend in Soviet policy whereby the Soviet Union is being transformed from an enemy into either a benign or incompetent source of competition to Western Europe.

These shifts in opinion occurred before the crumbling of the communist regimes in Eastern Europe in 1989.[18] The Soviet leadership debated within itself throughout the Gorbachev period about how to handle the future of Eastern Europe. This debate led to wide swings in Soviet approaches to Eastern Europe during the Gorbachev period. Nonetheless, by 1989, the Soviet leadership had reached the following conclusions:

1. Eastern Europe under Communist rule was more a liability than an asset in the reform process of the Soviet Union;
2. Reformist communist parties would energize change in the Soviet Union;
3. The failure of reform communism would not prevent Eastern Europe from pursuing deeper reforms;
4. Non-communist regimes would be acceptable to the Soviets as long as basic Soviet security interests were protected;
5. Soviet security interests in the region would be determined through interaction with West European regimes;
6. The Americans would be important interlocutors in the process of protecting Soviet interests.

As the Soviets began to let Eastern Europe reform, they shifted other elements of their policy as well. They embraced the concept of conventional parity. They began unilateral conventional arms reductions. They began to promote a concept of minimal nuclear deterrence. But above all, Gorbachev argued for the necessity of the Soviet Union becoming a key player in building the new Europe.

The Classic Paradigm

In the wake of the Revolution of 1989, the classic elements of Soviet foreign policy which have been designed and implemented by the Communist Party and the Soviet state, were crumbling. What are those classic elements, how have they changed, and what new elements seem to be emerging for Soviet foreign policy?

In retrospect, the classic Soviet foreign policy paradigm has consisted of ten key elements. First, there is an ideological basis to Soviet foreign policy, whereby regimes embracing Soviet-style socialism are the core allies of the USSR. Allies are determined at least in part on the basis of ideological affinity with the Soviet model of socialism.

Second, policy is defined with regard to the interests of the leading force in Soviet society, the Communist Party of the Soviet Union. The CPSU embodies the general will of the Soviet people, and the party leadership frames current definitions of the national will.

Third, the goal of foreign policy is to aid the development of the Soviet model of socialism. It is necessary to protect this model from contamination by outside forces, but limited involvement with the outside world is necessary for reasons of global economic development and competition.

Fourth, ideological and party objectives are blended with geopolitical ones. Allies are determined in part according to the importance of the given state or its political forces, not just on the basis of ideology alone. Any contradictions between ideological and geopolitical definitions of state interest are to be resolved by the party leadership. To a large extent, geopolitical considerations are considered temporary, whereas ideological ones are considered permanent factors dictating alliances.

Fifth, defense of the socialist commonwealth is critical to the vitality of the Soviet Union. The construction of an interdependent socialist system gradually supplanted socialism in one country.

Sixth, the defense of the empire in Eastern Europe was conjoined with defense of the empire at home. The Soviet Union was building a new Soviet people. Nationalism was being overcome in the creation of a new commonwealth of socialist nations. This experience at home was to be the basis of change in the Soviet-East European relationship.

Seventh, pragmatic compromises were possible with the West. Contradictions between the socialist and capitalist systems could be overcome by peaceful means, but it was necessary to have a substantial military capability to defend the interests of socialism against imperialist pressures.

Eighth, there was a centralized elite capable of making a coordinated national policy. Diplomatic, economic, political, and military instruments were combined through a highly centralized party-state system. Objectives could be set from above and enforced throughout the socialist community.

Ninth, the power of the Soviet Union was enhanced by the ability to have centralized control at home and the ability to split class enemies abroad. By pursuing an anti-coalition strategy against the West, the

Soviet Union could compete effectively with a far more powerful Western system.

Above all, the classic approach of Soviet foreign policy rested upon a careful balance between competitiveness and cooperation with the West, especially at the end of the 1970s and early 1980s. The West provided a model of progress in the economic sphere, but not in the cultural, political and military spheres. In other words, the West provided elements to emulate for economic, scientific, and technological progress, but at the same time challenges to the viability of the socialist system from a security and cultural standpoint.

The Changing Paradigm

Each of these elements of classic Soviet foreign policy has been challenged today. Most important, the viability of the Stalinist model of development became widely doubted within the Soviet Union and perhaps especially within the Soviet elite. The clear ideological guideline of the past no longer seemed relevant; if the autarchic model was not relevant, then what was the point of a separate socialist commonwealth? What is the meaning of a Soviet socialist model today? Gradually, the belief in a unique Soviet socialist model gave way to a search for a new model.

Next, the party organizatien began to crumble. The old system whereby the CPSU and its leadership embodied the will of the proletariat gave way to fragmentation of the political system. The will of the people seemed to dissipate into tribal political warfare. With the collapse of belief in the superiority of the Soviet model, elites began searching for new alternatives. Such intellectual and political quests require interaction with the outside world rather than defensive reactiveness. Geopolitical objectives remain important for the new USSR, but they have been overshadowed by the necessity to transform the Soviet polity. There is a quest for partners in development of the USSR, and this quest has become more significant at the beginning of the 1990s than the pursuit of the classic ideological or geopolitical objectives.

Not only have Soviet objectives shifted, but the old USSR is disappearing. The combination of the pressures for disintegration within the USSR and the collapse of the Soviet empire within Eastern Europe mean that the socialist commonwealth is collapsing at home and abroad. New elites are emerging within the USSR at the Union Republic and sub-regional levels and they are participating in the interaction with the outside world. This interaction is helping to shape the new Soviet system. The patterns of interaction between the emerging national and subnational elites in the USSR and their Western counterparts will become increasingly central to the definition of Soviet foreign policy itself.

Even though interaction with the outside world has been vastly expanded, the power instruments available to the Soviet elites to develop their country are not at all clear. Military power remains important. But how will the Soviet elites develop the economic power to participate in their own reconstruction within a global economic setting? How will the Soviets develop a culture compatible with twenty-first century modernization?

The difficulty is that the Soviets remain a great power within Europe solely on military terms and are struggling to find other ways to become key actors in the global arena. But even in the military sphere the Soviets are important more in a negative than a positive sense.[19] The Soviet military challenge continues, but less as a threat and more as a factor of danger. The Russians maintain the largest army within Europe and its size may grow proportionally as the arms control process bogs down. If the Germans cap their forces at low levels, the French continue to reduce forces, and the Americans withdraw significant forces from Europe for budgetary reasons, these unilateral Western actions might fundamentally alter the military balance in the Russians' favor. Indeed, the Russians will further justify large forces to deal with domestic difficulties.

In addition to the conventional weapons challenge, the nuclear challenge will continue. Even with reductions in forces, the Russians will deploy the largest nuclear arsenal by far within Europe. If the German connection with nuclear deterrence is decisively weakened, the Russians might be tempted to resort to nuclear blackmail in the years ahead. This would become more likely if the USSR were unable to participate effectively in the European construction process either by the fact or feeling of exclusion or by a structural inability to compete.

The tension between the centrifugal and centripetal forces within Russia and the Soviet empire will drive Russian definitions of security. Fear of outside pressures could return as a justification for isolation, which could lead to striking back at the Western world--a world the Russians admire but can never seem to emulate. The redefinition of the Russian character along lines which extol a Russian nationalism of discipline and spiritual superiority over the West could provide fertile grounds for remilitarization.

Trying to avoid the collapse of the Russians onto themselves is an important goal in the construction of the new collective security system in Europe. Indeed, it is a central goal for the European consultation process of the 1990s.

Quite obviously there is no centralized elite to coordinate the power instruments of the Russian state and thereby to enhance the capability of the Soviet Union to exercise influence on the world stage. One of the West's most important challenges will be to try to weaken further the Russian-Soviet legacy of a highly centralized elite maintaining the military predominance of Russia-Soviet Union in the world.

Can a new pluralism emerge in which diversity within the USSR sees a more flexible interaction with the outside world? Will this interaction lead to progress in European and Western development, or will it lead to nationalistic explosion within Europe? Will the difficulties of the new "sick man of Europe" (as Turkey was earlier this century) reduce the ability of Western Europe to build a new integrated structure?

Thus, the USSR remains central to the future of Europe and to the West as a whole. It no longer threatens the West by means of a cohesive national elite with awesome military might at its disposal and with the intention of crushing Western growth and development. Rather, it presents a challenge primarily in terms of whether it can overcome its past and join the modernization process. Can it develop a new model of development which revitalizes all or parts of the Soviet Union? What will be the foreign policy dimensions of this effort? How will foreign policy making change in the process? If the Soviets fail to find a peaceful transition to the future, the weight of the past will challenge the West once again. The dreams of building a new Europe and new world will be dashed by the inability of the Russians to leave their autocratic and autarkic past. This is the challenge the Soviet Union poses to itself and the rest of the world in the last part of the twentieth and into the twenty-first century.

Notes

1. For an overview of the evolution of Soviet foreign policy see Erik Hoffmann, "Soviet Foreign Policy Aims and Accomplishments from Lenin to Brezhnev," in Robbin F. Laird, ed., **Soviet Foreign Policy** (New York: The Academy of Political Science, 1987), pp. 10-31. Also see Frederic J. Fleron, Jr, Erik P. Hoffmann and Robbin F. Laird, eds., **Soviet Foreign Policy: Classic and Contemporary Issues** (Hawthorne, New York: Aldine Publishing, forthcoming 1991).

2. See chapter six in Theodore H. Von Laue, **The World Revolution of Westernization** (Oxford: Oxford University Press, 1987).

3. For a treatment of the Western debate about the role of ideology in Soviet foreign policy see part three of Erik Hoffmann and Frederic J. Fleron, Jr., eds., **Conduct of Soviet Foreign Policy** (Hawthorne, New York: Aldine Publishing, 1980).

4. Henry Roberts, "Maxim Litvinov: Soviet Diplomacy, 1930-1939," in Vernon Aspaturian, ed., **Power and Process in Soviet Foreign Policy** (Boston: Little Brown, 1971).

5. See von Laue, **The World Revolution**, chapter ten.

6. See part four in Hoffmann and Fleron, eds., **Conduct of Soviet Foreign Policy**.

7. Christopher Jones, **Soviet Influence in Eastern Europe: Political Autonomy and the Warsaw Pact** (New York: Praeger, 1981).

8. See Raymond Garthoff, **Soviet Strategy in the Nuclear Age** (New York: Frederick Praeger, 1958).

9. See Charles Gati, "The Stalinist Legacy in Soviet Foreign Policy," in Erik Hoffmann, ed., **The Soviet Union in the 1980s** (New York: Academy of Political Science, 1984).

10. Erik Hoffmann and Robbin Laird, **"The Scientific-Technological Revolution" and Soviet Foreign Policy** (Elmsford, New York: Pergamon Press, 1982).

11. See Karen Dawisha, **Eastern Europe: Gorbachev and Reform** (Cambridge: Cambridge University Press, 1988).

12. Erik Hoffmann and Robbin F. Laird, **Technocratic Socialism: The Soviet Union in the Advanced Industrial Era** (Durham, North Carolina: Duke University Press, 1985).

13. Robbin Laird, "The Impact of the West on the Soviet Union," in Helmut Sonnenfeldt, ed., **Soviet Politics in the 1980s** (Boulder, Colorado: Westview Press, 1985).

14. Erik Hoffmann and Robbin F. Laird, **The Politics of Economic Modernization in the Soviet Union** (Ithaca, New York: Cornell University Press, 1982).

15. See Dusko Doder and Louise Branson, **Gorbachev: Heretic in the Kremlin** (New York: Viking Press, 1990) and Robert Kaiser, **Why Gorbachev Happened: His Triumphs and His Failure** (New York: Simon and Schuster, 1991).

16. Robbin Laird and Susan Clark, **The Soviet Union and the Western Alliance** (London: Unwin and Hyman, 1990).

17. See William Garner, "The Soviets and Denuclearization," in Robbin F. Laird and Betsy Jacobs, eds., **The Future of Deterrence** (Boulder, Colorado: Westview Press, 1989).

18. Robbin Laird, "La Revolution de 1989," **Revue Des Deux Mondes**, May 1990, pp. 107-112.

19. See my treatment of the Soviet Union in Robbin F. Laird, **The Europeanization of the Alliance** (Boulder, Colorado: Westview Press, 1991).

2

The Soviets and the Western Alliance: The Classical Approach

The basic Soviet approach to the Alliance rested upon a specific judgment about the role of the United States within that Alliance and the balance of power between Western Europe and the United States. "Atlanticism," in the Soviet view, allowed the United States to exercise considerable influence over political and economic developments within Western Europe. From the Soviet perspective, an Atlanticized Europe was one in which American definitions of Western security needs dominated Western Europe's security interests and political and economic relationships with the Soviet Union. Such an Atlanticized Europe was able to exist only under the specific conditions of American predominance over Western Europe that existed in the late 1940s and early 1950s.

This type of Atlanticism was seriously undercut by the changing balance of power between the United States and Western Europe. The growth of West European economic power led to the emergence of the West European "power center" in the capitalist world, a power center that exercised growing assertiveness and independence from the United States.

The resurgence of the West European power center occurred most dramatically in the politico-economic realm. Economically, Western Europe has become a serious economic competitor as well as collaborator with the United States. West European scientific and technological capability was a significant factor in European economic development and provided the basis for significant progress in cutting-edge industries as well. The West Europeans have become major players in trade and capital transfer relations with the Third World, in many ways even more diversified than U.S. economic relations with the Third World. Politically, the West Europeans have collaborated to an unprecedented extent in the creation and development of intra-European economic relations. Strong Soviet skepticism about the European Economic Community (EEC) gave way over time to recognizing the significance of transnational European cooperation. Notably, the Soviets paid increasing attention to the economic transformation process of European markets associated with the 1992 target date for eliminating the remaining economic barriers in the Common Market. They also paid greater attention to the EEC role as a broker that managed the interaction between Western and Eastern Europe.

The emergence of the West European power center led to increasing assertiveness within West-West military-security relations as well. The West Europeans increased the scope and extent of intra-European security cooperation, notably in armaments development and production. Cooperation occurred among the major players in European security (e.g., Franco-German cooperation) in attempts to increase Europe's weight in Alliance policy. This weight was increasingly manifested in the development of West European policy and relations toward Eastern Europe and the Soviet Union. The West Europeans deployed the bulk of NATO's peacetime conventional forces in the European theater and a significant component of NATO's European theater-based nuclear forces. The European nuclear powers--Britain and France --have been undergoing a significant modernization of their forces and the Soviets have paid considerable attention to those forces.

In other words, a major shift occurred within the Alliance in the 1970s and 1980s. The West European countries played an increasingly critical role in the evolution of Western security policy. Indeed, in the wake of the revolution of 1989, the West Europeans emerged as key architects in framing a new European post-superpower security order. The Soviets have been especially interested in influencing West European policy as the West Europeans seek to craft a new European security order.

This chapter will focus upon the classic Soviet strategy in the 1970s and early 1980s in dealing with the Alliance. The next chapter addresses how the Soviets began to understand the Alliance situation in the mid-to-late 1980s, notably with regard to the expanding role of Western Europe within the Alliance. The challenge of dealing with the new security order--emergent from the process of German unification --will be addressed in the final part of the book.

The German Factor

Throughout the postwar period, the Soviets have pursued various policies toward West Germany. The basic Soviet effort to influence the evolution of West German policy has wavered between military pressure and diplomatic persuasion, the former playing an increasingly important role beginning in the second half of the 1970s. The three Soviet leaderships prior to Gorbachev apparently thought that forcing the pace of military competition in Europe and improving the Soviet preponderance in conventional and intermediate-range nuclear forces (INF) would make it possible to translate military power into political influence. The role of "nuclear hostage" was to be impressed on the West German mind as a way of lessening the West German attachment to the United States. Moscow viewed the rise of a powerful "peace movement" in West Germany as one of the main indicators that this approach was working.

What Soviet leaders until Gorbachev did not appreciate was that increased Soviet pressure produced counteractions. For example, this pressure, which raised international tensions, contributed to greater American-West German cohesion. In addition, in the early 1980s, the balance among West German political parties shifted toward a more anti-Soviet stance, a shift which was caused partly by Soviet intransigence on the INF issue.

Soviet political-military analysts of the FRG understood that the "forward defense" of West Germany was the key element of its political-military strategy. The stationing of foreign troops on West German soil was legitimate to defend West German territorial integrity from the outset of armed hostilities. The commitment to nuclear deterrence was ambivalent in the Federal Republic; only nuclear use outside West German territory was perceived to be legitimate, and the nuclear hostage fear was deeply rooted. Finally, West Germany's commitment to conventional defense placed it at odds with the other two major European powers (France and Britain), which relied on nuclear deterrence to defend their territory.

The political element of Soviet strategy took into account these main elements of specific West German interests. With regard to "forward defense," the Soviets linked such defense with offensive operations. The growing Soviet effort to paint their doctrine in defensive terms was designed partly to undercut the legitimacy of forward defense in West German minds. As if to underline a direct parallel with the Nazi past, the claim had been made that the West German Bundeswehr had expansionist territorial goals and an offensive military strategy.

The Nuclear Factor in the German-Alliance Relationship

With regard to nuclear weapons, the Soviets have underscored the "hostage" function of any U.S. use of nuclear weapons from West German territory. The Soviet handling of the INF crisis was especially reflective of this effort. From 1978 through 1983, Soviet analysts and leaders believed that Western Europe might not actually deploy the Euromissiles. During this period, they used Soviet Euromissile capability and the Western response to that capability to try to separate politically West European from American interests in NATO.

Throughout this phase of the crisis, the Soviets sought to exploit what they perceived to be a key pressure point in West-West military relations. Soviet analysts had noted that the centrality of American nuclear weapons to NATO defense underscored a fundamental contradiction between Western Europe and the United States. "The strategic calculations of the two centers of power make a strikingly different assessment of the character of a potential military conflict. In its endeavor to avoid destruction of its own territory the U.S. is oriented toward a limitation of operations to the European theater of action in the event of an armed conflict in this region, at least in its early stages. The West European military conceptions proceed from the necessity to ensure the broad participation of the U.S. in the conflict from the very moment of its inception. This diametrical opposition of their interests is breeding a chain reaction of fears in Western Europe and disagreements with the U.S. on such questions as the stationing of American troops in Western

Europe, the reliability of the U.S.'s nuclear guarantees, the role of NATO outside of its geographical bounds, the possible involvement of Western Europe in the military undertakings of American global politics."[1]

Soviet Eurostrategic capability contributed to this contradiction of interests between Western Europe and the United States. Parity in intercontinental systems tended and continues to deter the United States from using these systems to defend Western Europe and hence raised questions within Western Europe about the reliability of U.S. nuclear guarantees.

The modernization of Soviet Eurostrategic weapons contributed to the Soviets' ability to conduct a nuclear war limited to Europe. But when the United States sought to strengthen its European theater nuclear forces, the Soviets stressed the dangers of U.S. "limited nuclear war" doctrines. They did this in part to exacerbate West-West tensions and in part to impede Western military development.

To the United States, the Soviets emphasized the impossibility of containing a Eurostrategic war without escalating to intercontinental systems. Such a claim is designed to convince the United States to cease developing theater nuclear forces for NATO's flexible response strategy. To the West Europeans, the Soviets have stressed that U.S. emphasis on a limited nuclear war showed a lack of genuine American concern for West European security. The message had been that the United States was an offshore power not having the same security problems as the Soviet and West European "continental" powers, powers which share a "common home." By pressuring both the American and European components of the Alliance, the Soviets hoped to obstruct the construction of Western strategic power and to slow the further development of a Eurostrategic rung on the U.S. escalation ladder.

Thus, the Soviets hoped to increase their deterrent capability, to increase their leverage on Western Europe (especially on the Federal Republic), and to obstruct Western strategic development by maintaining their Eurostrategic superiority in the context of intercontinental strategic parity. NATO's firmness in rejecting Soviet pressures against the deployment of the U.S. missiles forced the Soviets to shift their approach. Under Gorbachev, the Soviet leadership now understood that the only way to eliminate the presence of new American missiles was to abolish completely the counterpart Soviet systems.

But the elimination of American systems through the INF treaty still served the purpose of conveying to West European elites that U.S. and

European interests were different. The Soviets had indicated to the Americans their desire for a condominium on global affairs, especially through the mutual reduction of the nuclear threat to both powers. At the same time, they had expressed a desire to enhance European security significantly by finding common interests in eliminating nuclear weapons from Europe and reducing the level of conventional forces on the continent.

The pursuit of American-Soviet cooperation and the enhancement of the "common home" of European security had converged in the effort to eliminate nuclear weapons from Europe. This convergence had been envigorated by the Gorbachev administration's recognition that only a plausibly serious effort in conventional arms control would permit the denuclearization campaign to proceed. Denuclearization in Europe was closely tied to the Soviets' political anti-coalition strategy; it was designed to encourage the Americans to rethink their military participation in Europe and to consider the serious threat which their presence posed to their own interests, narrowly considered. Furthermore, the pursuit of denuclearization in Europe divides the European nuclear powers from the non-nuclear ones, especially France from Germany.

Soviet analysts had underscored the centrality of the tension between the European nuclear powers and West Germany to impede West European defense cooperation. Intra-European security cooperation had become of increasing concern to the Soviets. Such cooperation supplemented the American role and might have resulted in the creation of a two-pillar Western Alliance. The Soviets wished to avoid such an outcome at virtually any cost. Soviet leaders had highlighted that Western Europe must choose between West European military cooperation and all-European detente. These two options were mutually exclusive from the Soviet standpoint.

The French Factor

The Soviets perceived the evolution of French policy to be especially troubling, as France increasingly strived to strengthen the Alliance via Europeanization. Such Europeanization was to be achieved by expanding conventional military cooperation with the Germans and nuclear military and arms control cooperation with the British. To the extent that France has encouraged greater European cohesion, the effectiveness of the Soviet effort to pressure the Alliance along transatlantic lines was reduced. The Soviets would have liked to pursue the anti-coalition strategy by exacerbating transatlantic tensions; they did not want this strategy to result in intra-European developments that would have challenged their interests. But this was precisely the situation faced by the Soviet leadership and with which it was increasingly preoccupied in the late 1980s.

The major political effect of French policy was to stimulate the "Europeanist" tendency in Western Europe. A. Utkin identified Europeanism as "an ideology of isolating Western Europe, of forming the West European alliance as an autonomous center in the world arena."[2] Utkin emphasizes that Europeanism had worked at cross purposes to Atlanticism. "Europeanism as an ideology focuses on greater independence from the hegemonic power of the capitalist world in the postwar period --the United States--which results in the definite anti-American trend of Europeanism."[3]

France has played a critical role in challenging American hegemony and encouraging the emergence of Europeanism as a practical ideology guiding the formation of a more independent West European power center.[4] Europeanism as a trend and France's critical role in promoting it were seen as a two-edged sword by Soviet analysts. Europeanism was a positive trend to the extent that Atlanticism or American hegemony was undercut, but a negative trend to the extent that a West European power center emerged as a result. The significance of France's security policy was perceived to be intertwined with the Europeanist trend.

The withdrawal of France from NATO's integrated military command meant to the Soviets that French compliance with American policy would have never be assumed by Washington. The French have operated as useful interlocutors between the Soviets and the Americans or between the Soviets and other West European states. From the Soviet point of view, it was better for France to be a "perturbator" in West-West relations than a consistent supporter of American positions.

The withdrawal of France from the integrated military command also had important consequences for U.S. military policy. First, the Americans had lost the "automatic" use of French territory in a war. Because France's geographical location is critical to the conduct of a conventional campaign in Europe, the fact that it was not available to the integrated military command was seen as an important loss for the Americans.

Second, the French had consistently rejected the U.S. doctrine of limited nuclear war. According to Soviet analysts, the Americans planned to fight various forms of limited nuclear war, whereas the French have planned for an all-out nuclear war. The clear implication was that French nuclear forces seriously complicate U.S. plans for exercising escalation control over Western nuclear forces. Third, the French example had encouraged other Western states, such as Spain, to only partial involvement in U.S. warfighting plans. Although the French policy of independence yielded benefits from the Soviets' point of view, they nevertheless perceived France's role in strengthening a West European power center as a largely negative one.

The sense that Atlanticism was irrevocably declining and the relative independence of Europe on the rise was at the core of Soviet analyses of France in particular and of European security more generally. For Soviet analysts, Western Europe's independence could have developed in one of two ways: Europe could have become more independent militarily, or Europe could have become more neutralist and embrace demilitarization. There was little doubt which of these two alternatives the Soviets favored. Equally certain was the fact that France was contributing to the emergence of the former.

For some Soviet analysts, even the detente policy of the 1970s and early 1980s has had an ambiguous effect on the emergence of the West European power center. As an authoritative group of Soviet analysts have noted, "detente is capable...of strengthening Eurocentric tendencies in the military policies of the West European powers, both within the framework of NATO and outside it. The Europeanization of NATO, i.e., the increase in the relative importance within it of its European participants, may strengthen."[5] The dark side of France's detente policy has also been noted: "The French government believed that the detente process had to parallel a strengthening of each West European country and all of Western Europe as a whole."[6]

Thus, the significance of French security policy to Soviet analysts was due largely to its contribution to the Europeanist tendency. Although France's example of independence was important in stimulating the West Europeans' quest for greater independence from the Americans, France's contribution to security interdependence within the West European power center has worried the Soviets more. Soviet analysts have noted a number of ways that the evolution of French policy would decisively affect the emergence of security cooperation within Western

Europe. First, to the extent that France developed its cooperation with Britain, a true European nuclear force (a Soviet term) might emerge.[7] Second, as the Franco-German security relationship became stronger, the Germans were more likely to acquire nuclear weapons, indirectly or directly.[8] Third, to the extent that the major Western European powers, perhaps through the West European Union, cooperated in joint armaments production, the possibility of greater cooperation in conventional force deployments was enhanced. Weapons standardization enhanced the probability of conventional military cooperation.

At least some Soviet analysts posed the possibility that Atlanticism and Europeanism might not be polar opposites at all. Rather, Europeanism might have provided the Americans with more room for maneuver in dealing with contingencies outside Europe. Actions taken by the Mitterrand administration to promote European cooperation and to reduce the anti-American thrust associated with traditional Gaullism were a manifestation of something approaching a worst-case scenario for the Soviets.[9]

The British Factor

The concern with the emergence of an enhanced European nuclear capability was reflected not only in Soviet assessments of the French but of the British as well. The British "special nuclear relationship" with the United States encouraged the British to be key supporters of the Americans in the European nuclear debate. Soviet analysts underscored that U.S.-UK nuclear sharing arrangements allowed the British to be the best informed of all America's European allies concerning U.S. nuclear policy. Also, the British had been able "to influence to some extent the United States' course in elaborating NATO's nuclear strategy, to receive information first-hand about a broad range of problems, and to participate in solving them."[10] Being kept in the nuclear ballgame through U.S. assistance, the British were generally the most pro-nuclear and pro-American of the U.S. allies within NATO. The British were especially strong supporters of maintaining the U.S. nuclear "guarantee" in Europe. Finally, by remaining a nuclear power, Britain not only supported U.S. nuclear policy, but rejected Soviet options for "reducing" tensions associated with the nuclear competition.

Not only has been the British emphasis on nuclear deterrence been troubling to the Soviets, so, too, was its growing interest in the Europeanization of NATO. Soviet analysts argued that the British had a two-fold approach to the Europeanization of the Alliance. On the one hand, the British tried to act as the interlocutor between Europe and the United States and used their position in NATO to generate greater influence within Europe.[11] On the other hand, the British sought to encourage the development of a "European pillar" within NATO. They helped to create the Eurogroup and the Independent European Program Group (IEPG) to facilitate this process. They developed extensive ties with other European states in joint armaments production in order to facilitate Europeanization as well.

In the Soviet view, the British played the preeminent European role in NATO, as illustrated in their high degree of representation within the command structure and in various NATO committees. The British approach to Europeanization was to draw on their strengths in NATO in order to assert their influence within Europe. Kolosov has argued that all this high-level influence, combined with "the significant presence of lower rank British officers and specialists in NATO's headquarters, commands, and various committees, is called upon to protect the specific interests of England's government and military leadership and not to permit a dimunition of its influence within the bloc's military organization."[12]

The British sought to Europeanize the Alliance through the formation of such institutions as the Eurogroup. According to Madzoevskii and Khesin, "A definite 'Europeanization' of its [Britain's] nonnuclear component is taking place under the auspices of the Eurogroup's programming, which is uniting the majority of the European members of NATO (without the participation of the U.S. and Canada)."[13] The NATO Eurogroup was perceived by Kolosov to play an "extremely" vital role in the coordination of collaborative efforts among the West Europeans and "contributed to the increase of their contribution to the build-up of NATO's military might and to the development among them of military-policy, military, and military-industrial ties."[14] The Eurogroup, however, acted only in certain spheres to promote collaboration, namely in military-technical rather than military-policy tasks.[15]

The linkage of the Eurogroup, Europeanization, and the significance of European--including British--conventional forces to greater inter-European cooperation has been clearly articulated by Kolosov. "In the military arena, England, the FRG, Italy and the other West European members of NATO provide the main portion of general purpose forces that are focused on executing the bloc's tasks.... There is a growing potential for developing more durable and long-term ties among the national ministries of defense, the armed forces in the most diverse fields --from their material-technical support to the conduct of joint maneuvers, and the elaboration of, to all intents and purposes, unified operational tactical plans for conducting a war."[16]

The British have not been receptive to Europeanization approaches outside of the NATO context. From the Soviet point of view, the reason Britain has rejected Europeanization outside NATO has been the priority which the British have placed on NATO's coalition military strategy. By and large, the British have perceived their forces to be most effective when operated jointly with NATO's forces. The British drew the Americans into a tighter nuclear "guarantee" by allowing deployment of U.S. nuclear weapons on British soil and promoting nuclear interdependence with the United States. The British did, however, retain the ultimate right to use their nuclear weapons to serve national interests.

The Soviets expected the British orientation towards Europeanization to emphasize the nuclear component of European defense. Many Soviet analyses of post-Reykjavik developments were struck by the extent to which the European conservative governments worked together to ensure that the Americans stayed on the nuclear path. For example, the Soviet press was quick to report on Mrs. Thatcher's visit to Paris in November 1986, when she sought to enhance her ability to influence the Americans on nuclear disarmament issues through a unified Franco-British stance.[17]

The Military Dimension

The classical Soviet approach to the Alliance attempted to combine a political-military and military-technical strategy. The political-military strategy revolved around an anti-coalition approach. It also underscored the salience of the political aspects of military competition with the West and the need to better leverage the Alliance in times of crisis and war. The military-technical policy emphasized the need to be able to prevail if war came in Europe through the use of conventional forces and the threat of immediate escalation in the event of nuclear use by NATO.

Marshal Sergei Akhromeev's formulation of coalitional strategy argued that the lessons of World War II were important and relevant to contemporary Soviet policy . "The main lesson of World War II, namely that war must be combated before it has begun therefore assumes special topicality today. Historical experience indicates that joint, concerted, and vigorous action on the part of all peace-loving forces against the aggressive actions of imperialism is necessary in order to defend peace."[18]

Central to Soviet thinking was the need to prevail in the initial period of any future war. The salience of political factors to such an effort were also taken into account. Among the critical political factors affecting success in the initial period of war were the following: the ability to mobilize forces; the ability to shift generally from a crisis to armed conflict; and the ability to deal with the issue of nuclear escalation. With regard to mobilization, the Alliance members would undoubtedly find themselves in conflict over whether or not to mobilize forces, over which forces to mobilize, and over whether the Soviet Union was really prepared to go to war. During the crisis period, the mobilization decision would become tantamount to shifting to war. General Gareev, for example, has argued that there was an almost irreversible nature inherent in the mobilization process, and that this process would be deeply affected by the political environment. "If a war generally is politics through and through, on the eve and at the start of a war its political aspects are even more prevalent."[19]

The general transition from peacetime to wartime would have been profoundly influenced by political conflict within the NATO Alliance. Differing national interests may well have come to the fore, which the Soviets would have seeked to exploit. A significant disinformation campaign would have been unleashed in the political arena to compound NATO's difficulties.

After hostilities had begun, the Soviets would have sought to prevail at the conventional level. Nonetheless, the campaign would have been fought under the constant threat of nuclear use. The political dimensions of the nuclear decision were very significant in Soviet thinking. Despite Soviet claims of an "all or nothing" strategy for nuclear deterrence, Soviet analysts had contemplated the use of limited nuclear strikes for political purposes.[20] Lectures at the Soviet General Staff Academy in the mid-1970s taught students that "political actions may affect the selection of the TVD [theater of military action] for action, the selection of the countries to be hit by nuclear strikes, or the nations not to be attacked by nuclear weapons."[21]

From the standpoint of an anti-coalition political-military strategy, the Soviets might have conducted their military campaign in such a manner as to put primary pressure on those states with forward deployed forces in West Germany. They would have concentrated on those countries that they perceived to be the weak links in NATO (the Netherlands, Belgium and Canada) and would encourage these states to withdraw from German soil. The Soviets might well have defined the threat as American "militarism" and West German "revanchism," the threats against which they "must" act. Soviet leaders would have conveyed through diplomatic and propaganda channels that they had no hostile intentions against other European states, especially those European states with forward-deployed forces. If the Soviets could have induced one state to withdraw these forces, they would have hoped to set off a chain reaction of withdrawal. They would especially hope, by means of such a chain reaction, to pressure the British to withdraw. Given the American-British "special relationship," a British withdrawal of forward-deployed forces might have been seen to be able to significantly affect U.S. attitudes and policies. Moreover, the Soviets could have more credibly offered "non-intervention" pledges to the British than to any other major European Alliance power.

The key Soviet objective would have been to isolate the Federal Republic of Germany as much as possible. If some forward-deployed forces could have been pressured diplomatically to withdraw, an isolation process would have been started. The Soviets would have hoped to freeze West German mobilization and West German willingness to support reinforcement efforts as long as possible. The Soviets would have conveyed to the German Chancellor that significant mobilization would have been considered an act of war, thereby raising the risk of mobilization from the outset.

The Soviets would have also sought to pressure France to follow its "traditional" strategy of protecting French territory. The Soviet leaders would have clearly encouraged the French to keep the Force d'Action Rapide (FAR) in French territory and would have encouraged the French to remove their forces from Germany in exchange for a non-aggression pledge. A key question for Soviet leaders would have been whether or not to attack French nuclear forces. Would frontal attacks or restraint be more effective in encouraging French acquiescence in West German neutrality?

The Soviets might have also prosecuted British and French SSBNs (nuclear ballistic submarines). They would have done so to reduce the nuclear threat against the Soviet Union. Also, successful prosecution would have increased the willingness of the two countries to withdraw from the conflict and pledge neutrality and support for the "demilitarization" of West Germany. Success in the destruction of French and British SSBNs might have also sent a useful signal to the United States, encouraging American leaders to husband SSBN assets rather than use them in limited nuclear strikes.

As the Soviets began military operations against NATO forces in West Germany, they would have hoped to encourage key Alliance states to revert to strictly national strategies. From the outset, they might have declared limited objectives against NATO forces in Germany and, if they were successful in capturing specific concentrations of national forces, they might have exchanged prisoners for pledges of neutrality by the specific country. Throughout the German campaign, the Soviets would have sought to influence U.S. policy and actions through Soviet successes on the battlefield. The Soviets would have attempted to destroy or isolate U.S. forces, and then perhaps sought U.S. pledges for West German demilitarization as well.

Nonetheless, conventional operations in the European theater would have been only quasi-conventional in character. The Soviets would have sought to eliminate as much of NATO's nuclear potential in Europe as possible. Their key goal during conventional operations would have been to degrade Western military forces in Europe, especially nuclear forces. The Soviets had become increasingly sensitive to the possibility and even the desirability of withholding nuclear strikes as long as possible or, in other words, of prolonging conventional operations in a war with the West as long as it were feasible to do so. Thus, a key military objective of Soviet nuclear weapons in Europe was to make a conventional war-fighting option more viable.

The Soviets might have contemplated the use of various types of nuclear weapons on the European battlefield to support limited war-fighting objectives. The Soviets might have used their short-range battlefield nuclear weapons to attack NATO ground forces, especially NATO's short-range battlefield weapons. The basic political objective would have been to raise the level of damage on West German territory and to thereby encourage West Germany to pressure NATO for an early end to nuclear hostilities.

The Soviets might have gone further, using their longer range theater nuclear force systems (notably their aircraft such as the Fencer and Backfire) to attack high-value NATO military targets in Europe. Among key NATO targets to be struck would have been airfields, ports, and tactical missile and warhead sites. In addition to the obvious military objectives of such an attack, there were a number of political objectives served as well. The Soviets would have been pressuring NATO for a termination of hostilities prior to conducting significant strategic attacks directly against the territories of the European nuclear powers, Britain and France. A subordinate goal might have been to try to "neutralize" France and Britain in order to undercut the will or need for France and Britain to use their strategic weapons against Soviet territory.

By such actions, the Soviets would have sought to influence U.S. escalation decisions. As European theater nuclear strikes occurred, the Soviets would have sought to assure the United States that the war could be confined to NATO Europe. Throughout, the Soviets would have sought to encourage the United States to desist from intercontinental nuclear exchanges.

Conclusion

The classical Soviet strategy toward the Western Alliance relied heavily on encouraging the development of serious tensions within the coalition of liberal democratic states. Soviet analysts were well aware of the voluntary quality of membership in the alliance as well as the increased national assertiveness among alliance members. They also recognized the collective strength of the alliance when cohesion prevailed. Hence, the maximization of Soviet power required the reduction of Alliance cohesion and the pursuit of an anti-coalition strategy to drive wedges and expand fissures within the alliance.

In their wartime strategy, Soviet analysts paid a great deal of attention to the coalitional nature of any future European war. Soviet emphasis shifted in the 1970s from simply studying the ability of the United

States to conduct combined operations with the North Atlantic Treaty Organization to the ability of the alliance to congeal politically in crisis situations. Soviet analysts of the alliance, especially of its European components, increasingly emphasized throughout the late 1970s and early 1980s the emergence of national strategies by major West European countries under the umbrella of a general alliance strategy.

In addition, a basic challenge for the Soviets was to manage as successfully as possible the "mediated nature" of their relationship with Western Europe. The Soviet-Western European relationship was shaped in part by the attempt to influence one another's allies. The Soviet Union made a significant effort to influence American policy toward the Soviet Union and to limit American foreign policy capabilities by attempting to shape West European foreign policy behavior. The West European powers, in turn, made a significant effort to shape Soviet foreign policy behavior by increasing West European ties with Eastern Europe. The West Europeans used trade and various forms of commercial relations as a key means of expanding their influence in the Eastern bloc.

Especially significant to Soviet peacetime strategy toward the Alliance was the need to influence the shape and direction of West European foreign policy as the West defined its position in East-West relations. The increased assertiveness of Western Europe provided the Soviets with opportunities to undercut American influence in Western Europe and to try to hinder the development of various kinds of Western relationships, such as strengthening the relationship between Germany and France, that could have damaged Soviet interests.

Notes

1. V. N. Shenayev, ed., **Western Europe Today** (Moscow: Progress Publishers, 1980), p. 306.

2. A. I. Utkin, **Doktriny atlantizma i evropeiskaya integratsiya** (Moscow: Nauka, 1979), p. 73.

3. Ibid.

4. V. P. Lukin, **"Tsentry sily": kontseptsii i real'nost'** (Moscow: Mezhdunarodnye otnosheniya, 1983), pp. 66-67.

5. V. N. Shenaev et al., eds., **Zapadnaya Evropa: ekonomika, politika, klassovaya bor'ba** (Moscow: Mysl', 1979), p. 261.

6. T. I. Sulitskaya, **Kitai i Frantsiya, 1949-1981** (Moscow: Nauka, 1983), p. 139.

7. For the fullest statement of the European nuclear force concept, see V. F. Davydov, "Discussion of the European Nuclear Forces," **SShA**, no. 3, 1976, pp. 28-38.

8. See, for example, V. Mikhnovich, "Calculations and Miscalculations," **Krasnaya zvezda** (hereafter **KZ**), June 14, 1984, p. 3.

9. See for example, Captain V. Kuzar', "NATO--An Alliance in the Name of Aggression," **KZ**, April 8, 1984, p. 3.

10. G. V. Kolosov, **Voenno-politicheskii kurs Anglii v Evrope** (Moscow: Nauka, 1984), p. 65.

11. **Ibid.**, p. 10.

12. **Ibid.**, p. 106.

13. S. Madzoevskii and E. Khesin, "Great Britain in Today's World," **Mirovaya ekonomika i mezhdunarodnye otnosheniya** (hereafter **MEMO**), no. 8, 1980, p. 56.

14. Kolosov, **Voenno-politicheskii kurs**, p. 178.

15. **Ibid.**, p. 184.

16. G. V. Kolosov in N. S. Kishilov (ed)., **Zapadno-evropeiskaya integratsiya: politicheskie aspekty** (Moscow: Nauka, 1985), p. 246.

17. Yu. Kovalenko, **Izvestiya**, November 23, 1986, p. 4.

18. Marshal Akhromeev in **Foreign Broadcast Information Service** (hereafter cited as **FBIS**), May 13, 1986, p. 8.

19. Colonel General M. Gareev, **M. V. Frunze--voennyi teoretik** (Moscow: Voenizdat, 1985), p. 242.

20. See the author's book coauthored with Dale Herspring, **The Soviet Union and Strategic Arms** (Boulder, Colorado: Westview Press, 1984).

21. "Principles of Strategic Action of the Armed Forces," **Lecture Materials of the Voroshilov General Staff Academy** (Washington, DC: U.S. Government Printing Office, 1989).

3

The Soviets and West European Security Cooperation, 1985-1989

The purpose of this chapter is to analyze Soviet views on the military integration process of Western Europe in the Gorbachev era, with special attention accorded to the security policy of Western Europe's three leading military powers: France, Great Britain and West Germany. The analysis is divided into two approximate periods that reflect significant shifts in Soviet positions. The first period runs from mid-1985 into 1987; the second period covers late 1987 to 1989.

Soviet General Perspectives on West European Security Integration, 1985-1987

During 1985-1987, the Gorbachev administration continued to uphold the classic Soviet view of Western European military integration as a variant of Atlanticism. They held specific assumptions that the U.S. strongly influenced the existing military framework in Western Europe, that is, NATO. Moreover, the assumption that a simple bipolar division of Europe operated, and that the United States led the Western allies in a concerted campaign against the socialist camp, was also operative.

Until the end of 1986 and through much of 1987, the dominant framework for understanding the military integration of the West was NATO, headed by the United States in a conscious policy of confrontation with the socialist camp.[1] Through this prism, NATO, from its conception, constituted a U.S.-dominated bloc which consistently sought over forty years to expand the boundaries of NATO's responsibilities in the campaign against socialism.[2] At a time when the United States could no longer act as the world's gendarme, it now sought, so argued the Soviets, to co-opt its NATO allies into assisting in police operations around the globe, including in the Middle East and Central America.

It was widely held that the Reagan administration explicitly pressured NATO members to change treaty language which defined NATO's zones of responsibility.[3] Part of this effort involved getting West Germany to agree to replace up to 80,000 U.S. ground troops so that the United States might make military forces available for action elsewhere on the globe.[4] It was also underscored that the U.S. aided the allies in their own operations around the world, such as British involvement in the Falklands and French action in Africa. Although the U.S. effort to create a multilateral NATO Rapid Deployment Force failed, France, Britain and Italy did create such forces.[5]

In 1985, Soviet coverage of NATO exercises in Europe reflected the basic accusation made against the bloc--that it planned for first strikes against the Warsaw Pact and envisioned European nuclear wars.[6] The basic bipolar image of the capitalist countries versus the socialist bloc dominated a series of collected essays published in 1987, which presented a history of post-war NATO aggressions against socialism.[7] Furthermore, the military periodical *Zarubezhnoe voennoe obozrenie* (*ZVO*) published an analysis of NATO strategy that fit into the above framework.[8]

To the extent that Soviet observers commented on independent European groupings, such as the Eurogroup within NATO and the newly reanimated (in 1984) Western European Union (WEU), they charged that these groups acted at the behest of the United States and NATO in its campaign against worldwide socialism.[9] The expansion of the European allies' activities in the security field was also interpreted as a reaction to U.S. pressure to increase Europe's contribution to Western defense.

The Soviet perception of European support for the United States was exemplified in the coverage of NATO's Eurogroup meeting in December 1985, which expressed its "satisfaction" with American missile deployments in Europe. It was also believed that the European ministers agreed to augment further NATO's military capability.[10] As the TASS military news commentator, Vladimir Bogachev, wrote: "The European NATO governments more and more often yield to Washington's pressure and timidly join, under the pretext of "bolstering Atlantic unity," U.S. military and political ventures which are against their own national interests."[11] Soviet commentators suggested that even when integrationist activity occurred within a purely European framework, it was designed to impart the impression of European sovereignty in matters of military and political integration in order to placate restless societies.[12]

This paradigm applied to the Soviet interpretation of the WEU's reanimation. V. Vladimirov explained in *International Affairs* that the revival of the WEU was a reaction to the public outcry over the U.S. diktat to the allies to deploy medium-range nuclear missiles. "In these conditions urgent measures were needed to spruce up the NATO facade and, at the same time, to neutralize and undermine the antimissile movement in Western Europe.... Thus, the Atlanticists focused on the WEU which, in their opinion, had not 'compromised' itself in the eyes of West European peoples."[13] The Soviets also depicted NATO and U.S. officials as pleased with Franco-German military cooperation and with general West European military integration, which lightened the burden on the U.S. and permitted it to pursue neo-globalist goals.[14]

In this period, Soviet observers were prepared to go to some lengths to place an American imprint on European actions, even when the Europeans disagreed with the United States on certain matters. In a late 1986 report, *Krasnaya zvezda* reviewed European unhappiness with American promises made at Reykjavik. Later in the same article, the Soviet commentator wrote that in the dissatisfaction of NATO's "Eurogroup, Washington's hand could be felt clearly. Scared by the historical prospects of Reykjavik, American hawks were pressuring their West European partners in the bloc to refuse the zero option, which would allow the United States to justify its retreat from the agreements made in principle [at Reykjavik]." In this context, the Eurogroup was represented as pushing for the further development of NATO's nuclear forces and moving to limit any removal of nuclear weapons by treaty.[15]

Soviet observers also cast doubts on the European ability to escape the dominant security framework based on American nuclear guarantees. The potential appearance of a European deterrent force, using UK and French nuclear forces as a response to the likely consequences of SDI and other developments, was dismissed as unrealistic by one Soviet analyst who believed that Western Europe would still need to rely on

American nuclear weapons. This observer saw Western Europe focusing its efforts on the Nuclear Planning Group (NPG) within NATO as the best means of influencing the United States.[16]

Soviet Perceptions of West European Military Institutions, 1985-1987

The major Western institutions perceived by Soviet observers to be capable of achieving West European military integration were the Western European Union (WEU), NATO's Eurogroup, the European Economic Community (EEC), and the Independent European Program Group (IEPG).[17]

Western European Union

In late 1986 *Izvestiya*'s Paris correspondent had noted growing support for the WEU out of concern for the consequences of the Reykjavik summit and the potential INF agreement. Use of the "Soviet military threat 'myth'" to Western Europe formed a crucial element for WEU support.[18] Vladimirov described the 1984 WEU restructuring initiated by France and West Germany as follows: "Both countries came to the conclusion that the WEU was the single West European organization having the right... to consider military-political questions, and Franco-West German cooperation [was] the basic condition for the rebirth of the WEU and its transformation into an effective European buttress of NATO."[19] After pointing to several WEU declarations in which the WEU's fealty to NATO was loudly declared, Vladimirov concluded that the recent changes had been mostly structural rather than effecting "real activity," and that the enthusiasm in Western Europe for the WEU had dissipated due to United States' dissatisfaction with this non-NATO grouping.[20] G. Kolosov considered the WEU an unlikely venue for further West European integration, despite French preference for this institutionally, without major structural changes in the Western Alliance.[21]

NATO's Eurogroup

In early 1987, Kolosov believed that NATO's Eurogroup had received the most attention from West European integrationists. He judged the situation as being the most optimal balance between Europeanism and Atlanticism.[22] Somewhat atypical for Soviet observers discussing West European military integration, Vladimirov did not cover NATO's Eurogroup in his autumn 1987 review.

European Economic Community

The potential for growing militarization of the European Economic Community also provoked Soviet criticism. In the 1980s, Kolosov criticized efforts by France and West Germany to promote military integration through the EEC and the acceptance of the body of their project for political cooperation in Milan in December 1985.[23] *Pravda*'s Paris correspondent, Vladimir Bolshakov, wrote in March 1987 of French efforts to arrange a common position through the EEC Commission on Soviet medium-range missile proposals. Bolshakov interpreted this move as an effort to change the nature of the EEC.[24] Vladimirov also briefly reviewed the potential for integrationists to use the European Community as a basis for future military integration.[25]

Independent European Program Group

This group, which is nominally independent, but in Soviet eyes serves NATO's interests, seeks to coordinate the production of arms by West European countries, including France. A Soviet review of the June 1987 meeting in Seville of this body noted a "dangerous tendency... gaining strength in the bloc through certain circles concerned with the perspective liquidation from Europe of medium-range nuclear missiles to engage in revanchism," through increased military integration and joint arms production.[26] Vladimirov pointed to the Independent European Program Group as a likely object of integrationist interest because of difficulties with reviving the WEU.[27]

Synopsis

One can see that Soviet analysts had focused on various institutions at various times to determine the most likely venue for future military integration in Western Europe. In each case, however, the conflicts and obstacles appeared greater than the actual integration achieved. Moreover, they wrote little of future development. Kolosov offered no definite conclusions to be drawn from the institutions he described, and he spoke weakly of the harm of West European military integration to European security. In a September 1987 article, Col. I. Vladimirov also considered Western integration but he, too, came to no firm conclusions as to which direction, specifically, European integration would take. In this, his assessment differed little from his analysis five years earlier of the same subject.[28] In the earlier article, Vladimirov discussed the WEU, NATO's Eurogroup, the Independent European Program Group and the EEC, but saw none as wholly successful in achieving military-political integration. He suggested a greater role for NATO's Eurogroup in the future and argued that the Eurogroup had been "transformed into a far-flung mechanism for coordination of the efforts of the member countries in military, military-economic, and military-political spheres."[29] In his 1987 article, Vladimirov did not even discuss the Eurogroup. While Vladimirov had dismissed the WEU in 1982 as a paper tiger, he had offered up the EEC as a likely military-political integrator for the future: "For the long range, the goal has been set to transform the EEC into a military political bloc--the European Union."[30] In 1987, Vladimirov focused mostly on the WEU and only briefly touched upon proposals to create unified European forces through the European Community.

Soviet Perspectives on West European Military Institutions, 1987-1989

During 1987, as the Soviet Union and the United States moved toward a nuclear arms reduction agreement, Soviet analysis of West European military integration changed. Whereas earlier integration had proceeded in conjunction with and was propelled by U.S. militarism, now integration advanced due to the West European fear that American disengagement from Europe would leave Western Europe vulnerable to the Soviet military threat. As a consequence of the INF agreement and other indications of American disengagement from Europe, the Soviets had noted a rapid increase in the pace of integration through channels not directly under U.S. control, such as the NATO Eurogroup, the WEU, the EEC, and other non-institutional bilateral and multilateral military cooperation, especially that involving France and Germany.

In contrast to the capitalism-in-crisis framework inherited by the Gorbachev era, we find in the more recent writings a realistic acknowledgement of the distance covered towards creation of a unified Western

Europe. While Soviet analysts were quick to point out divisions in Western Europe, the heavy hand of ideology has been lightened. An analysis of Soviet historiography on West European integration, mostly economic, provided a theoretical construct for understanding integration and offered none of the cynicism of earlier reports.[31] In its first 'theses' since 1962 on the European Economic Community, the Institute of the World Economy and International Relations had made fourteen points dealing mostly with the structural and economic integration of Western Europe.[32] The key difference from earlier analyses on the EEC was in tone: West European integration was a reality and was proceeding ahead.[33] *MEMO* also published a detailed history of the Single European Act. Despite the many difficulties involved in its genesis, this measure to strengthen EEC integration was adopted in January 1986.[34]

A similarly new, but limited, respect had been accorded to the development of a politically integrated Western Europe. Professor Yurii Rubinskii examined the position of the Council of Ministers of the EEC, which he viewed as an independent entity on regional issues, such as the Middle East, South Africa, and Central America. On the key issue of East-West relations, however, Rubinskii noted that the political apparatus of the EEC has yet to make a clear stand. Despite this hesitation, Rubinskii expressed his preference for EEC foreign policy rather than the more "blocish" nature of NATO's Eurogroup and the WEU. He wrote that the EEC "has demonstrated... relatively broader and more balanced assessments of the situation in Europe and the world."[35] Yu. Borko hailed Soviet initiatives which included "acknowledgement of the EC not only as an economic union, but also as an independent (samostoyatel'naya) political entity in the international arena."[36] V. Kremenyuk praised a book by V. Baranovskii on the European Community for its frank recognition of the reality of European integration.[37] V. Stupishin was less convinced of West European political integration. He characterized a future United States of Europe as "a voluntary alliance of nations yielding only specific parameters of their sovereignty in favor of supranational institutions, and every nation remaining the complete master of its own house."[38]

Concerning military integration, the defining event in this period was the signing of the INF accord in December 1987. For the previous year, the Soviet media had noted the efforts of the Europeans to adopt a unified stance on the missile talks and influence their progress. Now that the deed was done, it fell upon Europe to react. In Soviet eyes,

Europeans did so by speeding up their integrationist efforts on all fronts. Whereas earlier integrationist efforts had originated, according to Soviet observers, from Washington, now they emanated from the Europeans themselves.

For the taxonomy of historical change, the INF accord served as the precipitating cause, but there were long-term influences as well. Among Soviet analyses in this period, Baranovskii's monograph on West European military integration provided the most comprehensive assessment of these basic pressures. He wrote of the cardinal role played by East-West relations and the decline of Atlanticist sentiment on both sides of the ocean. In addition, the individual European nations were shown to have their own interests leading them toward integration, or in the case of Britain, to a very guarded position.[39]

West European military integration continued to be analyzed mostly through its institutional manifestations: the WEU, the NATO Eurogroup, the Independent European Program Group, and the EEC, often in that order. Soviet analysts also discussed non-institutional bilateral and multilateral cooperation.

The WEU

In the new context of West European military integration, those institutions with greater distance from the U.S. were depicted by the Soviets as increasingly active. Writing in early 1987, G. Kolosov had pointed to the Eurogroup within NATO as the most prominent institutional manifestation of West European military cooperation, but by early 1989, more attention had been focused on the entircly independent Western European Union.[40] The Soviets do not like this organization, and they have repeatedly criticized its reanimation.[41] Among the pressures contributing to its greater dynamism were U.S. pressure over burdensharing, U.S. threats to reduce the American presence in Europe, and a growing European consciousness of itself. In October 1987, the WEU approved a document, "Platform of Principles of European Security," which was drafted by the French and which foresaw a truly unified Europe that both the Soviet Union and the United States could not ignore. A Soviet analyst wrote that by promoting this charter, France sought to transform the WEU into a military-political organization independent of NATO.[42]

Baranovskii discussed two important factors, absent in earlier decades, which had made the WEU acceptable in the mid-1980s. The first was that France was trusted not to rend completely the Western Alliance; the second was that West Germany had matured into a sovereign, restrained nation and an equal partner within the Alliance.[43] The WEU also offered, according to Baranovskii, several specific advantages as a venue for integration: it was created to promote West European military cooperation, it included France, it did not harbor neutral or only marginally Western nations in its ranks (unlike the EEC with Ireland and Turkey), and it had the legal basis and institutional structure for greater military political cooperation. Still, despite these advantages and the upgrading of the WEU apparatus in 1984, Baranovskii was not fully convinced that the WEU would develop into the leading element of West European military integration.[44]

Eurogroup

Integration had also been seen proceeding through NATO's Eurogroup, which was considered increasingly active as part of the NATO effort to compensate for the losses of weapon systems due to the INF accord.[45] Baranovskii discounted the Eurogroup, however, as a powerful integrating force. He wrote that the Eurogroup concern not to upset Washington had precluded any chance for it to become a counterweight to NATO.[46]

A different analysis of the Eurogroup casted it in the light of U.S.-West European conflict over burdensharing. Reporting on the Eurogroup's meeting in December 1988, Yu. Kharlanov cited comments in Belgian papers that "for the Eurogroup, the main opponent now is not the USSR, but the American Congress."[47]

Even beyond the Eurogroup, NATO had been seen promoting closer cooperation of its European members. This was the conclusion of a report in *Krasnaya zvezda* on the June 1988 NATO meeting. *Krasnaya zvezda*'s writer reviewed support in the Western bloc for greater military cooperation and the proposals to form a "European division on the same principles" as the Franco-German brigade, "to create a European arms market," and to avoid costly repetition in arms development and deployment.[48]

EEC

Baranovskii chronicled the activity by the EEC, particularly the Europarliament, in political affairs. He concluded, however, that the European Community was not in a position to promote military integration on a practical level.[49] At most, it had facilitated foreign policy coordination and cooperation by EC members on major international issues, such as the medium-range missile negotiations and regional conflicts.[50] From other quarters, *Krasnaya Zvezda* critically received the Europarliament's growing interest in West European military integration. It reported appeals in March 1989 by the Europarliament to the European Economic Community "to devote themselves completely to questions of defense and the appeals to the Western European Union to create a 'European support for NATO'." The Soviet correspondent understood this to mean development "within the framework of the EEC and WEU of a joint military policy, forced military integration, the creation of a 'common market for arms,' and so forth."[51] He rejected this development for clashing with the "improvement of the situation in Europe that is currently in progress."

IEPG

Of the other institutions of West European military integration, the Independent European Program Group also continued to receive attention. A project of the group to create a single West European arms market was adopted by the relevant defense ministers in 1987.[52]

Eureka Project

Among the non-institutional bases for West European military integration, the Eureka project has been the most visible in the Soviet media. The potential for further military integration around the Eureka project has divided Soviet analysts, but in this period it was generally dismissed. *ZVO*'s description of Eureka in early 1988 and mid-1989 did not emphasize its military potential.[53] An IMEMO roundtable discussion on Eureka, held in early 1988, advanced a variety of views.[54] V. Presnyakov believed the Eureka project would inevitably involve military projects. In contrast, G. Kolosov and A. Chervyakov argued that Eureka was primarily a civilian project with insignificant military applications.

Writing in *SShA* six months later, V. Natalov gave little consideration to Eureka's military potential. He argued that Eureka had originally arisen out of the scientific-technological challenge to the West Europeans made by the United States through SDI. In the project's early stages, the potential had existed for it to develop along at least partially military lines. However, as it became clear that Eureka was not going to compete directly with SDI, the former project had become more and more focused on civilian projects aimed at overcoming Europe's technological backwardness from the US and Japan. "Changes in the approach to the Eureka program, as a result of which it ceased to be seen as an alternative to participation by the West Europeans in SDI research and to a greater degree its nonmilitary direction began to be traced through (proslezhivat'sya), which facilitated the vital acceleration of the process of creating a European technological community."[55]

European Arms Industrial Integration

Integration of the European arms industry was also depicted in Soviet publications as having matured. In a collection of essays on NATO arms production, the ideological emphasis was on the U.S.-led framework, but much of the information presented indicated the opposite: the coming of age of a coordinated and integrated European arms industry. France and the UK produced up to 90% of their armaments, either by themselves or in cooperative ventures; West Germany maintained a level of 80%.[56] The book also argued that while it was too early to speak of a transatlantic integration of arms production, one could certainly identify West European integration.[57] Among the most prominent examples was the announcement by West Germany, Britain and Italy to develop jointly and produce the next generation fighter.[58] France, West Germany, Italy and the Netherlands planned to produce a military helicopter for the 1990s;[59] France, Britain and West Germany had agreed to develop a tactical military transport aircraft.[60]

Soviet General Perspectives on Europeanization, 1987-1989

While the Soviet media paid increased attention to multilateral structures of military integration such as the WEU, they also focused on the expanding direct, bilateral and multilateral cooperation of the leading West European military powers. Preeminent in Soviet eyes was the ever quickening Franco-West German military integration, but this did not exclude the also expanding Franco-Anglo and Anglo-German cooperation, and discussion of a triangle of security based on the participation of all three. These themes will be addressed in the following sections of this chapter dealing with French, British and West German security policy toward integration.

The concomitant of Soviet analysis of European military integration and growing European independence in security matters was the disengagement of the U.S. from comprehensive management of European security. While earlier reporting discussed conflicts within a basically U.S.-led alliance, the new coverage reversed these terms and depicted a broad alliance in which the U.S. and Western Europe evolved in different directions. To the extent that this analysis highlights the differences between the U.S. and Western Europe, it continued in the vein of 'capitalism in crisis,' but the consensus of militarism and hostility toward the socialist world that previously overcame Western divisions had disappeared.

In the autumn of 1988, A. Utkin discussed the arguments put forward by Americans that Europe was no longer the economic center of the world, was no longer subject to Soviet attack, and should be able to pay more for its own defense. Utkin reviewed the pressure that SDI, the INF agreement and mounting calls to bring the troops home from Europe had on Atlanticism. For the future, Utkin foresaw Atlanticism continuing to fall into "siege" (*osada*).[61] A *Krasnaya zvezda* correspondent argued that "in Washington they can hardly have complete confidence in the desire of the European allies, on the basis of economic, political, and military integration, to acquire 'additional weight' in international affairs, including in relations with the United States."[62] One manifestation of the growing distance between Europe and the United States was the Soviet media presentation of a NATO fraught with internal division. Soviet coverage of the March 1988 summit in Brussels used this well-worn analytical framework of a divided NATO.[63]

Although there was a strong degree of disengagement of the U.S. from Western Europe explicit in Soviet coverage on integration, in some areas U.S. influence in Western Europe was stressed. Despite the increase in activity in exclusively European institutions of integration, NATO remained for Soviet observers the preeminent institution of West European military integration. "Within this alliance," Baranovskii wrote, "the mutual action in the military, political sphere of Western European nations has achieved a much greater scale than in any other institutional structure."[64] In the nuts and bolts of integration, NATO presented an integrated command structure from the level of "army groups" upwards. Baranovskii considered NATO's air forces and anti-aircraft forces the most integrated, but wrote of the "highly uneven development of military-political integration in the bloc."[65] If NATO provided the most integration and yet it descended only to the level of army groups, it must be recognized that the other institutions of integration rarely involved anyone lower than the Defense Minister and General Staff officers.[66] Departing from this pattern of high level but ineffectual integration, the creation of a joint Franco-German brigade indicated a break from the basic paradigm of West European integration.

In other areas as well, the U.S. factor retained prominence. A speaker at an IMEMO roundtable in early 1988 on West European participation in SDI and Eureka argued that the Pentagon sought to use SDI to buttress Atlantic solidarity and benefit from West European technology. Consequently, the West Europeans were seen as seeking to enhance their position in the bloc and to feed from the Pentagon trough.[67] *ZVO* reviewed West European participation in SDI from the perspective of technology and economic development. In both cases, Western Europe was shown to be at the giving rather than the receiving end.[68] In a different context, some Europeans, particularly the more Atlanticist oriented British and West Germans, were depicted as desiring closer ties with the United States.

In a review of British-German collaboration, E. Tsedilina summarized the arguments of the Western authors calling for better trans-Atlantic relations to improve European security. While the U.S. had raised some hackles by its plans for nuclear war in Europe, the British and German authors were shown to be interested in the U.S. nuclear guarantee based on MAD deterrence.[69] Baranovskii himself concluded that West European cooperation fits the "Atlantic system of coordinates."[70]

The shift in European affairs stemming from the INF accord, the preparation for conventional weapons negotiations and the move to military integration in Western Europe had spawned several interesting general analyses of Western European development.

One of the most provocative appeared in early 1988.[71] It was written by three young diplomats and is striking for its criticism of past Soviet policy and suggestion of alternatives for future Soviet action. Considering the consequences of the INF agreement for Western Europe, the diplomats wrote that the Soviet Union expected NATO's doctrine of flexible response to be abandoned for the lack of one rung on the escalation ladder. This assumption ignored, however, the presence of "Eurostrategic" weapons in France's arsenal and the prospective upgrading of overall French and British nuclear capabilities, which have been exempt from U.S.-Soviet negotiations. Moreover, they argued, this assumption was typical of a Soviet foreign policy that tended to look over Europe in order to achieve a dialogue with the United States. The Soviet Union, the diplomats charged, had failed to notice the rising power and strategic implications of an increasingly strong and united Western Europe. As U.S. and Soviet arsenals declined, the Soviet Union could no longer afford to ignore the West Europeans whose forces were shifting from being last resort protection of national territory to "an actively functioning factor in European and global strategy."[72] The article proceeded to list the many developments in the military integration of Western Europe, which, they wrote, had accelerated after Reykjavik. The diplomats further charged that the integration process was proceeding with popular support and that the Soviet Union could not expect it to cease with the election of an opposition party in any European capital.[73] The article specifically criticized Soviet analyses which emphasized only the divisions and difficulties in Western Europe. Despite these reports, they continued, 1992 and its consequences were coming. The diplomats also argued that further indifference to Western Europe played into the hands of continuing American leadership of Western Europe.

Another interesting analysis appeared in *SShA* in the summer of 1988. Yu. Davydov argued that the signing of the INF accord represented the culmination of a series of events from which the Europeans realized they could no longer trust the strategic American guarantee of European security. According to Davydov, SDI, the Reykjavik promises, and the INF accord "taken together, convinced the West European allies that the American leadership occupies a rather contradictory position on nuclear deterrence on which they [the Europeans] had constructed their entire security."[74] This doubt, in combination with economic friction and the Soviet arms initiatives, had led European leaders to reassess the situation. Davydov identifies three possible outcomes: 1) continued conservative loyalty to the United States based on the U.S. nuclear guarantee; 2) military integration of Western Europe based on the "myth" of the Soviet threat; or, 3) a new conceptualization of European security based on Soviet proposals. Davydov believed that the decision had not yet been made, but he directly linked the future direction of Europe to the course of Soviet-American relations. "If the current warming of Soviet-American relations does not move into a new, stronger and broader phase of detente," he wrote, "then most likely the military integration of Western Europe will begin to develop." If a new, stable climate was achieved, however, "the process of military integration might not develop or it could progress along the path of creating some sort of unified military system, built on the basis of non-offensive defense principles agreed to by East and West."[75]

Baranovskii's analysis of Western integration also foresees several outcomes. In the first, NATO relations remain basically as they are now. In the second, an integrated and independent West European bloc enters the stage. The third option entails further Europeanization of NATO. Baranovskii criticizes all three for continuing in the model of East-West conflict, and he calls for new political methods of achieving mutual security.[76]

The French Approach to Europeanization

Of all the West European powers, France was regularly and consistently identified as the main promoter and most frequent initiator of military integration in Western Europe. The emphasis over the years under Soviet review reflected contemporary influences, but the basic premise that France sought to promote and lead an integrated Western Europe remained.[77] Rarely do Soviet analyses of any substance fail to note, if only in passing, France's leading role in West European military integration.

While France was clearly identified as seeking to lead a Western Europe less dependent on the United States, a certain degree of schizophrenia characterized Soviet reporting through 1987. This followed the general pattern of agreement and conflict identified for the Western alliance as a whole in the first part of this chapter. On the one hand, France's *de facto* participation in NATO's military bloc, with all the Atlanticist connotations that such membership brings, was continually emphasized by Soviet analysts. The monthly journal *ZVO* was particularly strident on this matter. On the other hand, France's Gaullist heritage and insistence on strategic autonomy were also indicated, as were France's recurring conflicts with the United States over a variety of strategic issues. As the INF talks proceeded in 1987, France's historical role in Europe and current disagreements with the U.S. adumbrated the basis for a more narrow West European integration.

France's direct, military participation in NATO was indicated through examination of NATO exercises and strategy in which France played a role. Writing in late 1985, Col. G. Petrukhin noted close French cooperation with joint NATO forces during European TVD exercises. Petrukhin cited a French commander on the need to conduct more joint operations with the Bundeswehr that would "ensure the necessary merging of French forces into NATO operations in the event of a crisis."[78] In a discussion of NATO's strategic Atlantic command, the Soviet observer noted that the Atlantic command "considers France among joint naval groups in appropriate areas, particularly in the Eastern Atlantic," including possible deployment of French nuclear submarines.[79] The French participation in joint NATO air and sea exercises was noted during 1985 and 1986.[80] A review of NATO's airborne and air assault forces had presumed French participation.[81] A *ZVO* article late in 1986 on the French Air Force quoted both Mitterrand and Foreign Minister Claude Cheysson on French devotion to NATO. Cheysson said, "France will always remain a faithful NATO ally and no one may doubt this." In practical terms, the article continued, this meant "improvement and support of an operational NATO unified air defense system in Europe," NATO exercises in French airspace, and joint arms production.[82] A general description of France's military structure and forces in *ZVO* began with remarks placing France firmly in the NATO fold; French forces are considered a "basic NATO reserve force."[83] A review in early 1987 of France's Rapid Deployment Force noted that "France's non-participation in the military organization of the alliance is purely formal in nature," and that one of the RDF's main missions was to join combined forces in the Central European region, either as part of the French First Army or independently. The author also suggested that logistical difficulties for such a deployment had led the French to consider using the NATO rear supply network for their RDF.[84] A *ZVO* review of NATO military budgets in 1988 included discussion of French expenditures.[85]

While coverage of France in the Soviet military press left no doubt as to France's alignment within NATO, the academic observers painted a less certain picture. Writing in *SShA* in early 1986, V. Mikheev chronicled French agreement with the U.S. in military affairs and growing

French military capability in the first half of the article, and then proceeded to enumerate U.S.-French disagreements and Franco-Soviet cooperation. For the first argument, Mikheev pointed to the French turn in 1983 and 1984 toward a more U.S.-oriented foreign policy, including support for placement of U.S. medium-range missiles in Europe, nuclear and strategic coordination with the U.S., and the modernization of French nuclear forces. He also noted that French equipment and material operated on standards and measures common to NATO. Franco-West German cooperation was interpreted as meeting U.S. burdensharing demands and serving to control the growth of neutralism in the FRG. The inclusion of West Germany under the umbrella of French nuclear deterrence shadow was also noted as a possibility for the future. Mikheev claimed that French energy pouring into the WEU amounted to France militarily joining NATO through West European military integration. With France's inclusion in NATO achieved, Mikheev could have then proceeded to list French disagreements with the United States. These included France's *de jure* non-NATO status, SDI and France's own efforts to respond with a European technology consortium, regional conflicts, and tension over the reanimation of Soviet-French relations. Mikheev noted Mitterrand's refusal to attend Reagan's special conference of the Big Seven on the eve of the Soviet-American summit in 1985 because it would have appeared to subordinate France to the U.S. in the management of East-West relations.[86]

Perhaps the most prominent element of French integrationist efforts involved the intense cultivation of relations with West Germany. The importance of this relationship from the Soviet perspective was evident in the acute awareness Soviet observers had concerning further signs of Franco-German integration. Baranovskii devoted an entire section of his book to this relationship.[87] He asserted that Franco-German cooperation played an absolutely vital role in West European military cooperation, and he drew the outline of this cooperation in the post-war period. Despite several treaties and agreements, actual Franco-German cooperation remained low for many years due to West Germany's relations with the U.S. and substantive disagreements between the two nations. The 1980s had brought a new phase of greater meaningful Franco-German cooperation and the overcoming of past obstacles. This cooperation was now considered "compatible with West German participation in NATO's military organization and the independent status of French military forces."[88] Among the many other areas of cooperation, Baranovskii mentioned the intention to use France's Rapid Deployment Force as a quick reserve to be moved to West Germany's eastern borders during wartime.

TASS reported on Franco-West German consultations in May 1986 at which time Foreign Minister H. D. Genscher was quoted as saying, "France and the FRG have expressed the intention to put forward constructive proposals on disarmament and arms control at the forthcoming NATO council session."[89] Among other forms of cooperation in this period, joint arms production was mentioned, including Franco-German development of the new combat helicopter.[90] France's leader in the 1980s, Francois Mitterrand, was seen as a keen advocate of West European integration at all levels. A Soviet book review of Mitterrand's speeches noted his support for integration on all levels, and his dissatisfaction with a purely national approach to many scientific projects in Europe. Mitterrand was reported to have sought a new EEC treaty that would create a "political Europe," and he was shown advocating greater Franco-West German cooperation by breathing life into the 1963 Elysée Treaty between France and West Germany.[91] Baranovskii suggested that France sought to control West Germany's growth in power through a process that binds the two nations together.[92]

Franco-German cooperation in the form of joint maneuvers in the autumn of 1987 also resulted in Soviet criticism. *Krasnaya zvezda* reviewed the exercises, named *Kekker Spatz*, held on German soil in September, and noted that they reflected the joint statement by Kohl and Mitterrand, as reported in *Le Monde*, that "Relations between the two countries in the military field will henceforth be of the same nature as those between Bonn and Washington."[93]

Of particular interest to Soviet analysts was the ongoing discussion in the West of protecting West Germany with French nuclear forces. Few Soviet reports in recent years failed to note the possibility of such a move and to express their concern. In April 1987, Yu. Zhukov cited an editorial in *Le Figaro* calling for a Franco-West German bomb and a France-Germany-Britain axis that could be a "powerful link of the free world instead of being its 'soft underbelly' (*podbryush'e*)." He also noted statements in *L'Express* on the need to deploy French nuclear missiles in the FRG and accelerate the unification of French armed forces and the West German Bundeswehr even to the point of creating "mixed units." *Le Quotidien de Paris* was cited as well: "'it is necessary to strengthen the Franco-West German column of defense on the Elbe by advancing French missiles onto FRG territory."[94] *ZVO* also noted discussion in the West of extending the French nuclear umbrella over West Germany. Many Soviet reports have been critical of Western discussions to place neutron weapons under joint Franco-German control.

In September 1987, Mitterrand again visited Germany and spoke in favor of a "united Western Europe," including in security policy. Mitterrand appeared to back off covering West Germany with France's deterrence shadow. *Pravda* reported Mitterrand's statement that "France's nuclear potential serves the exclusive purpose of deterring a potential aggressor.... But France cannot defend the FRG. Only NATO, of which France is a member, can make war in Europe."[95] French insistence on maintaining absolute autonomy in regard to using nuclear weapons limits, for Baranovskii, the likelihood of further Franco-German nuclear integration.[96]

The French effort to promote military integration at all levels in Western Europe reached new levels during 1987. In the words of a *ZVO* commentator, "The year 1987 was marked in France by intensive efforts to build a definite 'European defense' based on the strengthening of military ties between France and West Germany, France and Spain."[97] Writing in the spring of 1987, G. Kolosov viewed the French as the most active integrationists, and he suggested that this activity stemmed from France's relative autonomy from NATO. France's efforts in 1987 to have the WEU adopt its proposed 'Charter of West European Security' were roundly criticized by Soviet observers for its conceptualization of European security in terms of a French-led, nuclear-armed, militarily integrated Western Europe. In October 1987, the WEU adopted the proposal in slightly modified form as the 'Platform Principles of European Security.'[98] In regard to arms production, A. Sergeev wrote in 1987 that in its cooperative arms development and manufacture ventures, Paris "seeks to use the specifics of its own military position to strengthen its leading role in Western Europe."[99]

Part of this flurry of Soviet coverage of French integrationist activity reflected France's concern for the potential consequences of an INF accord. As early as November 1986, Prime Minister Margaret Thatcher travelled to Paris for one day of consultations. The Soviet report on the visit noted both countries "concern" (*ozabochennost'*) about an INF accord that posed a threat to Western Europe because of the East bloc's conventional arms superiority. The French newspaper *Le Figaro* was quoted in regard to the impossibility of a full liquidation of nuclear arms in Europe and also wrote that future Reykjaviks must be avoided. The dispatch also noted Mitterrand's comment that France and Great Britain were very close to each other in strategic and military affairs.[100] In March 1987, Prime Minister Jacques Chirac travelled to the U.S., and, according to a Soviet report, rather than assist in the speedy conclusion of a medium-range missile agreement, he informed Washington that he "was distressed lest the security interests of the United States' European NATO partners might suffer with the elimination of the medium-range missiles."[101]

Foreseeing their security threatened by the consequences of a medium-range missile accord, some Europeans had begun to speak in early 1987 of creating a 'European nuclear bomb.' While Baranovskii considered a successful integration of French and British nuclear forces highly unlikely due to issues of sovereignty, other commentators took the proposals seriously enough to criticize them strenuously.[102] TASS charged that "Europe's chance to survive does not lie in the projects for a 'European nuclear bomb' or a British-French nuclear system."[103] In an article in *New Times*, Aleksandr Lebedev rejected the main argument in favor of a European bomb, namely that the Warsaw Pact enjoys an advantage in conventional weapons. He then went on to argue that European security would have been furthered by reducing French and British nuclear weapons, and that the "only sensible way is to lead things to their reduction and elimination."[104] In May 1987, the Soviet press noted French and West German efforts to reach a unified position in regard to Soviet proposals to eliminate medium-range missiles in Europe. Soviet accounts differed slightly in determining the results of these efforts.[105] Two weeks later, at the end of May, another round of Franco-German meetings was held with the same goal of achieving a unified position on the INF proposals. This effort appeared to fail due to internal differences of opinion in both countries, however, the leaders were depicted as "insisting on the necessity of developing a unified position of all the NATO member states to the Soviet initiatives."[106] In these consultations, Mitterrand was quoted to the effect that the French position on the proposals depended on the West German stance. One sticking point was the question of Germany's Pershing-1s. Another issue was the division between Mitterrand and Chirac over retaining American nuclear missiles in Europe.[107]

A Soviet report on the proposal by two former French defense ministers, C. Hernu and P. Messmer, that French neutron weapons be held under joint Franco-German control linked the project to individuals who sought to overcome the consequences of the elimination of American nuclear missiles.[108] In February 1988, *Pravda*'s Paris correspondent cited a Western journalist's conclusion that the revitalization of the Elysée treaty between France and West Germany was "undoubtedly affected by the Soviet-U.S. summit and the resulting [INF] treaty."[109]

The twenty-fifth anniversary celebration in February 1988 of the Elysée Treaty of Cooperation between France and the FRG provided the next opportunity to analyze French integrationist activities. In a long dispatch from Paris, *Pravda*'s correspondent, V. Bolshakov, reviewed the hopes of a unified Europe which had existed at the time of the treaty's signing.[110] He also noted more recent integrationist efforts, including the signing in January 1988 of a protocol on the creation of a Franco-West German Defense and Security Council and the decision to create a joint Franco-German military brigade commanded by French and German officers. Bolshakov turned next to the prospect of a French nuclear umbrella for West Germany. While then-Prime Minister Chirac had been quoted as favoring such an idea, Mitterrand was cited as firmly opposed. Bolshakov left this question open. He also raised the issue of France's role in the disarmament process. While in theory supportive of the INF accord, France, according to Bolshakov, continued to expand its nuclear potential. France also sought the cooperation of Britain in fulfilling the nuclear tasks being abdicated by the United States through the INF Treaty. This desire explained, according to Bolshakov, the Anglo-French consultations completed in December 1987 aimed at joint development of air-launched nuclear cruise missiles. These meetings also included discussion of Anglo-French military cooperation in regard to defense and wartime use of the Channel tunnel, strategic planning and joint submarine patrols.[111] Bolshakov concluded with reference to a Western journalist's commentary that "'the discussions within the framework of the Paris-Bonn-London triangle boil down to building a West European defense community which will remain bonded to the United States'." From this, Bolshakov viewed London and Bonn as placing pressure on France to rejoin NATO's military command.

By early 1988, France's reaction to the INF accords and to Gorbachev's propaganda offensive in Europe were clear enough to Soviet observers: France sought to lead a reinvigorated and hostile, militarily integrated West European community. A Soviet report on Mitterrand's plans to appear for the first time at a NATO summit, to be held in early

March 1988, interpreted this gesture as an indication of France's intention to increase military cooperation with NATO nations, although Mitterrand had absolutely excluded the possibility of a formal return to the NATO bloc military organization.[112] Whether within a hostile NATO or heading a more independent West European bloc, France's activity to promote integration were coolly received.

Several substantial denunciations appeared in the spring of 1988 and left no doubt how Moscow interpreted France's strategy. In a bitter critique of France, three officials from the European department of the Foreign Ministry focused on France's nuclear strategy.[113] They condemned French refusal to move toward a nuclear free Europe, French intransigence in regard to starting tactical nuclear weapons negotiations, and above all France's adherence to deterrence. They charged that the new political thinking had rendered deterrence obsolete and dangerous. Even within the framework of deterrence, France was unwilling, they argued, to move towards reductions in nuclear forces. France's bid to remain a world power had left it isolated after the superpower turn towards nuclear force reductions. They also argued that France's stance on SDI was hypocritical. While France has not participated directly in the project, French companies and the French government had been involved in military research in space. They chided the French claim to independence by pointing out France's desire for the American presence in Europe to remain and France's efforts to return to NATO. They berated France for its growing military cooperation with West Germany and for discussion of replacing U.S. missiles lost to the INF accord, including the possible full compensation by French and UK nuclear forces for those removed by the INF and any potential accord between the U.S. and USSR on strategic weapons. The authors further criticized the French military program for 1987-1991.

This document was examined in the spring of 1988 by A. Chervyakov who viewed its early adoption as a means by which the conservative majority in Parliament ceeded to themselves more foreign policy authority. Chervyakov reviewed France's program for militarization of space and the expenditures on increasing its nuclear capability. Then-Prime Minister Chirac was cited on the three goals of French military policy: 1) maintenance of France's position in the world as established by de Gaulle; 2) determination to modernize its forces; and, 3) to have a wide and public consensus behind French military policy.[114] While Chervyakov was not as stridently critical as Soviet Foreign Ministry officials, his emphasis on France's efforts in space and continuing reliance on deterrence clearly suggest the Soviet Union's dissatisfaction with French policy.

A further rebuke to France came in the spring of 1988 from yet another Foreign Ministry official--the Principal Advisor of the Evaluation and Planning Directorate of the USSR Ministry of Foreign Affairs.[115] V. Stupishin's article was essentially a rebuttal to charges made earlier that year in a published piece by three young diplomats.[116] Stupishin managed, however, to criticize the French for being behind the push to integrate Western Europe along military lines. He had spoken of Franco-centrism in Europe, French military cooperation with other nations, the "reanimation of the WEU," and French machinations involving the Independent European Program Group. Stupishin criticized these activities as likely to lead to a new era of military bloc division in Europe. Yu. Davydov also identified the French in 1988 as the main promoter of military integration. Davydov posited the French motive as seeking to retain a leading role in a united Europe against the challenges of an economically stronger West Germany.[117] An article appearing one year later on the Western European Union was highly critical of French activities in regard to the WEU. Writing of the likely future development of the WEU, G. Burduli saw France trying to turn it into a military-political organization independent of NATO, and he referred to an appeal in *Republique* by a Colonel B. calling for a new, non-NATO, security structure in Europe and NATO's rejecting outdated flexible response strategy.[118]

In the first years of the Gorbachev era, France occupied an ambiguous position in Soviet analysis. Perhaps this ambiguity made it the most likely candidate for Soviet efforts to reach out to Western Europe after Gorbachev came to power. Every article on Franco-Soviet relations during the 1985 to late 1987 period noted that Gorbachev's choice for his first visit to the West as General Secretary, in October 1985, was France. These same articles painted a Franco-Soviet rapprochement as absolutely vital to any broader improvement in European relations.

Immediately after Gorbachev's visit to France, the Soviet specialized and general media hailed a "shift," "turning point," "new page," etc. in European history. As part of this shift, Soviet analysts sought to depict the Soviet Union as paying greater attention to the West Europeans. A. Vtorov wrote that "The Soviet Union is not at all inclined to viewing the entire set of East-West ties through the prism of Soviet-American relations.... The Soviet Union is in favor of a heightened role for Europe in world affairs."[119] It would appear, however, that the Soviet wager on France as the key to its European policy had been reneged by 1988.

This conclusion is based on Soviet analysis of French security policy in 1988 and 1989. The hostile analysis discussed above, and the Soviet media's coverage of Gorbachev's visits in the summer of 1989 suggest that Soviet energy has been directed towards West Germany, just as it had been towards France in 1985 and 1986.

The British Approach to Europeanization

Soviet writing in the 1987 to 1989 period on British policy toward military integration in Western Europe has been very slight. This follows from the Soviet presentation of Britain under Thatcher as a devoted friend of America prepared to place Britain's "special relationship" with the U.S. before relations with the European allies. England was depicted as a hesitant and dilatory integrationist, especially when matters concerned non-NATO institutions of integration.

Following the pattern of earlier analysis, the Soviet military press continued in the first years of Gorbachev's rule to depict Britain as militarily all but dependent on the United States, particularly in regard to nuclear arms and nuclear strategy, and solidly supportive of the American-led NATO framework. On the British "special relationship" to the United States, there was a continuous stream of commentary indicating Britain's fealty and military dependence.[120] Even where differences between the United States and Britain were indicated, the continuing Atlanticist framework was affirmed.

Britain's Atlanticist orientation was linked explicitly with British efforts to stem the nation's decline. In late 1986, V. Matveev wrote that Britain's financial and material resources could no longer support the extensive strategic ambitions and overseas commitments that it had inherited from an earlier age.[121] Matveev charged that Britain's strident anti-Soviet ideology and the "special relationship" with the U.S. were seen as having hurt Britain's relationship with the West European allies. In a conflicting analysis, a different Soviet analyst averred that it was Britain's Europeanism, such as it was, that sought to halt the British decline.[122] Both authors saw England's power ebbing, but disagreed as to whether it was Europeanism or Atlanticism that the British government hoped would slow this process.

Despite this disagreement, most reports indicated Thatcher's preference for the NATO framework where Britain's 'special relationship' with the United States had given Britain greater authority. For example, on the issue of burdensharing, Col. V. Markushin in *Krasnaya zvezda* wrote that, "as pretender for the role of Washington's right hand in Europe, London as a rule sharply criticizes those NATO countries which, as it sees the situation, do not 'contribute sufficiently to their common tasks'."[123] Another element of this orientation reflected British concern over finding the country subject to French or Franco-German leadership in Europe.[124]

To the extent that Britain was portrayed as militarily integrated in Western Europe, it was through wholehearted support of the NATO alliance. This was particularly so in the early period of the Gorbachev era. Analyses of Britain's military published in *ZVO* repeatedly indicated Britain's commitments to the North Atlantic Alliance.[125] In a report on Britain's submarine force, N. Nikolaev wrote that "English SSBNs are intended for transfer to NATO Allied Armed Forces in the event of war, and that the targets against which they deliver strikes are determined by a single strategic, target, operational fireplan generated by a U.S. Chiefs of Staff Committee."[126] British ground forces, particularly the British Army on the Rhine, have been similarly integrated into NATO,[127] as have British air forces.[128] Britain was seen as a rear supply and transit facility within NATO wartime strategy.[129] A report on NATO military spending noted that ninty-five percent of the funds allocated to the British Defense Ministry went to meet its NATO commitments.[130]

The depiction of Britain and its security policy from 1987 to 1989 changed less markedly than Soviet coverage of France, but there was a distinct shift when it became clear in 1987 that the United States and the Soviet Union would be signing a medium-range missile agreement. Britain's movement towards greater military cooperation with France and West Germany could then be noted. Thatcher was depicted as concerned with the promises made by Reagan at Reykjavik,[131] and she sought to place restrictive conditions on any potential medium-range missile.[132] After the signing of the INF accord in December 1987, a flurry of reports in the Soviet press chronicled British and French efforts to react to the treaty through discussion of nuclear cooperation, possible compensation for nuclear arms lost to the treaty, and joint arms production.[133] While the likelihood of extensive nuclear cooperation between Britain and France was rejected, lower level coordination had been identified by the Soviets.[134] The potential development of a "European bomb" was criticized in regard to Britain as well as to France. Both nations were called to task for insisting on retaining their nuclear deterrence potentials, and augmenting them, in a period of disarmament.

In a dispatch from Paris in February 1988 that focused on Franco-German military cooperation, *Pravda*'s correspondent argued that France and Germany sought to bring Britain into their non-NATO joint "defense structures" because they needed Britain's nuclear weapons in order to create a European defense system. *Pravda* also spoke of Anglo-French nuclear missile coordination and joint development of an air-launched nuclear cruise missile.[135]

At the NATO summit in March 1988, Thatcher was shown as a particularly vocal advocate of "compensation" and "modernization" of NATO's tactical nuclear weapons.[136] Thatcher's suspicion of Soviet motives in Western Europe was noted in Soviet coverage of the summit, where she was cited as warning against Soviet "attempts to wrest Europe from the United States."[137]

While Anglo-German cooperation was perhaps less prominent in Soviet eyes than the Franco-German and Franco-British relationship, a Soviet book review in early 1989 of a Western collaboration on the subject reveals some basic Soviet propensities. In the review, the German and British authors of the articles disagreed more often than they agreed on the future direction of Anglo-German cooperation. The reviewer, E. Tsedilina, reported that both London and Bonn were frightened by Reagan's promises of nuclear disarmament made at Reykjavik. These concerns prompted German interest to strengthen British and French nuclear capability and to include the FRG within their deterrence shadow. This possibility appeared to be rejected by Lawrence Freedman (UK) who doubted whether British nuclear weapons would protect German soil; he also questioned further Anglo-French nuclear integration and argued that the U.S. nuclear guarantee should retain priority. In addition, the two sides disagreed over the future of the British forces on the Rhine. J. Alford (UK) argued that the way to maintain the quality and readiness of those forces during times of financial and demographic pressure was to reduce their number. The authors also noted that while West European military integration had proceeded under the impetus of U.S.-West European divisions, the UK had occupied a more reserved position. New pressure for integration, stemming from the improvement of U.S.-Soviet relations, had made military integration, according to Tsedilina, palatable even to the Tories. The reviewer considered the greatest difficulties for the West Europeans to be institutionalizing integration. The two articles on this subject (by V. Weidenfeld (FRG) and T. Taylor (UK)) reviewed the existing institutions and did not exclude the creation of an entirely new structure for integration. The closing essay of the book, by editors Karl Kaiser and John Roper, argued for closer West European-U.S. relations, an activated WEU, closer Anglo-French nuclear cooperation and greater UK-FRG bilateral cooperation. The reviewer rejected these planks as indicating that London and Bonn still consider achieving security through military means, rather than political resolutions.[138]

One Soviet analyst, M. Strezhneva, appeared to swim upstream against the prevailing Soviet consensus of British hesitancy toward European integration. In her monograph on Britain's move toward Europe, she depicts a Britain being dragged kicking and screaming to a more integrated Western Europe.[139] Strezhneva discussed the qualified nature of this movement and the many setbacks it had experienced. At times, these qualifications seem to overwhelm her Europeanist argument. For instance, Strezhneva pointed to Thatcher's "unqualified surrender" in the Westland affair and Britain's reaction to the SDI and Eureka projects.[140] In this framework, England's support for the NATO Eurogroup and the Independent European Program Group were seen as efforts to strengthen Europe's voice within NATO. Strezhneva also admitted that Britain's activity in the 1980s in regard to the Western European Union was designed to thwart further Franco-West German military cooperation through the WEU. She argued that the WEU served as an arena for Anglo-French competition for future leadership of Europe. As for Britain's relationship to the EEC, Strezhneva wrote that Britain saw the EEC as an unlikely venue for military integration, and that this situation suited the UK, which prefers NATO and its own nuclear forces as the basis for British authority in Europe. Despite Strezhneva's statement that "there are real prerequisites for a qualitative rethinking by England in the future of its position in NATO and, as a consequence, for a more favorable relationship by London to plans for formulating a military-political alliance, including one on the basis of the European Community,"[141] Strezhneva's argument in the final analysis falls victim to her own facts. She tried to show a Britain moving toward Europe, but Britain's hesitancy in this area and its continued adherence to Atlanticism comes through equally strong.

The West German Role

Soviet media coverage of West German participation in the military integration of Western Europe was limited in the period before the signing of the INF accord in December 1987. Like Britain, West Germany's conservative government was seen as an active supporter of the U.S.-led NATO framework.[142] West Germany was also regularly accused of using its increasing strength within the NATO bloc to pursue "revanchist" aims.[143] To the extent that they were observed, the FRG's efforts within the Eurogroup, the Independent European Program Group and the WEU were mostly understood as designed to strengthen West Germany's position within the Alliance. Along these lines, G. Kirillov wrote in early 1986, "The FRG government invariably emphasizes that the building up of West European cooperation in the military realm in no way signified any departure from its alignment with the USA and serves first of all to strengthen the European base of NATO."[144]

From the Soviet perspective, the common denominator in German policy in this initial period was revanchism and East-West hostility. An assessment of the WEU suggested the West Germany's goal of military integration with France through the WEU was designed to give Germany access to nuclear weapons.[145] Speaking of Germany's military industrial complex, E. Kondrashova wrote, "West German rulers hope to become leaders in a West European military structure and to use the combined resources of the region's countries to achieve their own goals."[146] The depiction of Germany acting both within and without the Alliance was consistent with the Janus-like treatment of European behavior in the period up to the INF accord.

It was from this perspective that Soviet analysts had begun in early 1987 to report West German government dissatisfaction with the prospect after Reykjavik of U.S.-USSR missile reductions in Europe.[147] One element of the West German reaction involved determining a joint West European stance on the medium-range missile negotiations.[148] Soviet coverage of the failure of France and West Germany to reach a joint position in May 1987 left no doubt of how important such a joint stance was perceived by the West Germans and the French. *Izvestiya*'s report on the meeting noted the differences in opinion by the West German defense and foreign affairs minister on the INF issue.[149]

Growing West German interest during 1987 in greater military cooperation with France, particularly in regard to the creation of some sort of European deterrent, merited consistent hostile Soviet coverage.[150] *Krasnaya zvezda*'s review of joint French-West German military exercises in 1987 noted that Germany was no longer being treated as a forward defense area for French troops and that there was support in some circles for placing French nuclear weapons under joint Franco-German control.[151] TASS criticized the West German Defense Minister's justification of Franco-German military cooperation and creation of a joint brigade.[152] The potential for a West European nuclear deterrent using French and English nuclear weapons integrated with West German forces had come under heavy fire from V. Bolshakov in *Pravda* in February 1988.[153]

Starting in late 1988, Soviet analysis of West German security policy underwent a transformation. Prospects for tactical weapons negotiations and cuts in conventional forces had led to a softening of Soviet criticism of West Germany.[154] By the summer of 1989, the improvement in relations had reached striking proportions. Part of this shift entailed perceived German support for the Soviet "common European home" slogan.

Still, Soviet analysis of military integration involving West Germany had been slow to change. On the one hand, *MEMO* published a speech by the SPD chairman, Vogel, in which he argued that "the task of military political cooperation of the Western European nations was a guarantee of military stability with less military participation by the USA," and that "the process of West European unification can be compatible with the prospects of the general European process."[155] On the other hand, Soviet analysts remained critical even in the 1988-1989 period of comity of what they understood to be West German efforts to attain access to nuclear weapons through military integration.[156]

An Alternative to West European Military Integration

Soviet analysis of West European integration often has had little to say about the alternatives to this process. To the extent that integration was viewed by Soviet analysts as structurally predetermined, there was not much they could say. In the years since 1985, however, the Soviet side has found and articulated a message designed to reach out to West Europeans. The theme of the "common European home" posed interesting challenges to Soviet perceptions of Western military integration, as we shall see below.

In the period up to 1987, Soviet writings did little more than criticize the status quo--an overarching positive policy was not present. The theme of "Europe--Our Common Home," although articulated by 1985, had not yet fully infected Soviet analysis and polemics.[157] Instead there were vaguer pronouncements in which the Soviet Union sought to reach out to the West European publics and governments. In these accounts, Soviet analysts unconvincingly stressed the centrality of Western Europe in Soviet foreign policy,[158] and spoke of an opportunity for West European leaders to break out of a cycle of confrontation by building on the "European process" as defined by the Helsinki accords.[159] After the Twenty-Seventh Congress of the CPSU and Gorbachev's arms reduction proposals of 15 January 1986, the Soviets depicted Western Europe at a crossroad where it must consider which path to take--one based on blocs or one based on general European security.[160] One specific Soviet proposal already put forward by this time was the establishment of official relations between the EEC and Comecon or CMEA.[161]

Rushing to fill the perceived void in European security after the signing of the INF accord, the Soviet-promoted theme of a "common European home" was intensively reported and advanced in the Soviet media. Its contours have become more specific over time, and the effort to win over Western Europe's trust, especially that of the West German public, appeared to be working if the West accepts the Soviet media's account of Gorbachev's visits to Western Europe in the summer of 1989.

Historical justification of the unified "Europe" appeared in a Soviet book, *The European Idea in History*, which was reviewed favorably in *MEMO*.[162] The means of achieving this ideal of the common European home involves continued diligent progress through the "European process," expanded trade and exploration of other all-European integrationist avenues.[163] The goal of mutual recognition and establishment of official relations between the CMEA and EEC was finally achieved in the summer of 1988.[164] While analyzing the Eureka project, Soviet scholars promoted joining Eureka and EEC science projects, on the one hand, and the "Comprehensive Scientific-technical Progress Program" of Comecon, on the other.[165]

As for the possible military characteristics of a united Europe, A. Shaskol'skii mentioned a proposal put forward in a British book he was reviewing--the removal of U.S. and Soviet troops from other countries in their respective blocs, and a "Finlandization" of Eastern Europe and "Swedenization" of Western Europe.[166]

Discussing in more general terms the different paradigms for West European integration, Yu. Borko held out hope that the model active during the period of detente could reappear and that the potential for "democratic influence" on the future development of the EC still existed. Out of this Borko foresaw the potential for a "coordination (uvyazka) of the processes of West European integration and all-European cooperation."[167]

The task of reconciling oxymoron images of a "common European home" and a hostile, militarily integrated Western Europe had not been ignored by Soviet analysts. In fact, in the 1988-1989 period, a certain optimism in Soviet writings can be observed. The Soviets had achieved this by denying the inevitability of a hostile Western military bloc arising in Western Europe.

A guarded optimism was evinced by O. Bykov as early as 1988 in an article on the "new political thinking." While most of the commentary concerned U.S.-Soviet relations, Bykov also observed that "not so long ago were heard dark prophecies in regard to the inevitable opposition of 'Europe' to the Soviet Union and the United States in terms of the irreconciliablity of geopolitical interests, which should sharply manifest themselves in connection with the prospective agreements on two classes of nuclear missiles. There was also no shortage of soothsaying about the inevitable collapse of negotiations in light of Western Europe's negative relation to them." He went on to note that these fears were unfounded and that Europe had set a model of cooperation for further disarmament.[168]

Stupishin wrote in early 1989 that while recent West European military integration contradicted the spirit of Soviet-initiated *razryadka*, this integration could be interpreted as a "political line" by which Western Europe was consolidating its position as a "center of power." He then claimed that military integration was not an absolutely necessary outcome of the integration process. Stupishin noted, in an almost approving tone, that the process had not yet extended far beyond the bounds of the traditional NATO framework and had been motivated by concerns over a weakened American security guarantee. If the fears of a "Soviet" threat were finally banished, the need for a U.S. security guarantee would be obviated. As for the future, Stupishin believed that two options existed--a lowering of European military confrontation, or increased tension through a continued, if altered, bloc division of Europe.[169] Stupishin appears to have softened his stance somewhat because in an article published less than a year earlier, he had clearly chosen the more pessimistic line. At that time, he acknowledged that the West European bloc may act as a check on the U.S., but he considered that its likely consequence would be the "split of Europe into opposed blocs" creating "new obstacles in the general European process, and the construction of a common European home will be impeded, to the detriment of our interests as well."[170]

In an analysis similar to Stupishin's more recent position, A. Rassadin argued in early 1989 that West European military integration was intended to safeguard European interests and that the Soviet press had been too quick in the past to assume that integration was designed to alter the European balance of forces or that Western Europe sought a global security role.[171] From his perspective, the recent shift in U.S.-Soviet relations had put Western Europe in a position to act nearly independently in regional security issues and to focus on conventional arms development, while global strategy would remain in the hands of the United States. Although this development reflected certain objective factors, it was also influenced by certain subjective pressures, and here Rassadin listed U.S. interest in shifting its resources to the Pacific basin, and the U.S.-Soviet accord on missiles which has led to an increased Eurocentrism due to the potential for U.S. disengagement.

While Rassadin considered a Europeanization of the bloc unavoidable, he did not conclude that an offensive entity was emerging. The only means through which the Europeans would be able to achieve a consensus, he argued, would be on a "defensive basis."[172] As the Soviet Union set the stage for lowering military confrontation in Europe, Rassadin concluded that the current increase in European military potential was not predetermined to continue in the future, and that integration could actually serve as a basis for lowering armed confrontation on the continent as part of "our common European home" through the "development of common approaches to security problems."[173]

In yet another discussion of the emerging "common European home" theme presented in this period, M. Amirdzhanov and M. Cherkasov wrote that the "system of security in Europe, obviously, will still be based for a long time on the existence of two military blocs. The growth of security will be achieved by correcting their relations, not by their dissolution."[174]

But the German unification process would reverse the order of overcoming the blocs--it would come through Westernization, not Soviet-style Europeanization. It was through coping with the German question that the new European security situation would emerge, not vice versa. It is the assessment of how the Soviets perceived the evolution of West German security policy to which we now turn. This would provide the prism through which the Soviets would have to cope with Western-style Europeanization.

Notes

1. For a representative newspaper article of this genre, see G. Vorontsov, "Vopreki zhiznennym interesam," **Pravda**, 11 July 1985 or a typically strident **Krasnaya zvezda** report: M. Ponomarev, "Real'nosti stuchatsia v dveri NATO," **Krasnaya zvezda**, 14 March 1987.

2. For the historical perspective, see Iu. Zhukov, "Evropa i NATO," **Mezhdunarodnaya zhizn'**, no. 9, 1986.

3. Yurii Zhukov, "As Far as They Can Reach," **Pravda**, 25 June 1986 (Foreign Broadcast Information Service, hereinafter FBIS).

4. This agreement is mentioned frequently in articles on NATO expansionism. For an example, see G. Arzumanov, "Oplot militarizma," **Krasnaya zvezda**, 2 September 1986.

5. Col. G. Melnikov, "NATO Expansion into Developing Countries," **Zarubezhnoe voennoe obozrenie** (hereafter cited as **ZVO**), no. 2, 1986, (JPRS-UMA-86-038), pp. 7-15.

6. V. Stroganov and V. Kulikov, "Exercise Autumn Forge-1985," **ZVO**, no. 5, 1986, (JPRS-UMA-86-065).

7. **Gosudarstva NATO i voennye konflikty: voenno-istoricheskii ocherk**, ed. by A. Zhilin, R. Briul', and K. Sobchak (Moscow: 1987)[signed to print 10/87]. This work's appearance so well into the Gorbachev period is somewhat surprising, in light of its ideological tone and manifest historical distortions, but the reason for this may lay in the fact that it is a book rather than an article and that it is a collaborative effort with scholars from Warsaw Pact nations.

8. Lt. Col. V. Stroginov, "NATO Military Strategy--An Implement of Imperialism's Aggressive Policy," **ZVO**, no. 6, 1987, pp. 3-10 (JPRS-UFM 87-008).

9. For a typical diatribe, see L. Vidyasova, "Zapadnoevropeiskaya integratsiia v agressivnykh planakh Vashington," **Mezhdunarodnaya zhizn'**, no. 5, 1985. A **ZVO** commentator on Western European military integration placed these institutions within a NATO-led framework. See Col. I. Vladimirov, "Novye tendentsii v voennoi integratsii stran zapadnoi evropy," **ZVO**, no. 9, 1987, pp. 7-13.

10. Capt. 2nd Rank V. Kuzar', "NATO: slova novye, kurs prezhnii," **Krasnaya zvezda**, 8 December 1985.

11. **TASS**, 1 July 1986, in FBIS, 2 July 1986.

12. See Vidyasova, **Mezhdunarodnaya zhizn'**, no. 5, 1985.

13. V. Vladimirov, "NATO's West European Buttress," **International Affairs**, 2, 1986.

14. Zhilin, ed., **Gosudarstva**, p. 27.

15. Capt. 2nd Rank V. Kuzar', "NATO protiv Evropy," **Krasnaya zvezda**, 14 December 1986.

16. G. Kolosov, "Voenno-politicheskie aspekty zapadnoevropeiskogo integratsionnogo protsessa," **MEMO**, no. 4, 1987, pp. 34-42.

17. The following review of institutions relies mostly on two articles on West European military integration that appeared in 1987: Kolosov in **MEMO**, no. 4, 1987 and Vladimirov in **ZVO**, no. 9, 1987.

18. Yurii Kovalenko, "Logika 'dinazavra'," **Izvestiya**, 3 December 1986.

19. Vladimirov, **ZVO**, no. 9, 1987, p. 8.

20. **Ibid.**, p. 11.

21. Kolosov, **MEMO**, no. 4, 1987.

22. **Ibid.**

23. **Ibid.**, pp. 40-42.

24. Vladimir Bolshakov, "Chto za initsiativa?," **Pravda**, 21 March 1987.

25. Vladimirov, **ZVO**, no. 9, 1987, p. 12.

26. Vladislav Drobkov, "Vot tak rychag," **Pravda**, 25 June 1987.

27. Vladimirov, **ZVO**, no. 9, 1987, p. 11.

28. Lt. Col. I. Vladimirov, "Basic Trends in the Military Integration of West European Countries," **ZVO**, no. 3, 1982 (JPRS-81925, 5 Oct 1982, USSR Military Report, # 1711).

29. Vladimirov, **ZVO**, no. 3, 1982, p. 125.

30. **Ibid.**, p. 128.
31. Yu. Borko, "O nekotorykh aspektakh izucheniya protsessov zapadnoevropeiskoi integratsii," **MEMO**, no. 2, 1988, esp. p. 47.
32. Institut MEMO, "Evropeiskoe soobshchestvo segodnya," **MEMO**, no. 12, 1988.
33. V. Stupishin, "Obshcheevropeiskii dom i lozung Soedinnennykh Shtatov Evropy," **Mezhdunarodnaya zhizn'**, no. 2, 1989.
34. Yu. Rubinskii, "Zapadnoevropeiskaya integratsiya na novom etape: institutsional'nyi aspekt," **MEMO**, no. 12, 1987.
35. Yu. Rubinskii, "European Community: 'Political Dimensions'," **International Affairs**, no. 2, 1988, pp. 48-49.
36. Yu. Borko, **MEMO**, no. 2, 1988, p. 50.
37. V. Kremenyuk, "Zapadnaya Evropa: integratsiya v sfere vneshnei politiki," book review of V. Baranovskii, **Evropeiskoe soobshchestvo v sisteme mezhdunarodnom otnoshenii** (Moscow: 1986), **MEMO**, no. 10, 1987, pp. 142-143.
38. Stupishin, **Mezhdunarodnaya zhizn'**, no. 2, 1989, p. 97.
39. V. G. Baranovskii, **Zapadnaya Evropa: voenno-politicheskaya integratsiya** (Moscow: Mezhdunarodnaya Otnosheniya, 1988), pp. 12, 18, 31ff, 181.
40. G. Kolosov, **MEMO**, no. 4, 1987.
41. See for instance, G. Burduli, "Vozrozhdenie zapadnoevropeiskogo soyuza," **MEMO**, no. 4, 1989.
42. **Ibid.**, p. 49.
43. Baranovskii, **Zapadnaya Evropa**, pp. 132-133.
44. **Ibid.**, pp. 138-139, 143.
45. Lt. Col. M. Kashirin, "NATO's European Group: On the Course of Militarization," **ZVO**, no. 8, 1988, p. 20 (JPRS-UFM-89-002).
46. Baranovskii, **Zapadnaya Evropa**, p. 55.
47. Yu. Kharlanov, "Nazhim na soyuznikov," **Pravda**, 6 December 1988.
48. Capt. M. Zheglov, **Krasnaya zvezda** 12 June 1988.
49. Baranovskii, **Zapadnaya Evropa**, pp. 91, 107.
50. **Ibid.**, pp. 95ff.
51. V. Pustov, "With Downcast Eyes," **Krasnaya zvezda**, 23 March 1989 (JPRS-UMA-89-008).
52. Major V. Surkov, "Nezavisimaya evropeiskaya gruppa programmirovaniya," **ZVO**, no. 3, 1989, pp. 72-73.

53. Col. V. Almazov, "West European Project Eureka," **ZVO**, no. 1, 1988 (JPRS-UFM-88-006); S. Smolnikov, "Uchastie stran zapadnoi evropy v programme 'zvesdnykh voin'," **ZVO**, no. 5, 1989, pp. 59-65.

54. R. Shchenin, A. Khlystov, "Kruglyi stol MEMO:Strany zapadnoi evropy v programmakh SOI i Evrika," **MEMO**, no. 2, 1988, pp. 129-135.

55. V. V. Natalov, "Otvet zapadnoi evropy," **SShA**, no. 8, 1988, p. 54.

56. **Gonka vooruzhenie v stranakh NATO: ekonomicheskii aspekt**, ed., by R.A. Faramazian (M: Voenizdat, 1988), pp. 99-101.

57. **Ibid.**, p. 121.

58. E. Grishin, "'Vozdushnyi potselui' Vernera," **Izvestiya**, 13 June 1989.

59. E. Grishin, "Memorandum voennykh kontsernov," **Izvestiya**, 18 November 1987.

60. Col. N. Nikolaev, **ZVO**, no. 8, 1988, pp. 39-41 (JPRS-UFM-89-002).

61. A. I. Utkin, "Sud'by 'Atlantizma'," **SShA**, no. 9, 1988, pp. 32-42.

62. V. Pustov, "With Downcast Eyes," **Krasnaya zvezda**, 23 March 1989.

63. See V. Drobkov, and Yu. Kharlanov, "Reassessment of Values? Certain Results of the Brussels NATO Summit," **Pravda**, 5 March 1988 (FBIS- SOV-88-044); and Col. V. Nikanorov, "Brussel'skie kruzheva Atlantistov," **Krasnaya zvezda**, 6 March 1988. Soviet coverage over 1988 of the debate within NATO on whether to modernize NATO's tactical nuclear weapons has provided yet another rich vein for this form of commentary.

64. Baranovskii, **Zapadnaya Evropa**, p. 40.

65. **Ibid.**, pp. 49, 57.

66. **Ibid.**, p. 183.

67. R. Shenin, A. Khlystov, "Strany zapadnoi evropy v programmakh SOI i 'Evrika'" (kruglyi stol IMEMO), **MEMO**, no. 2, 1988, pp. 129-135.

68. Smolnikov, **ZVO**, no. 5, 1989.

69. E. Tsedilina, "V pleny starogo myshleniia," book review of **Die Stille Allianz. Deutsch-britische Sicherheit-kooperation**, eds. Karl Kaiser and John Roper (Bonn, 1987), in **MEMO**, no. 1, 1989.

70. Baranovskii, p. 41.

71. S. Vybornov, A. Gusenkov, V. Leont'ev, "Ne vse prosto v Evrope," **Mezhdunarodnaya zhizn'**, no. 2, 1988. See also the rebuttal from a Soviet Foreign Ministry spokesman: Stupyshin, "Indeed, Nothing in Europe is Simple," **International Affairs**, no. 5, 1988.

72. Vybornov, **Mezhdunarodnaya zhizn'**, no. 2, 1988, p. 31.

73. The same point is made by Borko when he referred to the "European barometer" polls in Western Europe which showed consistently high support for general West European integration. Borko considered the reasons for this popular support to be poorly understood by Soviet analysts, and he suggested further study in this area. See, Borko, **MEMO**, no. 2, 1988, p. 36.

74. Yu. P. Davydov, "SShA, Zapadnaia Evropa i Dogovor po RSD-RMD," **SShA**, no. 7, 1988, pp. 8-16.

75. **Ibid.**, p. 14.

76. Baranovskii, **Zapadnaya Evropa**, pp. 185-7.

77. From the historical perspective, France's efforts were analyzed in a book review by A. Sidorov, "Evropeiskoi vybor Parizha," book review of Yu. A. Maevskii, **Frantsiya i malaya evropa: plany i realnosti**, 1987 in **MEMO**, no. 11, 1988.

78. Col. G. Petrukhin, "NATO Strike Forces in Europe," **ZVO**, no. 12, 1985, p. 7 (JPRS-UMA-86-027).

79. Capt. First Rank V. Khomenskii, "NATO's Strategic Atlantic Command," **ZVO**, no. 4, 1986, pp. 37, 42 (JPRS-UMA-86-062).

80. Capt. First Rank V. Khomenskii, "Combat Training of Combined NATO Navies in 1985," **ZVO**, no. 8, 1986; Col. V. Grachev, "NATO 'Tactical Fighter Meet' Tactical Air Exercise," **ZVO**, no. 8, 1987, pp. 31-36 (JPRS-UFM -88-002).

81. Col. L. Levadov and Lt. Col. V. Kholmogorov, "Combat Use of NATO Airborne and Air Assault Troops," **ZVO**, no. 3, 1987, pp. 19-25 (JPRS-UFM -87-005).

82. Col P. Ivanov, "The French Air Force," **ZVO**, no. 11, 1986 (JPRS -UFM -87-001).

83. N. Voronov and A. Isaev, "France (A Military-Geographic Description)," **ZVO**, no. 1, 1987, p. 115 (JPRS -UFM -87-003).

84. Major A. Vasiliev, "France's Rapid Deployment Forces," **ZVO**, no. 4, 1987, pp. 7, 9-10 (JPRS-UFM-87-006).

85. N. Voronov and L. Borisov, "Military Expenditures of Key European NATO countries in 1988," **ZVO**, no. 9, 1988 (JPRS-UFM-89-003).

86. V. S. Mikheev, "SShA-Frantsiia: sotrudnichestvo i protivorechiya," **SShA**, no. 1, 1986, pp. 26-36.

87. Baranovskii, **Zapadnaya Evropa**, pp. 167ff.

88. **Ibid.**, p. 178.

89. Victor Khrekov, **TASS**, 22 May 1986 (FBIS-SOV 29 May 1986).

90. Lt. Col. V. Nelin, "Combat Helicopters of NATO Armies," **ZVO**, no. 7, 1986, pp. 20-24 (JPRS UMA 86-070).

91. Yu. Borisov, "Prezident Frantsii o vneshnei politiki strany," book review of François Mitterrand, **Reflexions sur la politique exterieure de la France** (Paris, 1986), **Mezhdunarodnaya zhizn'**, no. 10, 1986, p. 139.

92. Baranovskii, **Zapadnaya Evropa**, p. 34.

93. Lt. Col. V. Nikanorov, "A Sparrow with a Nuclear Beak," **Krasnaya zvezda**, 24 September 1987 (JPRS-UMA-88-002).

94. Yu. Zhukov, "Security or Danger?" **Pravda**, 28 April 1987 (FBIS-SOV 6 May 1987).

95. I. Yakhontov, "In Search of a 'Common Strategy'," **Pravda**, 22 October 1987 (FBIS-SOV-87-205).

96. Baranovskii, **Zapadnaya Evropa**, pp. 35, 171-172.

97. Capt. 2nd Rank Yu. Shtokov, "Appropriations for Outfitting France's Armed Forces (1987-1991 Program)," **ZVO**, no. 1, 1988 (JPRS-UFM-88-006).

98. Vladimirov, **ZVO**, no. 9, 1987, p. 11; Burduli, **MEMO**, no. 4, 1989, pp. 47-49.

99. A. Sergeev, "Voenno-promyshlennyi kompleks Frantsii," **Mezhdunarodnaya zhizn'**, no. 9, 1987, p. 149.

100. Yu. Kovalenko, "Dve poezdki M. Tetcher," **Izvestiya**, 23 November 1986.

101. Yu. Gavrilov, "'Atlanticists' Resort to Tricks to Hamper Talks," **Sovetskaya Rossiya**, 1 April 1987 (FBIS-SOV 6 April 1987).

102. Baranovskii, **Zapadnaya Evropa**, p. 66.

103. **TASS**, 22 January 1987 (FBIS-SOV 22 January 1987).

104. Aleksandr Lebedev, **New Times**, no. 4, 2 February 1987 (FBIS-SOV 19 Feb 1987).

105. Yu. Kovalenko, "Vtrecha v Strasburge," **Izvestiya**, 5 May 1987, and **TASS**, "Taktika 'zatiazhek'," **Pravda**, 5 May 1987.

106. Yu. Kovalenko, "Vyrabatybaya obshchii podkhod," **Pravda**, 23 May 1987.

107. V. Bolshakov, "Reshenie otlozheno," **Pravda**, 24 May 1987, and Yu. Kovalenko, "Poka chetkosti net," **Izvestiya**, 24 May 1987.

108. Nikanorov, **Krasnaya Zvezda**, 24 September 1987.

109. Bolshakov, **Pravda**, 15 February 1988 (FBIS-SOV-88-030).

110. V. Bolshakov, "In the Shadow of the Dangerous 'Umbrella'," **Pravda**, 15 February 1988 (FBIS-SOV-88-030).

111. See Aleksandr Lyutyi, "Gotovyat 'kompensatsiya'," **Pravda**, 19 December 1987, and TASS, "Ukreplyayut voennye svyazi," **Krasnaya zvezda**, 22 December 1987.

112. Yu. Kovalenko, "Chto zhdet Parizh ot sessii soveta NATO?" **Izvestiya**, 24 February 1988.

113. N. Afanas'evskii, E. Tarasinkevich, A. Shvedov, "Mezhdu vchera i zavtra," **Mezhdunarodnaya zhizn'**, no. 4, 1988, pp. 24-36.

114. A. Chervyakov, "Novaya voennaya programma Frantsii na 1987-1991," **MEMO**, no. 5, 1988, pp. 116-120.

115. Stupishin, **International Affairs**, no. 5, 1988, pp. 69-73.

116. See Vybornov et al, **Mezhdunarodnaya zhizn'**, no. 2, 1988.

117. Davydov, **SShA**, no. 7, 1988, p. 14.

118. G. Burduli, "Vozrozhdeniya zapadnoevropeiskogo soyuza," **MEMO**, no. 4, 1989, pp. 44-49.

119. A. Vtorov, "USSR-France: Through a Dialogue to Greater Understanding and Detente," **International Affairs**, no. 12, 1985, p. 5. For an almost identical view, see V. Kravtsov, "CCCP-Frantsiya: novyi etap dialoga mezhdu Vostokom i Zapadom," **MEMO**, no. 12, 1985, pp. 16-21. See also A. Kudryavtsev, "Pressa Frantsiya o sovetsko-frantsuzskoi vstreche v verkhakh," **MEMO**, no. 2, 1986, pp. 112-117.

120. M. Yu. Bogdanov, "Voennye partnery," review of John Baylis, **Anglo-American Defense Relations, 1939-1984** (London: 2nd ed., 1984), **SShA**, no. 10, 1985, pp. 115-117; Col. A. Alekseev, "US Military Bases on UK Territory," **ZVO**, no. 6, 1986 (JPRS-UMA-86-066); Vladimir Bogachev, **TASS**, 1 July 1986 (FBIS-SOV 2 July 1986); V. F. Davydov, "Yadernoe partnerstvo," book review of Peter Malone, **The British Nuclear Deterrent**, in **SShA**, no. 6, 1986, pp. 105-107. See also for tangential comments on the same themes: N. Nikolaev, "Certain Aspects of Great Britain's Military Preparations," **ZVO**, no. 2, 1986 (JPRS-UMA-86-038); Sr. Lt. I. Dalin, "British Nuclear Submarines," **ZVO**, no. 4, 1986 (JPRS-UMA-86-062); V. Matveev, "Angliya i okruzhayushchii mir," **Mezhdunarodnaya zhizn'**, no. 10, 1986, pp. 100-109.

121. Matveev, **Mezhdunarodnaya zhizn'**, no. 10, 1986, pp. 100-109. For details of these overseas commitments, see Col. A. Alekseev, "Voennoe prisutstvie Velikobritanii za rubezhom," **ZVO**, no. 12, 1988, pp. 14-16.

122. M. Strezhneva, **Velikobritaniya i zapadnaya evropa: politicheskie aspekty** (Moscow: Mezhdunarodnaya Otnosheniya, 1988).

123. Col. V. Markushin, "Trubadory Atlantizma," **Krasnaya zvezda**, 18 August 1987.

124. **Ibid.**, pp. 127-130.

125. Lt. Col. I. Gavrilov and Yu. Antonov, "Great Britain (Physical-Geographic Conditions, State Organization, Economy, Infrastructure Elements, Armed Forces)," **ZVO**, no. 8, 1987 (JPRS-UFM-88-002).

126. N. Nikolaev, "Certain Aspects of Great Britain's Military Preparations," **ZVO**, no. 2, 1986.

127. Lt. Col. S. Anzherskii, "British Ground Forces," **ZVO**, no. 10, 1985 (JPRS-UMA-86-017).

128. Col. V. Artemiev, "Great Britain's Air Force," **ZVO**, no. 3, 1987 (JPRS-UFM-87-005).

129. Alekseev, **ZVO**, no. 6, 1986, pp. 75-79.

130. N. Voronov and L. Borisov, "Military Expenditures of Key European NATO Countries in 1988," **ZVO**, no. 9, 1988, pp. 61-69.

131. Yu. Kovalenko, "Dve poezdki M. Tetcher," **Izvestiya**, 23 November 1986.

132. A. Krivopalov, "Za ili protiv?" **Izvestiya**, 7 March 1987.

133. Aleksandr Lyutyi, "Gotovyat 'kompensatsiyu'," **Pravda**, 19 December 1987; **TASS**, "Ukreplyayut voennye svyazi," **Krasnaya zvezda**, 21 December 1987. For examples of joint military production, see Col. V. Artemiev, "Great Britain's Air Force," **ZVO**, no. 3, 1987.

134. Baranovskii, **Zapadnaya Evropa**, p. 68.

135. V. Bolshakov, "In the Shadow of the Dangerous 'Umbrella'," **Pravda**, 15 February 1988 (FBIS-SOV-88-030).

136. A. Krivopalov, V. Antonov, "Opredeliayut pozitsii," **Izvestiya**, 2 March 1988; Vladislav Drobkov, "S medvedem bylo proshche," **Pravda**, 2 March 1988; A. Krivopalov, V. Antonov, "Na slovakh i na dele," **Izvestiya**, 5 March 1988; Col. V. Nikanorov, "Bryussel'skie kruzheva atlantistov," **Krasnaya zvezda**, 6 March 1988.

137. V. Drobkov and Yu. Kharlanov, "Reassessment of Values? Certain Results of the Brussels NATO Summit," **Pravda**, 5 March 1988 (FBIS-SOV-88-044).

138. E. Tsedilina, "V plenu starogo myshleniya," **MEMO**, no. 1, 1989.

139. Strezhneva, **Velikobritaniya i zapadnaya evropa**.

140. **Ibid.**, pp. 127-130.

141. **Ibid.**, p. 46.

142. Reports on NATO exercises necessarily indicate the degree of NATO integration when describing the nationality of participating units. For a representative example, see Col. Yu. Vasiliev and Lt. Col. G.

Mikhalychev, "NATO Air Defense in the Central European Theater of Military Operations," **ZVO**, no. 6, 1988, pp. 31-36.

143. A. N. Yakovlev, "Opasnaya os' amerikano-zapadnogermanskogo militarizma," **SShA**, no. 7, 1985, pp. 3-15.

144. G. Kirillov, "Bonn: mirolyubivaya ritorika i militaristskaya praktika," **Mezhdunarodnaya zhizn'**, no. 3, 1986, p. 64.

145. V. Vladimirov, **International Affairs**, no. 2, 1986.

146. E. Kondrashova, "The Militarization of West Germany: Dire Consequences," **International Affairs**, no. 8, 1985, p. 87.

147. Major General F. Gontar', "V militaristskom ugare," **Krasnaya zvezda**, 18 January 1987.

148. Yu. Kovalenko, "Vstrecha v Strasburge", **Izvestiya**, 5 May 1987; "Taktika zatyazhek," **Pravda**, 5 May 1987; Yu. Kovalenko, "Vyrabatyvaya obshchii podkhod," **Pravda**, 23 May 1987.

149. Yu. Kovalenko, "Poka chetkosti net," **Izvestiya**, 24 May 1987.

150. Yurii Zhukov, "Security or Danger?" **Pravda**, 28 April 1987 (FBIS-SOV 6 May 1987); A. Zhakov, A. Mitropol'skii, "'Evropeiskaya oboronnaya initsiativa': tseli, sredstva, posledstviya," **MEMO**, no. 8, 1987, pp. 129-131.

151. Lt. Col. V. Nikanorov, "A Sparrow with a Nuclear Beak," **Krasnaya zvezda**, 24 September 1987.

152. Yurii Levchenko, **TASS**, 17 December 1987 (FBIS-SOV-87-243, 18 December 1987).

153. V. Bolshakov, "In the Shadow of the Dangerous 'Umbrella'," **Pravda**, 15 February 1988.

154. Yu. Yudanov, "FRG vo vtoroi polovine 80-x godov--osnovnoe problemy i poiski ikh resheniya," **MEMO**, no. 9, 1988; M. Maksimova, "Raskryt' potentsial sotrudnichestva," **MEMO**, no. 10, 1988, pp. 61-69.

155. G. I. Vogel, "Vneshnopoliticheskaya filosofiya SDPG," **MEMO**, no. 7, 1988, p. 35.

156. V. Pustov, "With Downcast Eyes," **Krasnaya zvezda**, 23 March 1989 (JPRS-UMA-89-008). See also G. Burduli, **MEMO**, no. 4, 1989, pp. 44-49.

157. See A. Grigoriants, "Evropa--nash obshchii dom," **Mezhdunarodnaya zhizn'**, no. 3, 1986.

158. Yu. Karelov, "USSR-Western Europe: Guidelines of Cooperation," **International Affairs**, no. 11, 1985; and A. Vtorov and Yu. Karelov, "Dinamizm evropeiskoi politiki SSSR," **Mezhdunarodnaya zhizn'**, no. 5, 1986.

159. "For Peace and Security in Europe (Tenth Anniversary of the Conference on Security and Cooperation in Europe)," **International Affairs**, no. 9, 1985.

160. See Zhukov, **Mezhdunarodnaya zhizn'**, no. 9, 1986.

161. TASS, **Pravda**, 28 January 1987.

162. V. Baranovskii, R. Varvaran, "Europeiskoe edinstvo: istoricheskii rakurs," a book review of A. D. Chubar'ian, **Evropeiskaya ideya v istorii** (Moscow: 1987), **MEMO**, no. 3, 1989.

163. Typical of this vision, see Yurii Rakhmaninov, "Europe: Approaching the Third Millennium," **International Affairs**, no. 4, 1988; Michal Dobroczynski, "Rapprochement of the Peoples of Europe: Difficulties and Prospects," **International Affairs**, no. 2, 1989.

164. V. Stupishin, **Mezhdunarodnaya zhizn'**, no. 2, 1989, p. 101, and many other references.

165. R. Shchenin, A. Khlystov, **MEMO**, no. 2, 1988, p. 135.

166. A. Shaskol'skii, "Evropeiskaya bezopasnost': alternativa antivoennogo dvizheniya," book review of **Prospectus for a Habitable Planet**, ed. by Dan Smith and E. P. Thompson (1987), in **MEMO**, no. 4, 1988.

167. Borko, **MEMO**, no. 2, 1988, p. 46, 49.

168. O. Bykov, "Novoe politicheskoe myshlenie v deistvii," **MEMO**, no. 2, 1988, pp. 15-16.

169. V. Stupushin, "Obshcheevropeiskii dom i losung Coedinennykh Shtatov Evropy," **Mezhdunarodnaya zhizn'**, no. 2, 1989, p. 99-101.

170. Vladimir Stupishin (Principal Advisor of the Evaluation and Planning Directorate of the USSR Ministry of Foreign Affairs), "Indeed, Nothing in Europe is Simple," **International Affairs**, no. 5, 1988, p. 73.

171. A. Rassadin, "Zapadnoevropeiskaya voennaya integratsiya--perspektivy i vozmozhnye posledstviya," **MEMO**, no. 2, 1989, p. 107.

172. Rassadin, **MEMO**, no. 2, 1989, p. 113.

173. **Ibid.**, p. 115.

174. M. Amirdzhdnov, M. Cherkasov, "Etazhi obshcheevropeiskogo doma," **Mezhdunarodnaya zhizn'**, no. 11, 1988, p. 30.

4

Soviet Assessments of West Germany, 1985-1987

This chapter identifies how Soviet perspectives on West German security and East-West policy evolved in the early Gorbachev period. Assessments of the 1985-1987 period were heavily colored by the experience of the East-West confrontation associated with the INF crisis during the early 1980s.

The fact that the Soviets paid a great deal of attention to the Federal Republic in this period is readily evident from the volumes of material published in the Soviet open literature about this country. In large part, Soviet analyses focus on foreign and security policy issues and the state of relations between the Soviet Union and the FRG. It is also worth noting that another indicator of the importance the Soviet leadership attached to West Germany is the fact that both *Pravda* and *Izvestiya* each had two correspondents in Bonn throughout the period under analysis.

Nuclear Weapons and the FRG

Not surprisingly, the subject of nuclear weapons received a significant amount of attention in Soviet newspapers, scholarly journals, and monographs. With respect to West Germany, the Soviets concentrated on several nuclear issues--its role in the deployment of U.S. intermediate-range nuclear forces (INF), the subsequent U.S.-Soviet agreement to eliminate these missiles, the debate surrounding the modernization of the short-range Lance system, and the FRG's own "nuclear aspirations."

NATO's Euromissile Decision

This decision, also known as the "dual-track decision," was formally adopted in December 1979. In Soviet analyses, the West German government's support for this decision was frequently contrasted with public opposition to this initiative. These analyses also noted the serious effect this decision had on individual West German political parties. For example, L. Bezymensky wrote, in the March 1985 issue of *International Affairs*, that three-quarters of the West German population opposed deployment of these missiles.[1] In an excellent book on U.S.-FRG relations, M. S. Ziborova identified the INF decision as having "serious political consequences for the SPD-FDP government." She argued that rise of the peace movement and the split between the party leadership and the masses effectively led to the fall of this coalition.[2]

Constant themes in Soviet writings with respect to INF were the implications for the international situation and negative role that West Germany played in this trend. L. Bezymensky, a political analyst at *New Times* who has written books on World War II, Nazism, and neo-Nazism, characterized the INF deployment in the following way: "West Germany is thus becoming a launching pad for American first-strike nuclear missiles, which means that for the first time since the war a threat to the Soviet people and Soviet allies will be emanating from German soil."[3]

Bezymensky was not alone in pointing out the threat to the Soviet homeland. In his 1986 book on revanchism, V. V. Pustogarov argued that the INF deployment would fundamentally change the situation in Europe; it was not just a matter of a disruption in the balance of forces. He stated that the FRG was turned into a base for delivering a first nuclear strike against the USSR, which led the Soviet leadership to conclude that "for the first time in postwar history, a military threat to the Soviet people once again emanates from German soil."[4]

Numerous others sources have also pointed to the FRG's role as a "bridgehead for a first nuclear strike."[5] G. Kirillov added a slightly different twist to the argument, reasoning that by accepting the INF missiles Bonn "is creating a situation where a new war could be launched from the territory of the FRG even without the knowledge of its authorities."[6] Kirillov further rejected Bonn's argument that these missiles brought the Soviets back to the negotiating table; he believed that the missile deployment only raised the level of nuclear confrontation and destroyed the political situation in Europe.

West Germany was, indeed, seen to share responsibility for the deployment decision with the United States. Writing in *Mirovaya ekonomika i mezhdunarodnye otnosheniya* in early 1985, I. Basova et al. stated that "having agreed to deploy American Pershing and cruise missiles in the country, the West German government acted, in effect, as one of the main initiators of the realization of NATO's decision to rearm."[7] In a 1986 book on West Germany's ostpolitik, I. S. Kremer similarly argued that "the FRG government--above all Chancellor Schmidt and Foreign Minister Genscher--not only did not restrain American plans to expand the U.S. nuclear presence in Europe and disrupt the existing correlation of forces between NATO and the Warsaw Pact Organization on the European continent, but even actively supported them [these plans]."[8] Because of this, Kremer reasons, the FRG "shares with the U.S. the responsibility for the serious complication in the international situation."[9]

Related to the issue of West German responsibility was the notion in Soviet writings that revanchism was again on the rise. Kremer wrote that it was not only the socialist countries, but also the FRG's allies, who were concerned about the revival of revanchism after the CDU/CSU-FDP coalition came to power "and especially after the beginning of the deployment of American medium-range missiles in the FRG, aimed at the Soviet Union."[10] Bezymensky's assessment of the situation was much stronger: "Detente was hit hard when new U.S. nuclear first-strike weapons began to be deployed in West Germany with the consent of the FRG government, in keeping with the will of the U.S. ruling elite.... Revanchism and the missile deployment appeared to be communicating vessels."[11]

Finally, Soviet analyses also paid considerable attention to the role of the peace movement in the INF controversy. For example, L. Istyagin argued that the United States and West Germany thought that the peace movement would fade away once the first INF missiles were actually deployed. On the contrary, these forces continued to oppose government policies.

> In the previous decade the Schmidt-Genscher "social-liberal" government made constant concessions to the opponents of detente, and beginning in the second half of the 1970s moved away from it [detente], having assumed a position of active complicity in the elaboration and realization of the American plans to 'rearm' that were dangerous for the cause of peace. It was precisely this turnaround that prompted West German anti-war forces to come out decisively against the SPD-FDP coalition's policy, and to an even greater extent against the course of Kohl's current conservative government that has intensified this policy, which has also led to the direct encouragement of militaristic and revanchist circles.[12]

Similarly, in his 1988 book, Istyagin noted that "the anti-missile campaign was marked by a very substantial expansion of the socio-political composition of anti-militarist forces."[13] Thus, from the Soviet perspective, the INF deployment decision was frequently identified as a negative turning point in West Germany's foreign and security policy. These sentiments continued to prevail during the U.S.-Soviet negotiations to eliminate these forces, at least until the Bonn government changed its position on the inclusion of the Pershing-1As in this agreement.

The Pershing IA-s Issue

The Reykjavik summit of October 1986 was identified as an important event in Bonn's thinking on the INF issue. It had been pointed out that prior to the Iceland meeting, Chancellor Kohl had supported NATO's zero option. Yet after Reykjavik, the Kohl government indicated grave concerns about the possibility of eliminating the INF missiles completely, calling instead for progressively lowering their numbers (but not abolishing them).[14]

Differences among the West German political parties and between the government and the public on the INF treaty certainly did not go unnoticed in the Soviet press and journals. For example, *Pravda* correspondent Yu. Yakhontov explained that the public supported a double zero solution, and the SPD and the Greens called for a serious approach to this proposal. Even Chancellor Kohl affirmed his support for the idea. But Yakhontov also pointed out existing opposition to the idea, namely from the Ministry of Defense, the Bundeswehr, and some highly-placed politicians.[15]

The real controversy surrounding the INF negotiations and West Germany came when the Soviets announced on 28 April 28 1987 that they wanted the Pershing-1As (P-1As) to be included in the treaty since, they argued, the warheads were under U.S. control. Bogachev elaborated the reasoning behind this decision: "Nuclear warheads for these systems are deployed on West German territory but are under the control of the U.S. military command. It goes without saying that the question whether it is nuclear or conventional warheads that will be used on these missiles will be decided primarily by the USA. That is why the Soviet draft treaty...provides among other things for eliminating also the American warheads for West German Pershing 1A missiles."[16]

It was also noteworthy that when Bonn rejected the Soviet insistence on including the Pershing-1As in the INF treaty, many Soviet articles attributed Bonn's position, at least in part, to West German nuclear aspirations. While this issue will be addressed in greater detail in a later section, another quote from Bogachev illustrated this Soviet attitude: "Are they acting out in Washington and Bonn a comedy of not understanding the substance of the Soviet proposals or has the West German Bundeswehr already become the owner of nuclear warheads contrary to international agreements signed by the USA? It is possible that West Germany has not given up hopes to be a nuclear power and sees control over U.S. nuclear warheads for its Pershings as the shortcut to realizing these hopes."[17]

Again, differences of opinion among the various political parties and even within the governing coalition were highlighted, this time with respect to the P-1A issue. *Pravda* correspondent Yu. Yakhontov described the debate held in the Bundestag on the Soviet proposal, where the CDU/CSU aligned on one side and the SPD and the Greens aligned on the other. Only later in the article did he mention that the FDP members "in effect have supported the government statements, although they have declared that a double zero solution...is considered desirable. But it, they say, requires careful study."[18] While the Bundestag eventually adopted the government resolution, Yakhontov noted that 33 of the 269 deputies from the ruling parties voted against it, demonstrating that "on the issue of disarmament, opinions within the coalition have diverged."[19] Another article by Yakhontov less than two weeks later again noted the division of opinion within the FRG coalition government: not only was the FDP split from the CDU/CSU on this issue, but even within the CDU/CSU block no unified position existed.[20]

In late May 1987, Kohl issued a special government statement on the INF issue, which according to the other *Pravda* correspondent in Bonn, Evgenii Grigor'ev, was designed in part to overcome inner-party differences of opinion and in part to calm public opinion in Europe, which saw the FRG's reaction to the Pershing dispute as a cause for concern. Grigor'ev noted that, in contrast to Kohl's reaction after Reykjavik, he apparently supported the elimination of INF; to this extent, Bonn's policy had undergone "positive movement." Grigor'ev posed the question: Will the West German government be realistic and not let the opportunity pass?[21]

The West German government did agree to the inclusion of the Pershing-1As in the INF treaty, but not before the Soviets had ample opportunities to criticize FRG and U.S. policy throughout the summer months of 1987. Essentially, many Soviet commentaries during this time portrayed the United States as wanting to circumvent the INF treaty by retaining the P-1As. For example, according to Viktor Levin.

> The USA asserts that these [P-1As] are--as they say--the weapons of third countries and therefore there can be no discussion of them. But the nuclear warheads for such missiles belong to the USA. What kind of third-country weapons are these? And what kind of zero in operational-tactical missiles is it if there are 72 missiles remaining on the NATO side? Moreover, in the FRG itself now no particular secret is being made of the fact that in the very near future the Pershing-1A missiles are supposed to be replaced by Pershing-1B missiles, which are nothing other than one step short of Pershing-2. The Soviet Union cannot close its eye to open attempts by the USA to insert into the agreement on the elimination of missiles a loophole which allows it to circumvent the accord.[22]

In an article published in *Krasnaya zvezda*, Yu. Lebedev explained that the Pershing-1B was a "one-stage version of the Pershing-2" and that the procedure required to convert the former into the latter takes about 48 hours. Lebedev reasoned that "Bonn is thus trying to secure a loophole for *upgrading* the Bundeswehr with improved operational and tactical missiles capable of being easily and quickly converted into medium-range missiles. At the same time it can please the United States, which wants to keep nuclear weapons in Europe on the false pretext of *meeting its NATO allies* needs."[23]

President von Weizsaecker visited the Soviet Union in July 1987 and provided Andrei Gromyko with the opportunity to make known his views on the West German stance in this controversy: "The position taken by the FRG regarding the Pershing-1A missiles on its territory gives cause for regret. Such a position is capable of spoiling things--the vessel might be wrecked before it is launched."[24] The foreign minister at the time, Eduard Shevardnadze, offered his own assessment of the situation in early August, echoing many of the arguments that had already been made, with the added twist of the East European reaction: "If, as certain American leaders and their West German partners pretend, the Pershing 1-As belong to a third country, let us ask once again why and with what right does West Germany have nuclear weapons." Shevardnadze said that if West Germany had nuclear weaponry in its arsenal it would be creating a "world political crisis," which would jeopardize the Soviet-U.S. talks and create a situation where "our allies could demand the installation of similar systems on their territory and the Soviet Union could respond to their demand."[25] The article concluded that "either the Pershing 1-As belong to the United States, and should be included in the INF negotiations, or they belong to West Germany, which has neither the legal nor moral right to possess them."[26]

When Chancellor Kohl announced on 26 August 1987 that "under certain conditions" the Pershing-1As could be eliminated rather than modernized, Soviet press reaction was mixed. *Pravda*'s correspondent Evgenii Grigor'ev made a favorable assessment of this shift, while *Izvestiya* paid more attention to all the conditions Kohl had attached to this statement.[27] Finally, following the agreement and signing of the treaty, at least one observer, writing in the more liberal weekly publication *New Times*, felt compelled to recognize the ultimately positive role Kohl had eventually played and the occasionally negative role other West German political parties had played in the INF issue:

> At the critical moment when the fate of the treaty was at stake, Helmut Kohl--who by no means commanded unanimous support on the issue within his own party--displayed political realism and farsightedness by removing the barriers which obstructed progress towards the treaty. Nevertheless, doubts as to the

correctness of this move still persist in the CDU, let alone CSU. Social Democrats celebrate the "double zero" as a personal victory. Indeed, they have more reason to do so than the conservative parties. Let's not forget, however, that it was the Social Democrat Helmut Schmidt, who, as Chancellor, "godfathered" the NATO decision on rearmament. Later the party's stand on Euromissiles was not always consistent either, and all but led to a split in the party.[28]

West Germany's Nuclear Aspirations

Soviet analysts frequently argued that the West Germans had an interest in acquiring nuclear weapons--either through production of their own or through some kind of joint agreement, most likely with France or the United States. With respect to the U.S. connection, the issue of a German hand on the "nuclear button" was raised during the controversy over the Pershing-1As and West Germany's reluctance to include them in the INF negotiations. For example, according to Bovin appearing on the *News Today* program,

> I think the issue of Pershing-1A missiles goes beyond the framework of the arms control negotiations. It has crucial political implications for the future of Europe, and not only of Europe. You know that Federal Germany is forbidden to have nuclear weapons. I think that any attempts to upset this and to give Bonn any hopes of possessing its own nuclear potential is fraught with grave consequences. But Pershings are American-made missiles, and their warheads are under American control. But nonetheless I see in Bonn's position not a lack of logic but the deep-seated ambitions to join the nuclear club.... It is clear that through a European nuclear fighting force, Bonn is seeking to gain access to nuclear decisions and nuclear arms.[29]

Evgenii Grigor'ev had suggested that such nuclear aspirations ultimately threatened the security of Europe:

> Why does Bonn need these 72 missiles and, the main question, the nuclear charges for them? It is sometimes said that this is the "bone" which the chancellor has allegedly been forced to

> throw to the "steel helmet" (the militarist Christian Democratic Union/Christian Social Union faction) for domestic policy reasons. But can the "pacification" of the far right in any NATO country at the expense of European security be tolerated? Can it be allowed to objectively become a demand for unilateral military advantages, moreover in the nuclear sphere? It appears that while officially renouncing nuclear weapons, Bonn actually wants to be a "near-nuclear power" with its finger on the button of nuclear missiles.[30]

Writing in *International Affairs*, Igor Borisov argued that either the Pershing-1A warheads were under U.S. control and should therefore be eliminated under the treaty or they were under West German control, which would have been a gross violation of the nonproliferation treaty. He continued his argument: "What would be the reaction in the FRG if the USSR's allies had similar carrier missiles and the nuclear warheads for them were stored close to the launching positions in Soviet depots? In this case, perhaps, Bonn would look at the issue of third countries' weapons in a different way."[31] Borisov also postulated that West Germany feared that without the P-1As, it would lose some of its influence concerning NATO's nuclear policy and, he further argued, the FRG had not relinquished its aspirations for its own nuclear weapons.[32]

In addition to the Pershing-1A issue, Soviet analysts also underscored the nuclear component of the Franco-German relationship. Here, they argued, West Germany sought access to nuclear weapons through a bilateral arrangement. For example, one *Pravda* article noted Franz Josef Strauss's comment that "the time has come when it is necessary to create a joint European nuclear arsenal." The article further alleged that there were increased West German aspirations to have France and, if possible, Britain, provide a nuclear umbrella for the FRG and that Paris had no objections to moving in this direction.[33]

Another account drew the explicit connection between the INF agreement and a French nuclear guarantee: "This is not the first time Bonn has shown its nuclear ambitions, and there is thus no surprise on that score. What is surprising, however, is the exceptional readiness with which Paris wants to satisfy the nuclear appetite of the West German military."[34]

Both the West German and French governments were portrayed as seeking to counter Soviet peace initiatives with a "Eurodefense." According to TASS military specialist Vladimir Chernyshev, "All this seems to be closely linked with Paris' stubborn commitment to nuclear weapons and Bonn's long-standing aspiration to join the 'nuclear club'."[35]

German Relations with France

Following the signing of the INF agreement, V. Pustov wrote that Franco-German defense cooperation had been expanding and that France was acting as the main instigator in the process. According to Pustov, France was playing the FRG off against the United States, saying to West Germany that the U.S. was pulling out of Europe, so it should rely on cooperation with France more, and saying to the United States that with neutralism increasing in the FRG, the United States should count more on France.[36] It might also be noted that prior to the INF agreement, the Soviet daily press gave considerable coverage to meetings between the French and West German leaders as they sought to develop some common West European approach to the issue. For the most part, these analyses underscored the lack of consensus within both of these countries, which clearly impeded their ability to develop a common line between them.[37] But in this context, then Defense Minister Giraud was under no illusions about the need to establish a common position, as reported in *Pravda*. Giraud argued: "It is precisely the Soviet-American disarmament talks that have shown France and the FRG how close their solidarity must be."[38]

More broadly, Franco-German defense cooperation was perceived by the Soviets to be the main impetus in the West European military integration effort. In an article published in July 1985 in *Kommunist Vooruzhennykh Sil*, Lt. Colonel V. Konobeev analyzed the reasons behind this evolving cooperation, explaining that, aside from the benefits to be derived for both countries' military-industrial complexes, it is seen as a way of strengthening the European pillar in NATO. He also suggested that some believed that France could not have ensured its own security without assistance, so it had turned to West Germany as a partner. In addition, Konobeev raised the question of the reliability of the U.S. nuclear umbrella; given the doubts surrounding the U.S. guarantee, he argued that a system of European defense must be created, which can only be done through the unification of French nuclear weapons and West German industry.[39]

As already indicated, the subject of nuclear weapons was raised frequently in Soviet discussions of the Franco-German relationship. According to *Pravda*'s correspondent in Paris, V. Bol'shakov, this bilateral defense cooperation showed "the obvious determination of the French ruling class to use French nuclear weapons to ensure its command position in the future 'united Europe'." For its part, the FRG "perceives France's 'nuclear payment' as a certain condition of the proposed alliance."[40] In September 1987 the military newspaper *Krasnaya zvezda* argued that this cooperation was entering a new level: "As an important step on this path it is proposed to station on FRG territory French tactical nuclear weapons--future missiles of increased range with neutron warheads." The author further stated that the FRG would be able to participate in the decision on their use and that one should not rule out the possibility of the Bundeswehr being outfitted with French nuclear missiles.[41]

Similarly, Gusenkov had argued in 1986 that the emphasis on military cooperation and the creation of a bilateral commission which discussed "strategic coordination" matters placed the nuclear issue clearly on the agenda:

> It is known that Bonn long ago sought pledges from Paris concerning the possible use of French nuclear weapons on West German territory. These are the Pluton tactical missile and the Hadés missile, which is under construction, as well as the Mirage and Jaguar aircraft, with which France has equipped its Air Force. According to press reports, the French government has agreed to hold consultations on these questions with the FRG. It is true that Paris immediately declared that the agreement to hold consultations by no means meant an agreement to FRG participation in deciding on the use of nuclear weapons. The right to use it, they said, remains as before the exclusive prerogative of France's supreme political and military leadership. A question arises in this connection: Will not French-West German consultations be a prelude to the admission that "France's vital interests" also extend to FRG territory? After all, there is only one step between this admission and the pledge to expand the French "nuclear umbrella" to the other side of the Rhine.[42]

But Gusenkov also recognized the continued differences between the two countries on certain issues, such as the Strategic Defense Initiative (SDI).

> France and the FRG have different views of Western Europe's place in the current interdependent world. Paris, which by no means questions the leading role of the United States in the Western camp, regards Western Europe as one of the "centers of power,"-by depending on its own economic potential and political influence--to be able to more boldly defend its specific interests in the face of its mighty transoceanic ally. Bonn does not share this philosophy. It increasingly counts on Western Europe's direct entry into the global strategy of the United States. Does not the so-called "European defense initiative," which is being nurtured by FRG ruling circles, testify to this? It envisages the creation of an antimissile defense system in Western Europe--a kind of adjunct to the SDI.... The Bonn coalition will not make any decision that could create the impression that it is dissociating the FRG from the United States. The Rhine clearly does not intend to sacrifice its close ties with the United States for the sake of strategic cooperation with France.[43]

In a May 1988 article that appeared in *International Affairs*, Afanasyevsky et al. differentiated between the political and military aspects of this bilateral relationship: "Nobody can reasonably object to stronger good-neighbor relations between the two countries, particularly in view of their poor record in mutual relations. But what is one to make of the fact that France and the FRG are increasingly "militarizing" their cooperation? What or whom are these efforts directed against? Why is it that closer ties between them are not a generator of constructive proposals for ending division and confrontation in Europe and for building a common European home?"[44] Clearly, the Soviets did not see the relationship evolving in a direction favorable to their interests.

Germany's Role in NATO

Within the Alliance framework, the two issues to which the Soviets generally paid the most attention were the FRG's close relationship with the United States and the country's role in West European integration efforts. As for the U.S.-FRG link, M. S. Ziborova dedicated an entire book to the subject, entitled *Bonn-Vashington: 70-80 gody.* This excellent and in-depth analysis provided a useful sense of how relations between these two important countries were viewed by Soviet scholars.

Briefly encapsulated, Ziborova argued that in the 1970s, Bonn developed its *ostpolitik*, which led to a change in its relations with the United States from complete dependence to mutual dependence. In the mid-1970s, Bonn's relative independence was seen to emerge. But then, Ziborova noted, in the 1980s there was a gradual movement to subordinate West German interests to those of the United States. The reasons for this were identified as being: the INF deployment, Ronald Reagan's style of pressuring U.S. allies, the increase in the strength of the West German right wing, and so on.[45]

The question of the FRG's independence--or lack of independence-- in its relations with its transatlantic ally was a frequent theme in the Soviet literature of the period. Two 1985 assessments were considerably more pessimistic about West Germany's independence, laying particular blame on the INF issue, than was Ziborova writing in 1988. According to Basova et al.:

> The Kohl-Genscher government is turning the country from an equal partner into the U.S.'s faithfully servile assistant. National interests are being sacrificed for solidarity with the Reagan administration. This was manifested above all in the deployment of American medium-range missiles in the FRG's territory, aimed at changing the strategic balance of forces in the U.S. and NATO's favor. At the same time, Bonn is seeking to use relations with Washington to strengthen its own position in the European Economic Community.[46]

Similarly, Bezymensky emphasized the FRG's willingness to play the role of servile ally: "There has not been a single issue on which the West German authorities would not toe the Washington course towards building up world tensions and stepping up military preparations. The only exceptions are instances when the USA unscrupulously demands too much of the FRG budget."[47]

With the INF controversy resolved, Ziborova was able to give more credibility to West German independence, although this was still qualified:

> The United States of America is the leader of the capitalist world with global ambitions and possessing colossal military might. The Federal Republic of Germany is a West European country which has emerged in the position of the leading power in the region. Despite Bonn's continued military-political dependence on Washington, the FRG has acquired such a solid position in NATO that a kind of reverse dependency has arisen--ensuring the participation of the Bundeswehr in its military-political measures has become an integral element of the American strategy for the Atlantic Alliance."[48]

In conclusion, Ziborova wrote that "despite the bursts of contradictions on a wide range of problems, these relations are dominated by the tendency to support and develop cooperation, cultivated by the ruling circles of both countries."[49]

Finally, with respect to the Federal Republic's role in integration efforts, Soviet analyses generally carefully pointed out the balance of West German interests between wanting such efforts to succeed but not wanting them to affect the U.S. commitment to the Continent. Ziborova provided one of the best assessments of this issue:

> As a whole, the West German government strives to be the "motor" of West European integration, not relinquishing this to French leadership. It seeks to step up the activities of all the organizations that see their task to be coordinating the West European countries' approaches to today's military-political problems. But this policy is also aimed at increasing its [the FRG's] role and potential in its relations with the US; it is being worked out in such a way so that cooperation by West European states in the military-political sphere does not contradict, at least in the foreseeable future, NATO objectives. Coordination of military-political issues by the West European states and an increase in their military contribution should, according to the calculations of the FRG's ruling circles, lead to the transformation of NATO's West European component into a most important

> integral part of the bloc, indispensable for the US, which will ensure close military-political ties between Western Europe and the US and the conformity of the bloc's policy to West European interests, and in the long-term will prepare the foundation for a military-political community of West European states, especially in the event of a reduction of the US presence in Western Europe. At the same time, the special significance which Bonn accords to military-political cooperation with the US inevitably limits the possibilities and restrains the tempo of development of the integrational processes in the military-political area within the West European framework.[50]

In the final analysis, the Soviets recognized that West Germany had a multi-dimensional role in Western Europe --within the NATO alliance, in its bilateral relations, especially with the United States and France, and within the framework of other European institutions--all of which impacted on the Federal Republic's relations with the Soviet Union.

Soviet-West German Relations

Soviet-West German relations experienced prolonged periods of strain in the 1980s, in large part because of the INF disputes and also because a conservative government (CDU/CSU-FDP coalition) came to power in 1982. Writing in *International Affairs* in late 1985, Kirillov provided a straight-forward assessment of the status of their bilateral relations:

> Summing up, one is bound to conclude that the relations between the USSR and the FRG have become noticeably more complex in the 1980s as compared to the 1970s. But this is not to say that they have come to a standstill. The impetus given to the Soviet-West German relations by the Moscow Treaty is still at work. The two states continue political contacts at various levels. The two countries maintain a relatively high level of trade and economic ties.... There is no doubt, however, that both business and, above all, political relations between the two countries could have been far more effective if the FRG government pursued a constructive policy on security matters.[51]

In I. S. Kremer's 1986 book which examined the FRG's ostpolitik, it is noted that the FRG sought to continue economic relations despite negative trends in the two countries' political relations: "the West German government, even during the period of worsening relations between East and West, sought to continue cooperation with the socialist countries in the economic area."[52] In assessing the general state of Soviet-West German relations in the 1980s, Kremer included the economic dimension as well as differentiated among the German political parties:

> The tendencies toward reviving the trade-economic and other ties between the FRG and the socialist countries testifies to the fact that the FRG did not want to completely throw away the positive experience of cooperation in the 1970s. But, in examining the main aspects of *ostpolitik*, above all connected with the FRG's military-political strategy, the approach of its leadership to the problems of ensuring national and European security, it must be admitted that the ruling CDU/CSU-FDP coalition has greatly moved away from the course which had contributed to an improvement in the situation in Europe and has supported Washington's dangerous course of forcing the build-up of military preparations.... One should also note the substantial positive changes in the foreign policy views of the leaders of the Social Democratic Party. Having lost their governmental responsibility, the leaders of this largest opposition party began to much more fully reflect the mood of the rank and file of the SPD members and the country's democratic public.... On the whole, the development of events in the first half of the 1980s has shown that the ostpolitik begun by the Moscow Treaty has put down deep roots and contrary to the actions of the rightists and the pressure from the outside, it is finding support from the overwhelming majority of the population of the Federal Republic of Germany.[53]

An interesting comparative assessment was provided by Yulii Kvitsinskii when he became the Soviet Union's ambassador to the Federal Republic; he contrasted the then state of affairs with the period 1978-1981, when he was last in Bonn. In true diplomatic fashion, he indicated that the potential was there for cooperation, the times were obviously more difficult now, but nothing must allow the relations to deteriorate further.[54]

However, Kohl's unfortunate remarks which likened the Gorbachev leadership to Goebbels brought about a marked deterioration in relations.[55] This statement, combined with the controversy surrounding the INF systems, created perhaps the worst strain in Soviet-West German relations in recent memory. The July 1987 visit of President von Weizsaecker to Moscow signalled at least a first step toward better relations, although the INF dispute over the P-1As would continue for a few more months. During this visit, Gorbachev assessed the situation in the following way, making reference to Foreign Minister Genscher's trip to the Soviet Union the previous year: an "agreement seemed to have been reached on 'opening a new page' in relations between the two countries. However, to date, it has remained unfilled, and at one time there was even a threat that it would be shut. Fortunately, this did not happen."[56] Thus, the worst seemed to have passed, but there was still a long way to go.

Naturally, the FRG's subsequent decision to allow the Pershing-1As to be included in the INF negotiations further contributed to the development of more positive relations. Of particular significance in the bilateral relationship was the visit of conservative politician Franz Josef Strauss to Moscow in December 1987. Gorbachev used this opportunity to express "the hope that the new year 1988 would be marked by more intensive, constructive political dialogue between the USSR and the FRG, and broader contacts and meetings between the two countries. Both sides showed understanding of the importance of making Soviet-West German relations a matter of practical policy."[57]

The German Question and Revanchism

Soviet articles focusing on West German "revanchism" had begun to appear in 1984, following the decision to deploy the INF systems, the lifting of the ban on West German production of strategic bombers and long-range missiles by the WEU, and the GDR's initial steps toward improving relations with the FRG.[58] Reflective of the tone of the revanchist articles during strained Soviet-FRG relations in the early Gorbachev period was an article by Bezymensky in *International Affairs*. In it he criticized those who believed that revanchism was a nostalgic reaction with no immediate policy relevance. "All this is far from the truth. And the more attempts to belittle the scope of revanchism there are, the clearer the ideological, propaganda and other aims of those who are behind this campaign become."[59] He also distinctly linked the INF deployment with revanchism: "Revanchism of both forms--territorial and social--has been growing since the start of the Pershing deployment and an anti-communist 'crusade'.... As a result of the deployment of new U.S. nuclear missiles on West German soil, forces were again rearing their heads in the FRG which were calling in question postwar political and territorial realities in Europe."[60]

Just one month later, another article published in *International Affairs* by D. Davidovich used strong and colorful language to describe this trend:

> Today's filthy froth on the surface of West Germany's political life whipped up by the insolent revanchist propaganda is obviously just reconnaissance in force foreboding more dangerous actions. As is shown by the course of the events, it has in mind a strategic objective to undermine all aspects of the postwar peaceful settlement. A coalition of neo-Nazism and revanchism and the militaristic policies of the USA in Western Europe is considerably aggravating the threat to peace.... Provocative neo-Nazi and revanchist rallies attended by the FRG's government leaders convey a serious warning, especially in view of the fact that revanchism becomes particularly dangerous at a time when the FRG is being turned into a bridgehead for a new world war through the deployment of American first-strike nuclear missiles on its territory.[61]

In another statement published in September 1986, this time in the more authoritative but military-oriented journal, *Zarubezhnoe voennoe obozrenie*, the stridently anti-German tone persisted: "A necessary condition for stability in the positive processes in Europe and in other regions is a respect for the territorial-political realities which came about as a result of the Second World War. The CPSU will quash any appearance of revanchism. This serious reminder is directed primarily to the FRG where revanchism became a component part of state politics of the ruling coalitions CDU-FDP."[62] In fact, throughout Soviet analyses was the constant theme of the Kohl government's support for revanchist tendencies.

Not surprisingly, President Reagan's visit to West Germany in June 1987 during which he called for the tearing down of the Berlin Wall, precipitated additional Soviet articles about revanchism. For example, political commentator Aleksandr Bovin cautioned that Reagan "should realize that in present conditions trying to undermine the 'wall' and blow it up politically can have only one meaning--that of putting West Berlin back into the position of a 'frontline city,' sharply intensifying the danger of crisis in Central Europe and wrecking hopes for disarmament."[63]

In September 1987, the long-delayed visit of East German leader Erich Honecker to West Germany finally took place. The improved international atmosphere, especially in Soviet-West German relations, was evident in Soviet coverage of this event. The trip was portrayed as an event capable not only of improving inter-German relations, but of making a positive contribution to East-West relations as a whole. Only passing mention was made of Kohl's commitment to the "unity of Germany."

In short, by the end of 1987, Soviet analysts had seemed hopeful of an improvement in Soviet-West German relations in the wake of changes in East-West relations more generally. But what now needed to be defined was the role of West Germany in this effort for change and the possibilities for generating a Soviet-West German partnership to encourage change. These topics would become much more salient in the period ahead.

Notes

1. L. Bezymensky, "The Wild Dreams of Modern Revanchists," **International Affairs** (hereafter **IA**), no. 3, 1985, p. 32.

2. M. S. Ziborova, **Bonn-Vashington: 70-80-e gody** (Moscow: Nauka, 1988), p. 79.

3. Bezymensky, **IA**, no. 3, 1985, p. 33.

4. V. V. Pustogarov, **Zapadnogermanskii revanshizm i mezhdunarodnoe pravo** (Moscow: Nauka, 1986), p. 98.

5. See, for example, **Krasnaya zvezda**, 28 April 1985; Parkhitko, as reported in Foreign Broadcast Information Service, **Daily Report: Soviet Union** (hereafter **FBIS**), 31 December 1985, p. Cl.

6. G. Kirillov, "Bonn: Peaceable Rhetoric and Militaristic Practices," **IA**, no. 4, 1986, p. 60.

7. I. Basova, L. Volodin, S. Sokol'skii, and V. Shenaev, "The FRG: Dangerous Tendencies," **Mirovaya ekonomika i mezhdunarodnye otnosheniya** (hereafter **MEMO**), no. 1, 1985, p. 57.

8. I. S. Kremer, **FRG: etapy "vostochnoi politiki"** (Moscow: Mezhdunarodnye otnosheniya, 1986), p. 172.

9. **Ibid.**, p. 191.

10. **Ibid.**, p. 195.

11. Bezymensky, **IA**, No. 3, 1985, p. 29.

12. L. Istyagin, "The Invincibility of the Ideas of Peace," **MEMO**, no. 2, 1985, p. 131.

13. L. Istyagin, **Obshchestvenno-politicheskaya bor'ba v FRG po voprosam mira i bezopasnosti** (Moscow: Nauka, 1988), p. 110.

14. See, for example, **FBIS**, 28 October 1986, p. G2 and **FBIS**, 6 November 1986.

15. Yu. Yakhontov, **Pravda**, 3 April 1987.

16. Bogachev, **BBC: Summary of World Broadcasts** (hereafter **SWB**), 5 May 1987, p. A1/2.

17. **Ibid.**

18. Yu. Yakhontov, **Pravda**, 9 May 1987; see also E. Bovkun, **Izvestiya**, 3 June 1987.

19. **Ibid.**

20. Yu. Yakhontov, **Pravda**, 18 May 1987.

21. E. Grigor'ev, **Pravda**, 21 May 1987.

22. Viktor Levin, Moscow Home Service, 22 June 1987, as translated in "FRG's Pershing Missiles Being Used to 'Emasculate' INF Agreement," **SWB**, 26 June 1987, p. A1/3. See also, Gerasimov, as translated in "Gerasimov: Space Arms, Pershing-1A, Conventional Arms, Seoul Olympics," **SWB**, 26 June 1987, p. A1/1; Viktor Karpov, as translated in "'Alliance Commitments' No Excuse for Refusal to Eliminate Pershing-1A Warheads," **SWB**, 6 August 1987, p. A1/3.

23. Yu. Lebedev, **Krasnaya zvezda**, 21 July 1987, p. 3.

24. As reported in **Pravda**, 9 July 1987, p. 2.

25. As reported in **FBIS**, 10 Aug 1987, p. AA3.

26. **Ibid.**, p. AA4.

27. E. Grigor'ev, **Pravda**, 1 September 1987; **Izvestiya**, 28 August 1987. Other favorable assessments can be found in Serov, **Sovetskaya**

Rossiya, as translated in **FBIS**, 8 September 1987, p. 27 and Gerasimov, **FBIS**, 9 September 1987, p. 1.

28. Nikita Zholkver, **New Times**, no. 52, 1987, p. 3, as translated in Joint Publications Research Service, JPRS-TAC-88-005, 16 February 1988, p. 7.

29. Borin, 5 June 1987, as reported in "Borin Views Bonn's Nuclear Arms Objectives," **FBIS**, 10 June 1987, p. H4.

30. E. Grigor'ev, **Pravda**, 15 June 1987, p. 6. Other articles that link the Pershing-1A dispute with West German nuclear ambitions include: **FBIS**, 12 August 1987, pp. AA3-4; Karpov statement in Kuvshinnikov, **Izvestiya**, 13 August 1987, p. 5.

31. Igor Borisov, "Bonn: Words and Deeds," **IA**, no. 10, 1987, p. 45.

32. **Ibid.**, pp. 45-46.

33. **Pravda**, 23 June 1987.

34. **FBIS**, 29 June 1987, p. H1.

35. Vladimir Chernyshev, as reported in "FRG-French Military Ties Viewed," **FBIS**, 28 September 1987.

36. V. Pustov, "The Nuclear Zeal of Paris and London," **Krasnaya zvezda**, 7 February 1988, p. 3.

37. See, for example, **Izvestiya**, 5 May 1987; **Pravda**, 23 May 1987; **Pravda**, 24 May 1987.

38. **Pravda**, 9 July 1987. See also, **Izvestiya**, 22 July 1987.

39. Lt. Col. V. Konobeev, "In the Spirit of 'Atlantic Solidarity'," **Kommunist Vooruzhennykh Sil**, no. 13, 1985, pp. 85-86.

40. Bol'shakov, **Pravda**, 28 August 1987.

41. **Krasnaya zvezda**, 13 September 1987.

42. Gusenkov, **Sovetskaya Rossiya**, 15 February 1986, p. 3, as translated in **FBIS**, 20 February 1986, pp. G2-3.

43. **Ibid.**, p. G4.

44. Afanasyevsky et al., **IA**, no. 5, 1988, p. 27.

45. Ziborova, **Bonn-Vashington**, pp. 8-9.

46. Basova et al., **MEMO**, no. 1, 1985, p. 49.

47. Bezymensky, **IA**, no. 3, 1985, p. 33.

48. Ziborova, **Bonn-Vashington**, p. 5.

49. **Ibid.**, p. 237.

50. **Ibid.**, pp. 115-116.

51. G. Kirillov, "The Moscow Treaty: A Basis for USSR-FRG Relations," **IA**, no. 9, 1985, pp. 34-35. For a more negative assessment and one that

concentrates more on the security policy aspects, see Pustogarov, **Zapadnogermanskii revanshizm**, pp. 97-98.

52. Kremer, **FRG: etapy "vostochnoi politiki,"** p. 184. For a good summary of the connections between trade relations and political relations and between Soviet-West German and East-West relations generally, see the conclusion in L. M. Chetvertnoi, **SSSR-FRG: problemy torgovo-ekonomicheskogo sotrudnichestva** (Moscow: Mezhdunarodnye otnosheniya, 1988), pp. 150-154.

53. Kremer, **FRG: etapy "vostochnoi politiki,"** pp. 202-204.

54. Yu. Kvitsinskii, **FBIS**, 25 April 1986, p. G2.

55. For Soviet reaction to this statement, see, for example, the frot-page editorial in **Pravda**, 27 November 1986.

56. M. S. Gorbachev, **Pravda**, 8 July 1987, p. 1.

57. **FBIS**, 30 December 1987, p. 36.

58. See, for example, Bezymenskii, **Pravda**, 27 July 1984, p. 4; D. Davidovich, "Revanchism and Neo-Nazism in the FRG," **IA**, no. 4, 1985.

59. Bezymensky, **IA**, no. 3, 1985, p. 30.

60. **Ibid.**, pp. 35, 37-38.

61. Davidovich, **IA**, no. 4, 1985, pp. 145-146.

62. Col. A. Tsvetkov, "West German Special Services--Weapon of Aggression and Revanchism," **ZVO**, no. 9, 1986, as translated in JPRS-UMA-87-015, p. 1.

63. A. Bovin, **Izvestiya**, 18 June 1987.

5

Soviet Assessments of West Germany, 1987-1989

This chapter will carry forward the evolution of Soviet assessments of West German developments in the 1987-1989 period. The division between this chapter and the last is an approximate one and there is overlap between the two. This chapter covers Soviet assessments only through the summer of 1989 and stops short of making judgments about Soviet perspectives during the year of the unification process or concerning the Revolution of 1989, which will be dealt with in chapters seven and eight.

In this chapter Soviet perspectives are constructed from the general Soviet literature published during the 1987-1989 period. But in addition, materials taken from the leading Soviet military journal which deals with foreign military events during both periods are used throughout this chapter. The reason for some overlap from the military literature is due to the absence of a serious difference of perspective within the military literature in the two periods. This is in contrast to the foreign policy and general newspaper literature, which did show marked shifts in the treatment of West German security and foreign policy issues in the two periods.

During the 1987-1989 period, the tone and approach toward the West Germans changed. Whereas the West Germans were characterized by most Soviet analysts as forces for revanchism and obstructionism in the earlier period, in the new phase the West Germans were treated as possible partners in building a new Europe. Notably, the task of building a "common European home" was linked explicitly with the effort to change the Soviet-West German relationship. But this change was still conceived within the framework of a divided Europe, with the Soviet-West German relationship being critical to building a new Europe overarching the old.

Soviet policy in this regard was best symbolized by Gorbachev's speech to the Council of Europe in July 1989. This speech called for overcoming the division of Europe by a new detente process. It did not suggest the end of socialism in the East and certainly did not support the Westernization of Eastern Europe and the Soviet Union. The Soviets were soon confronted with this challenge in the context of the Revolution of 1989. It was a rare Soviet analyst indeed who understood the magnitude of the task confronting the reconstruction of Soviet European policy.

This chapter will conclude with a remarkable set of statements by a leading Soviet analyst of Germany--Vyacheslav Dashichev--which were outlined in an unpublished paper presented in early 1989. The forecast of changes needed on the Soviet side was very accurate, but even Dashichev, who was criticized by many in the Soviet hierarchy for his "radical" views, understated the magnitude and pace of change to come.

The West German Role in the World

Soviet assessments during the 1987-1989 period focused upon West Germany as a country in transition from traditional thinking (whether conservative cold war or left-wing detente thinking) to a more dynamic reassessment of what was possible in European and East-West affairs. Increasingly, the West Germans were portrayed as eager to see a new order in Europe in which they would play a leading role in carrying out Western reconciliation with the "legitimate aspirations" of the Soviet Union.

The Soviets paid special attention in this period to the role of the Social Democratic Party (SPD). As did many of their Western counterparts, Soviet analysts at the time saw the SPD as having a real opportunity to attain power (within a coalition with the FDP) in the 1989 election. Typical of the Soviet assessment was how they presented an interview with SPD party leader Vogel in May 1988. The Soviet journal *Mirovaya ekonomika i mezhdunarodyne otnosheniya* interviewed Vogel and quoted him as saying the following:

> The task of West European military-political integration is to ensure military stability with less military participation of the United States of America. Success in accomplishing this task can not only improve Western Europe's political position vis-a-vis the East European countries and contributes to its self-determination vis-a-vis the leading world powers. In the SPD's opinion, cooperation among the West European countries should also stimulate the deepening of the all-European policy of detente.[1]

Soviet analysts underscored that the West German role within NATO was expanding. Presumably, the ability of the West Germans to reshape the objectives of NATO in line with broader changes in East-West relations was growing as well. As Maksimova wrote in 1988, "From all this it follows that future East-West relations, including the all-European process, and the development of cooperation between the CEMA and the EC will depend to no small extent on the position of the Federal Republic of Germany."[2]

She also argued that this was due in no small part to the FRG's expanded role within the Alliance.

> The FRG's position within the North Atlantic Alliance is changing. The new situation that has taken shape in the world as a result of the INF treaty, Soviet-American strategic arms talks, and the prospects for reducing conventional arms and armed forces in Europe affect the FRG's interests considerably more than the other European participants of NATO. There is therefore reason to assume that in the changing situation, the FRG's role in formulating the future policy of this organization will grow.[3]

Notably, the central role of West Germany within the European construction process was especially significant to Russian analysts. That is, some analysts perceived that there was a reciprocal process underway whereby the enhanced significance of the European construction process to the USSR for its own development in turn elevated the importance of West Germany to Soviet foreign policy, since it was the key nation shaping the European construction process. Again, Maksimova clearly noted that "the transition of the EC countries to the creation of a single market in the 1990s, the intensification of supranational elements, the strengthening of political cooperation, and, finally, the plans for West European military integration all meet the FRG's aspirations and will be widely used by its ruling circles to further consolidate its weight and influence both in Western Europe and beyond its borders."[4]

Associated with the expanded "objective" role of the FRG within the Western and East-West systems was change in the "subjective" perceptions of the West Germans of their role. West Germans were becoming increasingly resistive to the limitations placed by other Western countries on Germany. As Pleskov noted, "The West Germans now do not see the likely dangers as coming from the usual, 'red' side. In their view, those which can begin to act on the FRG's territory at their own, not at Bonn's discretion, are its closest allies--the U.S., Britain, and France."[5]

Yurii Kvitsinsky, the then Soviet ambassador to Bonn, was particularly adamant in underscoring the changing perceptions within West Germany of that country's role within the West and in the East-West system. His comments were published in early 1989; the thinking behind them was to become even more significant in the next period.

> One should see also that the FRG was, and will remain a reliable component of the present system of Western alliances for many years to come. But this is not contrary to our own strategic interests: we are interested in [a] stable FRG, stable GDR, and stable Europe as a whole. The problem for the FRG is not that it wants to "flee" from the Atlantic alliance and "rush into the Russians' embrace," as the critics of its policy in the West allege. It is not going to do that because it feels ever more at home in the upper echelons of West European communities. The point is, however, that the FRG has clearly outgrown the role assigned to it at the time it was being formed and when it was admitted to NATO.[6]

In short, during the 1987-1989 period, Soviet analysts were coming to the conclusion that West Germans were seeking to expand their role within the Western world. As the West Germans tried to do this, they would be seeking to expand their leadership role as well within the East-West system. Therefore, the Soviets needed to sort out how to redefine the Soviet-West German relationship as the West Germans sought to reshape their East-West role.

West Germany's Relationship with the Superpowers

West Germany was viewed by the Soviets during the 1970s as the key European state for the Soviet Union as the latter tried to construct a detente system within Europe. The INF struggle in the early 1980s and the return of the conservatives to power in the FRG altered the German-Soviet relationship. The West Germans were becoming more "subservient" to American thinking and less in tune with Soviet approaches and efforts to restructure the European security environment. As Ziborova commented with regard to Bonn's East-West policy in the early-to-mid 1980s, "The inconsistency of West German policy is to a significant extent the result of American pressure, which the West German government feels sharply on issues connected with relations with the USSR and other socialist countries."[7]

Nonetheless, Bonn responded to Washington's pressure by trying to expand its role within the West European system. Ziborova added:

> At the beginning of the 1980s, when American-West German relations were complicated by differences over East-West problems, Bonn made new attempts to improve the process of coordinating the West's foreign policy activity in NATO in the context of international crises, which made it possible to avoid situations when unilateral steps by the US administration did not find support from the West European countries' governments.... Bonn's interest in creating a mechanism which would put the actions of centrifugal tendencies in NATO under control, were manifested to a particular extent when inter-imperialist contradictions arose over problems of East-West relations.[8]

Bonn then used its position within Europe during the 1987-1989 period to reinforce its ability to influence Washington to move in directions commensurate with Bonn's definition of Western interests. As Ziborova further argued,

> The United States of America is the leader of the capitalist world with global ambitions and possessing colossal military might. The Federal Republic of Germany is a West European country which has emerged in the position of the leading power in the region. Despite Bonn's continued military-political de-

> pendence on Washington, the FRG has acquired such a solid position in NATO that a kind of reverse dependency has arisen--ensuring the participation of the Bundeswehr in its military-political measures has become an integral element of the American strategy for the Atlantic Alliance.[9]

The expansion of West Germany's influence on the American approach to Europe during the 1987-1989 period enhanced the significance to the Soviets of trying to alter the Soviet-German relationship. Perhaps a German partner in changing Western policy would have provided a better means for Moscow to connect with the European development process, than simply seeking to use the West Germans as influence agents inside the Western camp.

But for Moscow to be able to play a German card, they would have to change their approach to Bonn and to forge a new Soviet-German relationship. Such an effort would have required a real change in how the Soviets had historically treated Bonn and a recognition of the threat which Moscow posed to Bonn in following classic Soviet anti-coalitional politics. In other words, the Soviets would have to develop a policy toward Bonn as part of a reconstruction of Soviet European policy and not simply try to use Bonn as a tool to implement Soviet influence within the Western community.

The clearest statement that connect Moscow's Bonn and European policies in the 1987-1989 period was made (not surprisingly) by Moscow's ambassador to Bonn. Kvitsinsky argued the following:

> Europe today is a broad and beneficial area of activity for our diplomacy. This truism is not as banal as it may seem at first. For a few decades we, unfortunately, too often looked at the world through the windows of the Soviet embassy in Washington.... There is no need to say that the FRG by its significance is a central state in Western Europe and a major power in the capitalist world. Our relations with it have been changing for the better over the past years.... Both countries are determined to open a new chapter in their relations, and the important thing is that there is a consensus on this question practically among all political parties in the FRG.[10]

He then added that, along with "vast possibilities," there were also difficulties that did not exist in Soviet relations with other European countries, namely the German question. He then warned that "to clean Soviet-West German relations entirely of the alarming cold war vestiges remains a major task.... This is not a return to past disputes. This is a continued advance into the future."[11]

The effort by Bonn to redefine its relationship with Washington and to expand its role within Western Europe required Bonn to enhance its relationship with Moscow. By developing positive relations with Moscow, Bonn would be able to stake out its role as a leader in redefining the Western system, rather than as a broker between East and West. As Maksimova argued,

> Bonn's appraisal of the Soviet Union is also changing [in the 1987-1989 period]. For many decades the FRG stubbornly clung to the outmoded idea that it was necessary to weaken the USSR economically in order to thereby undermine its military potential and international position. It is now coming to understand that it is in the fundamental interests of the FRG and, incidentally, all the rest of the West, to have the USSR not be an illusory weak opponent, but a really strong partner.... It is well known that certain circles in the West are not at all interested in the development of Soviet-West German ties, which would go beyond the existing framework.[12]

In other words, Maksimova had underscored direct conflict between West Germany's interest in building a partnership role to expand their influence and the interest of West Germany's allies in both containing West Germany and in limiting their relationship with the Soviet Union. The dynamic highlighted by this Soviet researcher would become increasingly significant for Soviet analysts and policymakers in responding to the Revolution of 1989.

The Franco-West German Relationship

Throughout the 1987-1989 period, the Soviets paid continuing attention to the Franco-West German dynamic. The Soviet concern continued to be that the French and the West Germans might find a way to strengthen a West European pillar to the Alliance or the West European development process in a manner that would exclude the Soviets. Increasingly, Soviet analysts and policymakers focused on the importance for the Soviet Union in joining the European development process. West Germany (and then Germany) were increasingly perceived as central to this process. The Franco-West German dynamic was seen in this light to be a threat to an emergent Soviet-German partnership.

The linkage between the Franco-West German dynamic and the kind of Europeanization process which might emerge was made explicitly by one Soviet analyst in the following terms:

> Nobody can reasonably object to stronger good-neighbor relations between the two countries, particularly in view of their poor record in mutual relations. But what is one to make of the fact that France and the FRG are increasingly "militarizing" their cooperation? What or whom are these efforts directed against? Why is it that closer ties between them are not a generator of constructive proposals for ending division and confrontation in Europe and for building a common European home?[13]

The potential Franco-West German nuclear relationship was of clear concern to Moscow, less for its military than political implications. "While rejecting the NATO doctrine of "flexible response" as well as the idea of the permissibility of a limited nuclear conflict, Paris speaks more and more often of France and the FRG having a "common strategic space," of the desirability of drawing Bonn into choosing targets for French tactical nuclear weapons or even of supplying the FRG with a "second key" to them."[14]

The relationship between Chancellor Kohl and President Mitterrand seemed to be strengthening the Bonn-Paris dynamic in the 1987-1989 period. For example, the Soviet press characterized the October and November 1988 meetings between the two leaders as pushing France toward greater European integration and solidarity with Bonn. If the Bonn-Paris relationship deepened, military integration within Europe might become inextricably intertwined with the general European integration process, a development which Soviet analysts clearly opposed. As one Soviet analyst wrote,

> The WEU sees its official objective in converting itself into a European Union (this would move it close to becoming a United States of Europe). The military integration trend, still a rather feeble rivulet, is gradually merging with the general integrational process that is going on within the EC, swelling to a more and more powerful stream. The military integration trend is now motivated above all by the likelihood of a slackening of the U.S. commitment to defend Western European against the "Soviet military threat."[15]

The Nuclear Issue

As was evident in the treatment of Soviet perspectives in the previous chapter, the INF controversy--surrounding both NATO deployment and treaty negotiations--occupied a central place in Soviet writings during the mid-1980s. Within this context, the FRG consistently played a prominent and frequently negative role from the Soviet perspective. Yet it seems that no sooner had this controversy been resolved than the issue of tactical, or short-range, nuclear weapons emerged.

The nuclear issue, notably the follow-on-to-Lance (FOTL) debate, became central to Soviet analyses during the development of West German foreign and security policy in this transitional period. The Soviets increasingly believed that the West Germans would resist Lance modernization and would thereby lay down the groundwork for the reworking of NATO's approach to nuclear issues. Again, positions developed during this transitional period clearly foreshadowed changes in the upcoming bargain to be reached in 1990 for the emergence of a unified Germany.

Just as INF had been a dominant theme in Soviet treatments of West Germany, so now was the Lance modernization issue and the question of eliminating tactical nuclear weapons in Europe, as these themes took center stage in many Soviet daily reports coming from Bonn in Spring 1989. In fact, a sampling of the writings from *Pravda*'s and *Izvestiya*'s correspondents in the FRG highlighted both the internal and the external pressures placed on the West German government in this debate.

Both *Izvestiya*'s E. Grishin and *Pravda*'s E. Grigor'ev covered the appearance of Chancellor Kohl in the Bundestag in late April 1989 following the reshuffling of his cabinet, during which the issue of tactical nuclear weapons was also debated.[16] Grishin's article had a more positive tone and focused more on Kohl's statements about the importance of Soviet-West German relations. He also devoted more attention both to Kohl's position and the ensuing debate, namely the position developed by SPD party leader Vogel. As Grishin assessed the situation, the debate "reflected deep differences between the government and parliamentary parties," and the government had come to recognize that the West German people did not see a threat from the East.

Grigor'ev also saw the internal pressures evident in the FRG on the nuclear modernization issue. He argued that the debate showed that the government was trying to change public sentiment in its favor by correcting its policy and making new promises, but Kohl had not, in fact, said much new.

The other *Izvestiya* correspondent, E. Bovkun, interviewed Karsten Voigt of the SPD on foreign policy and disarmament.[17] Voigt noted the commonality of all the FRG's parties on two issues -- they were for a sharp reduction in battlefield nuclear weapons and for beginning talks with the Warsaw Pact to reduce short-range missiles. But he also noted their differences: 1) the SPD was for a third zero; 2) the CDU insisted on modernizing the tactical nuclear weapons; and 3) the FDP wanted to keep the question open at least until 1991. Bovkun also pointed out that, with Bundestag elections pending, the current government did not wish to perpetuate a new arms debate. But in addition to the domestic side of the issue, Bovkun's article also addressed the factor of foreign pressure being applied to West Germany, citing the various visits Bonn's allies had been paying to the capital to push the government toward accepting the modernization decision. In two later articles, Bovkun underscored the pressure being applied to the West German government.[18]

Another article by Grishin similarly focused on American (and British) pressures and the West Germans' reaction to this.[19] The United States resorted to "overt blackmail," according to Grishin: "Irritated by the obstinacy of its Rhine ally, the U.S. administration set the strongest operating means in motion. U.S. Ambassador to the FRG Walters threatened: if Bonn does not display 'solidarity,' then Washington will raise the question of withdrawing U.S. troops from West German territory." Grishin then noted that Helmut Schmidt's reaction to this "threat" was that they had been hearing such threats for years; and Egon Bahr characterized the U.S. and British actions as "irresponsible." Finally, Grigor'ev posed the question bluntly: Will Bonn give in to the United States in the name of Atlantic solidarity in the face of support for negotiations by the overwhelming majority of the public and the main political forces in West Germany.[20]

In other words, Soviet analysts focused on the direct confrontation between the United States and West Germany over the FOTL issue. After the INF issue had bonded the American and West German governments on the nuclear deterrence issue, the FOTL issue promised to place serious strain on their bilateral relationship. Clearly, Soviet analysts saw this as an opportunity to reinforce the Soviet-West German dynamic at the expense of the American one in a zero-sum relationship. For the Soviets at this time, the "common European home" held the promise of becoming a nuclear free one, at least with regard to the American guests in that home.

The Role of FRG Military Forces in Western Defense

Particularly on the pages of the military journal *Zarubezhnoe voennoe obozrenie*, Soviet analyses consistently highlighted the important role the Federal Republic has played in the NATO Alliance and in Western defense efforts more generally:

> The FRG's military-political course at the present stage is aimed at further increasing the country's role in NATO, comprehensively strengthening its ties with the U.S., expanding and deepening Franco-West German military cooperation, and constantly building up the Bundeswehr's combat might. The FRG's leadership is actively participating in the elaboration and implementation of a coordinated military policy for the North Atlantic bloc vis-a-vis the Warsaw Pact, is taking upon itself the basic obligations to build up the combat potential of the bloc's allied forces, and is constantly pressuring the West European allies to increase their contribution to collective militaristic preparations.[21]

The same author, V. Lyudchik, wrote several months later a quite similar assessment, this time emphasizing the Bundeswehr's role:

> Completely approving and supportive of the aggressive foreign policy course of the U.S. and NATO ruling circles, the FRG is actively participating in augmenting the bloc's military prepa-

> rations. This is reflected, in particular, in the further increase in the Bundeswehr's striking might through the constant improvement of its organizational structure and the outfitting of formations and units with modern weapons and combat equipment. According to foreign specialists' appraisals, the Bundeswehr is presently the largest and most combat ready armed force in Western Europe. Thus, in Central Europe it accounts for 50 percent of the ground troops, 60 percent of the tanks, 30 percent of combat aircraft, and 30 percent of naval men and materiel.[22]

Soviet analysts in the 1987 to 1989 period identified the prevailing characteristics of the West German approach to military issues. First, a number of Soviet military analysts continued to identify a persistent militaristic attitude in Bonn's ruling circles, especially within conservative ones. As one analyst bluntly wrote, "No, to believe that fascism in the FRG has disappeared or is impotent is, without a doubt, premature. It is still alive and active."[23] This particular analyst perceived even West German efforts to expand West European military ties towards a hard-line direction. "It has recently become clear that the FRG is making concerted efforts to hook up to the so-called 'European army' and French armed forces. What is this, if not a super-Wehrmacht?"[24]

Second, Soviet analysts underscored the continued existence of the West German "military-industrial complex" and its steady influence on West German foreign and security policy. Notably, the orientation of the FRG "military-industrial complex" was to reopen the German question. "The build up of the FRG's military-economic potential, the increased strength of its military-industrial concerns, and the stepping up of aggressive revanchist forces demanding a reexamination of territorial-political realities in Europe, represent a serious threat to the peaceful future of European states and peoples."[25]

Third, the West German state continued to provide a high-level of support to the "military-industrial complex." According to an article by Shitov in *Zarubezhnovoennoe obozrenie*,

> The military-political leadership of the FRG is continuing to build up the Bundeswehr's combat might by outfitting it with new types of weapons and military equipment, increasing the number of personnel, especially officers and non-commissioned

> officers, and improving the combat training of the troops. These militaristic aspirations are reflected in the constant growth of military expenditures, whose share of the state budget is more than 20 percent.... Military development will be conducted both in the interests of the Bundeswehr and in order to develop the infrastructure according to the NATO program. The increase in the FRG's military expenditures for 1987 demonstrates the determination of the country's militaristic circles to further increase the combat capability of its armed forces and to pump up military tensions in the center of Europe.[26]

Finally, the West Germans were characterized as continuing to harbor covert nuclear aspirations.

> Having agreed to turn the FRG into the U.S.'s main nuclear base in Western Europe, Bonn persistently put forward demands to establish a "dual key" system over the nuclear weapons located in its country: one of them would be in the hands of the American masters, the other in the hands of the West German generals. The FRG military-industrial complex has also not abandoned the idea about the possibility of receiving access to French nuclear weapons. With this aim, it has intensively sought to strengthen military-political and military-economic cooperation with France. At the present time the West German military-industrial complex, through participation in the American "Star Wars" program, is holding out its hands to control third generation nuclear weapons and to create its own means of mass destruction.[27]

In addition to identifying a set of general propensities for the West German "military-industrial complex," Soviet analysts also highlighted a number of key elements in West German military strategy in the 1987-1989 period. First, the West Germans remained committed to the concept of forward defense regardless of the allied military framework which might evolve.

> The development of West European military-political integration can open up additional possibilities for the FRG. Mainly, this is explained by its favorable attitude toward such integration

> plans.... But the FRG's position on the issue of West European military-political integration is also motivated by geostrategic considerations. Its location in the region of direct NATO-Warsaw Pact contact...and the relatively small operational depth of West German territory (200-300km) makes, in Bonn's eyes, the reliability of "forward defense" of paramount importance. And any schemes to organize military-political cooperation--within the NATO framework or outside of this bloc, with the active participation of the U.S. or with the growing role of the West European component of "unified defense"--is viewed above all with this criteria in mind. Such projects of West European military-political integration which even theoretically could undermine or weaken "forward defense" provokes an extremely guarded attitude in Bonn.[28]

Second, the desire by West Germany to shift away from excessive reliance on nuclear weapons called for the enhancement of the role of conventional forces in Western strategy. In such a shift, Bonn would have to play a critical role. "In the context of the scheduled reduction of the U.S. nuclear arsenal in Europe, it is planned to concentrate the main efforts on building up the Bundeswehr's conventional arms during its modernization."[29]

Third, West Germany would have to expand its technological capabilities in the conventional area, for example in air defense. "NATO military experts believe that after refitting and reorganizing of West German Air Force SAM units and completing the program for modernizing FRG air defense control entities, the tactical capabilities of its air defense system, and of the NATO allied air defense system in the Central European Theater (of which it is the basis) on the whole, will increase considerably and will meet modern requirements."[30]

Finally, the West German military was seen as shifting its strategy in a more offensive direction. As the West German military worked toward improving its capability to fight maneuver warfare, the line between defense and offense had become blurred and the challenge to the Soviet military had expanded.

> The FRG's ground troops are intended to conduct both offensive and defensive actions. In the opinion of the Bundeswehr command, the offensive is the basic type of combat action, as

> a result of which the opponent is routed, seizure of his territory is ensured, and favorable circumstances for further successes are created. According to the views of West German military specialists, success in offensive actions will depend to a considerable extent on firmly suppressing the opponent by means of nuclear destruction, artillery and tank fire, air strikes, and on decisive actions by formations and units in the depths of the opponent's defense.... Defense, as FRG military specialists believe, is also one of the basic types of combat action, to which the troops will temporarily transition in order to break the opponent's offensive, economize men and materiel on certain axes and create superiority over the opponent on others, maintain important borders and regions, win time, and create the conditions for a transition to the offensive. The underlying principle for conducting defense today is, in their opinion, the skillful combination of maneuvers by formations and units and the effective use of all types of weapons, above all nuclear and high precision weapons.[31]

The West German state was perceived to be seeking during the 1987-1989 period to balance interests in maintaining a close military tie with the United States and transforming the Alliance into a European defense organization. In other words, the West Germans sought to use their military assets to anchor the Western allies to support West German national aims.

Close ties with the United States remained significant. "The FRG's military policy has become an integral part of the U.S. policy to 'destroy socialism,' reinforced by gigantic military programs aimed at undermining the existing balance of forces and obtaining military-strategic superiority over the socialist countries. Today the Bundeswehr has been turned into a shock force of the aggressive NATO bloc."[32]

Nonetheless, the West Germans sought to expand their European military ties as well, as Ziborova details.

> As a whole, the West German government strives to be the "motor" of West European integration, not relinquishing this to French leadership. It seeks to step up the activities of all the organizations that see their task to be coordinating the West European countries' approaches to today's military-political

> problems. But this policy is also aimed at increasing its [the FRG's] role and potential in its relations with the U.S.; it is being worked out in such a way so that cooperation by West European states in the military-political sphere does not contradict, at least in the foreseeable future, NATO objectives. Coordination of military-political issues by the West European states and an increase in their military contribution should, according to the calculations of the FRG's ruling circles, lead to the transformation of NATO's West European component into a most important integral part of the bloc, indispensable for the U.S., which will ensure close military-political ties between Western Europe and the U.S. and the conformity of the bloc's policy to West European interests, and in the long-term will prepare the foundation for a military-political community of West European states, especially in the event of a reduction of the U.S. presence in Western Europe.... At the same time, the special significance which Bonn accords to military-political cooperation with the U.S. inevitably limits the possibilities and restrains the tempo of development of the integrational processes in the military-political area within the West European framework.[33]

In other words, Bonn was pursuing a contradictory policy of Atlanticism and Europeanization. Soviet analysts implied that only a turn away from classic Atlanticism and a partnership arrangement with the Soviet Union could provide for genuine Europeanization. The negative side of this was most often noted by Soviet military analysts.

> The West German government's readiness to play the role of a special connecting link, vitally necessary for both Western Europe and the United States, in fact complicates the process of Western Europe's acquiring its own identity in the world arena. "Atlanticism" in West German policy constricts and limits "Europeanism." Bonn's policy of ensuring the cooperation of West European states with the U.S. contributes to the retention of Western Europe's dependency on the U.S. and not only does not motivate Washington to reject an open restriction of the West European allies' interests but it also multiplies Washington's attempts to create new problems and difficulties for the European Community.[34]

The more positive side of Europeanization was the focus of attention by diplomats, politicians and political analysts. Usually framed as the quest for the common European home, the goal was to promote "genuine" European cooperation, not West European integration which revolved around military and security issues.

Germany and the Common European Home

The most remarkable presentation of the linkage between the "common European home" theme and Soviet policy toward West Germany was contained in an unpublished paper by Vyacheslav Dashichev. This paper was presented at a conference in West Germany in early 1989 and was subsequently widely distributed in the West German government. In this section, the main points Dashichev outlines in his paper are presented.

Dashichev began his assessment by noting that many indicators pointed to the end of the post-WWII split in Europe. A new European order was on the horizon "free from the dangerous and exceptionally costly confrontation" between the Warsaw Pact and NATO.[35] Major changes "are putting under question the previous political objectives and strategy of NATO and the Warsaw Pact."[36]

The United States was increasingly searching for ways out of the heavy obligations of underwriting West European security. For the United States, continuation of the status quo encompassed the risk of involving American territory in nuclear strikes. The United States had consistently sought ways to modify NATO's strategy in order to reduce the risk of being drawn into a nuclear exchange over European affairs, notably the shift from massive retaliation to flexible response. Moreover, the economic burden of U.S. military obligations in Western Europe "is one of the important reasons for the noticeable weakening of the U.S. economic position in the world and for the country's financial difficulties."[37]

The Western Europeans were not satisfied with the status quo either. They wished to expand their role in global affairs, which required a change in their relationship with the superpowers. Among other things, this required ending Soviet supremacy in Eastern Europe.[38] For the West Germans, the emphasis was upon the German question; for the other West Europeans, the task was to change the status of Eastern Europe as a whole. Dashichev argued that "the FRG is, naturally, advocating to the greatest extent a change in the existing status quo; its political circles link the resolution of the German national problem with this. For France and England, freeing the East European countries from Soviet control is of paramount importance."[39]

But there was a noticeable tension among the West European powers. The French and British feared that West Germany might eventually be unified with the GDR, which would make it the dominant political and economic power in Western Europe, would make NATO's existence impossible, and West European economic and miliary-political cooperation difficult.[40] The French and the British feared that West Germany might pull out of NATO and the GDR out of the Warsaw Pact because they would lose political control over West Germany. The FRG would have then been able to dedicate all its economic potential to civilian development, becoming an economic giant like Japan. In addition, Dashichev argued that the smaller countries of Western Europe shared British and French concerns.

West Europeans were reexamining their position in East-West relations in part bacause of changes in the Soviet-East European relationship. There was a "profound erosion of the political, economic, and moral-psychological positions of the Soviet Union in Eastern Europe."[41] The Brezhnev doctrine had become the symbol of weakness in Soviet policy toward Eastern Europe. The Soviets had virtually no political, economic or ideological influence in East European countries. Military force had also lost its importance as a direct or indirect influence on internal developments in Eastern Europe. The results have been that Eastern Europe has shifted from being a security zone to an area plagued with danger and instability.[42]

As a result of weaknesses in Soviet influence over Eastern Europe, the Soviet Union was forced to reassess its policy in the region. Such reassessments were reflected in "new political thinking." Dashichev argued that the West was still not convinced that these ideas would actually be implemented. For the West to be convinced of the serious rethinking of Soviet foreign policy, the Soviet Union had to renounce completely the Brezhnev doctrine.[43]

In addition, the Soviet Union had to alter its policy on the German question. Dashichev forcefully underscored that "in our land the opinion firmly took root that the division of Germany into two German states serves Soviet interests best and the maintenance of European security.

But this view carries the imprint of one-sidedness and conservativism...."[44] Soviet policy on the German question in the postwar decades had been "very contradictory and inconsistent." This was explained by the fact that in this policy, "the interests of security closely neighbored systemic-political considerations." Dashichev further pointed out that one can not ignore the role of great power or "imperial" ambitions in Soviet foreign policy as well.[45]

Conditions had changed in Europe and the Soviet Union. Today, the West German public would like to see a shift in Soviet policy. They wanted to have their national interests more effectively taken into account. Increasingly, West German political order coalesced around a commitment to detente. "The concept of the common European home is viewed in Bonn most favorably... from the viewpoint of resolving the national tasks of *ostpolitik*."[46] Notably, the West Germans were increasingly viewing nationalism and overcoming the East-West divide as two aspects of the same effort. "Thus, whereas before among West German politicians and ideologues there were arguments about whether it were a priority task of FRG policy to overcome the division of Germany first and only then the division of Europe, now an overwhelming majority of them are of the opinion that national reunification can occur only within the framework of gradually overcoming East-West antagonism, above all between the USSR and U.S."[47]

Changes in West German policy as well as in Eastern Europe allowed for the possibility of change in Soviet foreign policy. It was especially important for the Soviet Union to stop confronting all the leading Western powers. The logic underlying this policy was lost long ago, but it has still continued. Perestroika opened up new possibilities for stopping confrontation and creating a common European home. "For this, it is necessary once and for all to free the countries of Eastern Europe from Soviet tutelage, and moreover not to allow any kind of diktat as was established by Stalin and practiced in subsequent decades."[48]

To generate the process of constructing a common European home required dealing with the German question as well. "It is time to renounce a narrow approach to the 'German question' through the prism of interests of some one state. It is of all-European importance and all European states must join efforts to resolve it in order to put an end to the abnormal situation in the center of Europe. By most reckonings, this is in the interests of all European peoples, their security and close cooperation."[49] It would be a mistake to try to resolve the question according to bloc thinking, to the detriment of East or West European countries. "An all-European approach is necessary."[50]

No matter how the German question might be resolved in the future, it was obvious that the FRG economy would remain closely tied to Western Europe. This shouldn't be viewed as a tragedy for the East for East European countries have also "grown up" and are no longer obtaining all their raw materials and energy resources from the USSR, Dashichev noted.[51] A key question was whether the EC members would be sufficiently "wise" to not close their market, especially after 1992. They needed to allow free entry of goods from the East and they should not use their economic might as a political counter to USSR and Eastern Europe. If this occurred, the old antagonisms would develop again which would make the creation of a common European home very difficult.[52]

An expansion of East European economic cooperation with Western Europe, above all with West Germany, would help stabilize the economic situations of the East and move their economies forward. For the Soviet Union, deepening cooperation with West Germany and other Western countries could solve many economic tasks associated with perestroika. This would seriously alter the position of East Germany. "It must be assumed that the processes of economic opening to the West, especially to the FRG, will also affect the GDR sooner or later.... The GDR could become an important mediator in deepening economic and scientific-technical ties between the FRG and countries of Eastern Europe."[53]

When the East-West confrontation gives way to all-European cooperation, when dangers disappear, one can expect the formation of a confederation of the two German states or the emergence of other forms of close cooperation between the FRG and the GDR, Dashichev postulated. It was very important that this process would take place in a stable domestic and international environment.

In short, the resolution of the German question and of the constructing process of a common European home should be interwoven. Both of these issues would occur in a process of gradual change of breaking down blocs and overcoming the division of Europe, such was the image projected by Dashichev.

> If one regards the idea of a common European home seriously and does not view it as some kind of propaganda slogan--and it, in our opinion, meets the deep national interests of the USSR--then it follows that the settling of the "German question"

> must occupy the central place in its realization one way or another. As soon as the situation around this question is cleared up and is normalized and the dissociation of the German nation is overcome, one of the main reasons for political and military confrontation on the European continent will disappear. Then the peoples of Europe will stop senselessly spending enormous material and spiritual resources on dangerous confrontation; their division into two camps will be stopped; the need to maintain U.S. troops in Western Europe and Soviet troops in Eastern Europe will fall away; and they will be able to be put into their own borders, the European people will be freed from the fear hanging over them and the possibility of free development will finally be found. As for the Soviet Union, for it this will bring an historic deliverance from the heavy, back-breaking burden of opposing the coalition of West European states, the U.S. and Canada.[54]

Conclusion: The Strasbourg Synthesis

In an historic presentation, President Gorbachev addressed the Council of Europe in Strasbourg, France on 6 July 1989 on his administration's new thinking. This speech represented a synthesis of rethinking which his administration had undertaken in the late 1980s. In this sense, the Strasbourg synthesis is the culmination of Gorbachev's thinking about Soviet European policy prior to the Revolution of 1989. The speech brought together in one place the various elements of the "new thinking" as it applied to Soviet foreign policy toward Europe.

There were six major elements of the Strasbourg synthesis. First, there was the assertion that capitalist and socialist Europe would continue to exist and that it would be illegitimate for the West to put the socialist system into question. Gorbachev commented that "I know that many in the West see the presence of two social systems as the major difficulty. But the difficulty actually lies elsewhere--in the widespread conviction (sometimes even a policy objective) whereby overcoming the split in Europe means 'overcoming socialism.' But this is a policy of confrontation, if not worse. No European unity will result from such approaches."[55]

The second element was an emphasis upon a process of gradually overcoming the differences between the two social systems, perhaps by creating a new synthesis or a new European civilization. Not in the cards was an expectation that Westernization would spread East and rapidly engulf "socialism."

Third, the European states have the right to determine for themselves the nature of their social systems. Asserting this right was correlated with Gorbachev's belief that "socialism" in the East had taken root and would continue to exist after the Brezhnev doctrine was allowed to lapse. "The fact that European states belong to different social systems is a reality. And recognition of this historical given and respect for the sovereign right of every people to choose a social system at its own discretion constitute the most important prerequisite for a normal European process."[56]

Fourth, the military factor will become less and less determining in relations among the European states. The military factor's reduced significance is especially significant in determining the Soviet Union's place within the European system. "The colossal burden of armaments and the atmosphere of confrontation were not only hindering Europe's normal development, but at the same time, were obstructing--economically, politically and psychologically--the full-fledged inclusion of our country in the European process and were introducing deforming impulses in our own development."[57]

Fifth, along with the decreased salience of the military factor there is the increased importance of economic, cultural and political interdependence among the European states. Gorbachev makes a comment on the metaphysics of historical development in these words: "In today's interdependent world, geopolitical notions born of another epoch as just as useless in real politics as the laws of classical mechanics are in quantum theory."[58]

Finally, the common European home is defined as the residuum of all of the above--an interdependent, less militaristic, freer and more dynamic world whereby East-West differences are gradually overcome. "In essence, we are talking about restructuring the existing international order in Europe in such a way that common European values will come firmly to the forefront and it will become possible to replace the traditional balance of forces with a balance of interests."[59]

Not only is it assumed that gradual East and West transmutation will occur, but that the Alliances crystallizing the interests of Eastern and Western states will gradually change over time. Not only did

Gorbachev underscore this point in his Strasbourg speech, but the Warsaw Pact meeting reinforced the point in its July 1989 meeting.

> The conference participants called for directing relations between the Warsaw Treaty Organization and the North Atlantic Alliance into a nonconfrontational channel, for establishing a constructive dialogue between them in the political and military spheres, and for turning that dialogue into a factor of security and cooperation on the Continent. At the same time, the Warsaw Treaty member-states' fundamental position that Europe should be rid of military blocs, that the two alliances should be simultaneously disbanded, and that their military organization should be dismantled as a first step remains in force.[60]

Notably, in an authoritative statement on the common European home concept made in May 1989, Gorbachev's central point concerning the need to build new structures while taking into account the realities of the divided Europe was underscored. V. Zhurkin, head of the European Institute of the Academy of Sciences, argued that "the search for new forms of European cooperation should be carried out very thoughtfully and cautiously, taking into consideration traditions and emerging realities, so that the stability in the European situation that has been achieved in recent decades with such difficulty is not disrupted, but strengthened."[61] He then went on to provide the following working definition for the European common home: "It is a new system of security and cooperation growing out of the all-European process and extending it, a system based on gradually eliminating the military-political and economic division of Europe and replacing it with effective and mutually beneficial forms of coexistence among states with different social systems, based on a balance of interests and involving political, military, economic, humanitarian and other areas."[62]

Notwithstanding Soviet aspirations, history was to take a sharp turn. Instead of gradualism, there would be a series of explosions. Instead of an evolutionary path, there would be a revolutionary one, albeit a peaceful one. Instead of the gradual forging of a new East-West synthesis, Westernization would explode Eastward. The Soviets would need to confront a serious crisis of analysis, policy and redefinition of themselves.

Notes

1. H. Vogel, **MEMO**, no. 7, 1988, p. 35.
2. M. Maksimova,"To Uncover the Potential for Cooperation," **MEMO**, no. 10, 1988, p. 62.
3. **Ibid.**
4. **Ibid.**
5. Pleskov, "On FRG's Sovereignty," **IA**, no. 2, 1989, p. 82.
6. Yu. Kvitsinsky, "An Embassy on the Rhine," **IA**, no. 5, 1989, p. 37.
7. M. S. Ziborova, **Bonn-Vashington: 70-80-e gody** (Moscow: Nauka, 1988), p. 235.
8. **Ibid.**, pp. 204-205.
9. **Ibid.**, p. 5.
10. Kvitsinsky, **IA**, no. 5, 1989, pp. 35-37.
11. **Ibid.**, p. 38.
12. Maksimova, **MEMO**, no. 10, 1988, pp. 62-63.
13. N. Afanasyevsky, Eduard Tarasinkevich and Andrei Shvedov, "Between Yesterday and Today," **IA**, no. 5, 1988, p.27.
14. **Ibid.**, p. 28.
15. V. Stupishin, "Common European Home and the Slogan for a United States of Europe," **IA**, no. 3, 1989, p. 93.
16. E. Grishin, **Izvestiya**, 28 April 1989; E. Grigor'ev, **Pravda**, 28 April 1989.
17. E. Bovkun, **Izvestiya**, 7 April 1989.
18. E. Bovkun, **Izvestiya**, 19 May 1989 and 23 May 1989.
19. E. Grishin, **Izvestiya**, 10 May 1989.
20. E. Grigor'ev, **Pravda**, 24 May 1989.
21. V. Lyudchik, "The Armed Forces of the FRG," **Zarubezhnoe voennoe obozrenie** (hereinafter **ZVO**), no. 12, 1988, p. 7.
22. V. Lyudchik, "The Ground Troops of the FRG," **ZVO**, no. 3, 1989, p. 19.
23. E. Genri, **Za stsenoi v Bonne** (Moscow: Mezhdunarodnye otnosheniya, 1986), p. 99.
24. **Ibid.**, p. 78.
25. A. V. Shishaeva, **Voenno-promyshlennye kompleksy v zapadnoi evrope** (Moscow: Mezhdunarodnye otnosheniya, 1988), p. 140.
26. Shitov, **ZVO**, no. 2, 1987, pp. 91-92.
27. Shishaeva, **Voenno-promyshlennye kompleksy**, p. 123.

28. V. Baranovskii, **Zapadnaia Evropa: voennno-politicheskaya integratsiya** (Moscow: Mezhdunarodnaya Otnosheniya, 1988), p. 33.
29. Lyudchik, **ZVO**, no. 12, 1988, p. 7.
30. Viktorov, **ZVO**, no. 2, 1988 in JPRS-UFM-88-008, p. 58.
31. Lyudchik, **ZVO**, no. 19, 1989, pp. 24-25.
32. Shishaeva, **Voenno-promyshlennye kompleksy**, p. 123.
33. Ziborova, **Bonn-Vashington**, pp. 115-116.
34. **Ibid.**, p. 140.
35. Dashichev, "The Common European Home Conception and the German Question," unpublished paper, 1989, p. 1.
36. **Ibid.**
37. **Ibid.**, p. 2.
38. **Ibid.**, p. 4.
39. **Ibid.**
40. **Ibid.**, p. 5.
41. **Ibid.**, p. 6.
42. **Ibid.**, p. 7.
43. **Ibid.**, p. 8.
44. **Ibid.**, p. 10.
45. **Ibid.**
46. **Ibid.**, p. 16.
47. **Ibid.**, p. 19.
48. **Ibid.**, pp. 28-29.
49. **Ibid.**, p. 30.
50. **Ibid.**
51. **Ibid.**, p. 33.
52. **Ibid.**
53. **Ibid.**, p. 35.
54. **Ibid.**, pp. 36-37.
55. M.S. Gorbachev, "All-European Process Moves Ahead," **Pravda**, 7 July 1990, in **The Current Digest of the Soviet Press** (hereinafter **CDSP**), vol. xli, no. 27, 1989, p. 6.
56. **Ibid.**
57. **Ibid.**
58. **Ibid.**
59. **Ibid.**
60. Communique of the Conference of the Political Consultative Committee of the Warsaw Treaty Member-States, **Pravda**, 9 July 1989, in **CDSP**, 8 July 1989, p. 3.

61. V. Zhurkin, "A Common Home for Europe," **Pravda**, 17 May 1989, p. 4, in **CDSP**, vol. xli, no. 22, 1989, p. 15.

62. **Ibid.**

6

Soviet Public Diplomacy Toward West Germany, 1985-1989

This chapter examines the Soviet approach toward the Federal Republic of Germany under Gorbachev, especially Soviet public diplomacy from 1985 through the Gorbachev visit to Bonn in the summer of 1989. The chapter is based upon interviews of key German officials and observations of Soviet behavior in the Federal Republic in the period during several visits from 1985-1989.

The New Dynamism Under Gorbachev

Although broad Soviet objectives toward Western Europe did not change much initially, the Soviet leadership under Gorbachev quickly injected a new dynamism and vigor in Soviet foreign policy. The Soviet leadership initially sought a "breathing space" in East-West relations to aid their domestic reform efforts. In order to get that "breathing space," however, Gorbachev believed it necessary to convince the West that he was seeking fundamental reform in the Soviet Union.

Soviet foreign policy changed most in the area of public diplomacy; particularly illustrative was the new leader's ability to tap more deftly than previous leaders the evolution of objective capabilities. Gorbachev proved himself the first Soviet leader to make effective use of the electronic media. He instinctively understood how to use the media to his political advantage. This was true both of his domestic and foreign policies.

But the Gorbachev phenomenon signified more than the ascension of a media personality to the Soviet leadership. The Soviet foreign policy apparatus overall had grown increasingly sophisticated. A new foreign policy elite had emerged over the previous fifteen years that was better trained and better informed than its predecessors. Nonetheless, Andrei Gromyko's dominance in foreign policy and the general aging of the Soviet elite had impeded the emergence of this new generation. Gorbachev's ascension enabled the new elite to rise to positions of power, including in the foreign policy system. Furthermore, Gorbachev and Shevardnadze were aware of the benefits of a flexible leadership style and good public relations at home and abroad, in stark contrast to the increasingly inflexible and dour Gromyko.

Shaking up the foreign policy elite and opening up the system to new faces led to a ferment in foreign policy activity. It also allowed the Soviets to rethink some old positions and to move forward more flexibly. It is clear in retrospect that the inflexibility of the Soviet negotiating position on the INF forces was largely due to Gromyko. Gorbachev was willing to rethink the Soviet position and to accept the legitimacy of Western demands for Soviet reductions in nuclear forces.

An important component of Soviet foreign policy under Gorbachev has been a new "realism." Rather than just focusing on political forces more favorable to Soviet interpretations of Western interests (e.g., the peace movement), Soviet leaders began to recognize the staying power of more conservative elements in Western Europe; namely because of the conservative party victories in both the United Kingdom and West Germany in the late-1980s. Since it was clear that in many of the key countries conservative governments would remain in power into the 1990s, the Soviets recognized the need to reach out to a broader elite than before in Western Europe. For example, in the West German case, Soviet officials moved beyond their past courting of SPD officials, to the point that a conservative politician such as Franz Joseph Strauss was welcomed in Moscow. Nor were they disappointed for their efforts. The strikingly positive attitude Strauss adopted in his December 1987 visit to Moscow was a clear victory for this new style of Soviet diplomacy.

Another important dimension of the exercise of public diplomacy under Gorbachev was the general effort to bring words more into line with deeds. Rather than relying on wishful thinking, cliches or bombastic propaganda alone, the Soviets began to recognize that changes in Soviet actions were required to affect changes in West European and American perceptions.

This was especially true in the arms control area, where the Soviets sought to carry out actions which the West would recognize as significant; ones which would indicate that the Soviets were "serious" about lowering the level of confrontation in East-West relations. The acceptance of the single zero option, the promotion of the double zero option, and then the acceptance of the Western insistence on an on-site verification regime--all led to enhancing significantly the Western perceptions that the Soviets were seeking genuine reconciliation in East-West relations.

An important by-product of the arms control effort was the desire to legitimize the ideas of the European left on security ideas. During the INF deployment struggle of the early 1980s, the left opposed not only nuclear but conventional modernization. Their opposition to conventional modernization was grounded in the concept that defense should be "genuinely" defensive, not oriented toward "provocative" offensive operations. Under Gorbachev several Soviet spokesmen accepted the legitimacy of these ideas under the rubric of "reasonable sufficiency." There is an explicit connection between the Soviet argument about the need to shift Soviet doctrine and forces to a posture based on "reasonable sufficiency" and the West European left's promotion of the idea of non-provocative defense.

Above all, Soviet spokesmen began underscoring that there was a growing and more realistic possibility of East-West reconciliation if Soviet initiatives were met with correspondingly serious proposals by the West. Simply put, the message was as follows: "We are now reasonable; work with us and we can put the old confrontations behind us and live in a more peaceful and interdependent world."

The Soviet Approach to West German Elites, 1985-1988

Gorbachev's approach toward the Federal Republic was designed to deal with the most troubling trends in West German security policy. "Revanchism" was to be deflected by encouraging the West Germans to return to their detente policy of the 1970s, a policy which accepted the territorial and political status quo in Europe. To deflect "revanchism," Gorbachev emphasized a new detente with the Alliance in which the

Soviets accepted the "realities" of the foundations of Western security policy in exchange for a recognition of the "realities" of Eastern security policy.

To reduce "militarism" in West German policy, the Soviet leadership emphasized the possibilities of serious reductions in the Soviet military threat. In fact, the Soviet goal was to minimize the ability of the West German conservatives to use the "excuse" of the Soviet military threat to justify West German military expenditures. Furthermore, the Soviets emphasized the possibilities of shifting East-West military policy to a "defensive" basis, a policy which would allow the SPD to move back toward the center of the political spectrum on security issues.

To reduce Atlanticism and Europeanism, the Soviets emphasized the primacy of the common European home, but without European military integration. The emphasis on the common European home suggested a distancing from the Americans, although the new "realism" in Soviet policy led to a recognition of the durability of NATO and the legitimacy of some form of American military presence in Europe. The goal was simply to reduce the cohesion of the Alliance and the nature of the American military presence. But the Soviets did not want to see a reduction in the American role lead to an enhancement of the European role in the Alliance, a process which could occur only with vigorous West German involvement. While the Soviets emphasized the legitimacy of developing West European economic and even political integration (some even said they could accept a West European role in Eastern Europe), they clearly denied the legitimacy of West European military integration. The common European home would be possible only if there were no military integration of Western Europe, according to the Soviets.

Prior to the Gorbachev administration, the Soviets targeted their efforts at groups opposed to the mainstream policies of the Federal Republic, especially the peace movement and the SPD (after the party moved toward the rejection of mainstream policies during the INF crisis). The Soviets under Gorbachev shifted their approach to try to deal directly with mainstream groups, including prominent conservative politicians who had hitherto been considered anathema to the Soviets.

The Soviets fostered a dialogue with mainstream groups by openly discussing issues and demonstrating a publicly self-critical attitude. When in the presence of American representatives at common forums in the FRG, the Soviets focused on the political context of security policy whereas the Americans were more likely to discuss military-technical issues. The Soviets came across as more interested in peace than the Americans precisely because military-technical discussions are so rare in the West German public domain that the mere discussion of security in these terms showed a blatant American misunderstanding of how to influence the West German public. By dealing with the main political factors of security policy in their presentations and discussions with West Germans, the Soviets revealed a greater sensitivity to West German opinion. The Americans did have a major asset in influencing West German opinion due to their candor in discussing issues and admitting mistakes which had been made in the past. But, the new Soviet leaders sought to eliminate this advantage and to capture it for themselves. By opening up a dialogue with mainstream groups, Soviet discussions with other groups, such as SPD politicians critical of mainstream politics, became less marginalized. Discussions with the SPD became just one more strand in West German-Soviet discussions, rather than something standing out for public attention.

Also, the Soviets tied discussions of reasonable sufficiency to alternative defense concepts in the FRG. To the extent that the reasonable sufficiency concept could become the coin of the realm in discussing security issues, alternative defense concepts would become less marginalized and gain respectability and plausibility.

The Soviet approach in trying to influence West German elites was well adapted to that effort. Whereas in the United States, Soviet spokesmen had the opportunity to operate as commentators directly on American news programs, the operation of the West German media made such an approach difficult. Considerably more important to the effort to influence elite opinion was direct work with the network of elites in discussion groups and fora, as well as trying to affect positions of West German journalists. West German print media has been very influential in shaping elite understandings, much more than television.

Typical of the Soviet effort to participate in meetings and round tables was the invitation extended to the Bergedorfer Gesprachskreis group to visit Moscow in March 1987. This group included Egon Bahr (SPD), Horst Teltschik (then advisor to Chancellor Kohl), Lothar Ruhl (State Secretary in the Defense Ministry) and former Chancellor Helmut Schmidt. The round table has been a politically bipartisan association of important figures from West German politics, economy and society, meeting on an ad hoc basis to discuss critical contemporary issues. The Soviets invited this group to Moscow and took the opportunity to present their views on the course and implementation of perestroika and the new thinking.

The Soviets actively participated in conventions, meetings and forums held in the Federal Republic as well. For example, Soviet Ambassador Kvitsinsky participated in a 1987 conference on foreign policy which was organized by the CDU. At this meeting, Kvitsinsky emphasized that the Soviet Union was willing to alter its East-West policy and to alter especially its position on the presence of the United States in Europe. He even suggested that the American military presence in Western Europe was legitimate; the Soviet dissatisfaction with this presence centered merely on how the Americans used their presence to influence the course of progress.

Also typical of the Soviet diplomatic effort was a discussion by Valentin Falin, former Soviet ambassador to the Federal Republic. Early in 1988, Falin held a press conference in West Germany in which he urged the West Germans not to rush ahead with short-range nuclear modernization. He asked the West Germans to give the Soviet Union time to realize the promise of perestroika and not to force the Soviet leadership to react to a new round of arms modernization on West German soil. He urged the West German government to build on its responsible performance in resolving the Pershing IA problem. But if the West Germans ignored this advice, of course, Falin indicated the Soviet Union could harden its policy toward the Federal Republic. Thus, the former Soviet ambassador to the Federal Republic combined an effort to woo West German elites with a clear warning. This combination was typical of most Soviet attempts in dealing with West German elites, although the attempt to woo predominated during this period.

Kvitsinsky and Falin were the most visible representatives of the Soviet Union in the Federal Republic. Both speak fluent German and were very adept at presenting the proper mix of wooing and cajoling in their effort to influence West German elite perceptions. Kvitsinsky became the much more visible figure of the two.

The then Soviet ambassador was perceived to be a very ambitious man who was on the rise and therefore influential with Gorbachev. Contrary to his predecessor (Semyonov), he was perceived to have much greater authority in Moscow. While Semyonov was seen to be a representative of the "old way of thinking," Kvitsinsky was strongly in favor of the "new political thinking," glasnost and perestroika. While in American eyes he was first and foremost a specialist and leading figure in arms control, he belonged as well to the so-called Germanisty. He was a protege of Politburo member Yakovlev and a close friend of Nikolay Portugalov (a senior Soviet Germanist) and Valentin Falin. He was definitely not an Amerikanist, which meant that in the International Department of the CPSU, he was linked more to Zagladin than to Dobrynin. He also had close connections to TASS and was a friend of the chairman of the Gesellschaft BRD-USSR, Losev, who was also affiliated with TASS.

Kvitsinsky was not only a candidate member of the Central Committee but also one of the relatively few foreign policy specialists given the opportunity to speak before the Central Committee. Prior to Kvitsinsky's tenure, it was impossible to contact people from the Central Committee apparatus via the Soviet embassy. But under Kvitsinsky, the embassy acted as an intermediary agency with regard to the Central Committee apparatus as well. The Soviet embassy officials under Kvitsinsky were given relatively wide latitude in dealing with West German elites and tried to use their embassy like the Americans had used theirs, as a place where frank discussion could be held.

Falin remained an important player as well and used his position as the head of Novosti to try to help promote Soviet public diplomacy in West Germany. Most notably, he was the guiding force behind the decision to publish a West German version of *Moscow News*. This paper was not a German translation of the Russian-language paper, but rather was a monthly publication of the most prominent examples of glasnost and new thinking. The paper did not focus on German-Soviet relations but rather dealt mainly with Soviet domestic policy issues associated with perestroika.

The German version of *Moscow News* was written in a chatty style. The Soviets wanted to use this publication to suggest subliminally that press freedom had been significantly expanded in the Soviet Union. Most West German readers of *Moscow News* had no idea that it was not a literal translation or that the Russian language version had a limited circulation in the Soviet Union itself. The English title and the use of the word "news" was intended to convey to the reader that this publication was something akin to an American newspaper.

There was a curious mixture of the old thinking among the German hands in the Foreign Ministry and the new thinking of the International Department of the Central Committee. The West German officials at the working level continued to experience frustration in dealing with their

Soviet Foreign Ministry counterparts. Typical was the Soviet effort to challenge the recognition of West Berlin in negotiating the bilateral agreement between the EC and Comecon. In contrast, officials of the International Department evidenced much greater flexibility and openness in dealing with West German elites, especially outside of government.

Thus, the behavior of Soviet officials was somewhat contradictory in the 1985-1988 period and as such limited the prospects of successfully influencing West German elite opinion. Most notably, West Germans perceived a consistent anti-German feeling among high-ranking Soviet officials (excluding Gorbachev). For example, during Dobrynin's first visit to West Germany in 1987, SPD officials clearly discerned anti-German feelings by Dobrynin, although by the end of his stay he was demonstrating greater openness to West German concerns. His speech delivered to the SPD also demonstrated the limits to innovation on the Soviet side, since it was a speech about the U.S.-Soviet relationship which would have been more appropriately given in Washington than in Bonn.

Following Strauss's visit to Moscow in December 1987, Gorbachev conveyed his desire to accelerate progress in the bilateral relationship. He met with virtually every prominent West German visitor who came to Moscow. During the Strauss visit he was frank and open with this representative of "revanchism." He met for four hours with Brandt in April 1988 and communicated the important stake which the Federal Republic had in the success of the Soviet reform effort. Gorbachev told Brandt that it would take twenty years before perestroika could be successful. In May, Gorbachev met for one hour with the then head of the FDP and Minister of Finance (Mr. Bangeman) and indicated the important economic stake which the West Germans had in a revitalized Soviet economy. The importance of economic reform to the Soviet Union was a key theme articulated by Gorbachev in his meetings with West German leaders and also pounded home by Soviet representatives in the Federal Republic. The Soviets clearly perceived the West Germans to be key players in shaping Western policy toward East-West trade.

The Soviets attempted to use various commissions with the West Germans as fora to convince West German businessmen of the seriousness of change on the Soviet side. For example, the first meeting of the West German-Soviet Commission for Scientific and Technological Cooperation met in April 1988. The meeting focused on questions of nuclear reactor safety, bio-technological research and public health improvements. By focusing on issues seemingly outside the Cocom restriction area, the Soviets sought to defuse the political dimensions of East-West trade, opening up a new chapter in West German-Soviet trade. An important innovation was reached with a West German loan to the Soviet Union for a factory to produce consumer goods, with the financing supported by bonds that could be purchased by West German citizens.

The Soviets sought to conduct a dialogue with the West German parties as well. The SPD remained the Soviets' preferred party in this period, because the SPD was seen to pursue policy preferences more compatible with Soviet definitions of their security interests in the West. But after the change of government from the SPD to the CDU/CSU in 1982, the Soviet Union tried to strengthen its contacts with the new Kohl government and with the Christian Democratic Party. For example, Volker Ruhe (then security policy spokesman of the CDU) visited Moscow and met with high-ranking Soviet officials, including Vadim Zagladin.

The most significant example of this changed attitude towards the CDU/CSU unquestionably was the invitation to the Bavarian prime minister and chairman of the CSU, Franz Josef Strauss to visit the USSR. Although Strauss had been the very personification of revanchism for the Soviets, he was accorded all the honors of a state visit. He was also shown a special favor. He was allowed to fly his private jet into the Soviet Union, thus becoming the first Westerner to be given permission to fly to the national capital (although not all West Germans seemed to have sought such permission prior to their flight!). This example of a deft touch left a profound impression on Strauss; such flexibility was a key dimension of the new Soviet public diplomacy.

The Free Democrats (the FDP) and especially Foreign Minister Genscher were seen by the Soviets as the co-founders of ostpolitik policy. Genscher's oft repeated theme that it was in the Western interest to help Gorbachev succeed in his reforms matched well with Gorbachev's basic message to the West, a message reinforced by Soviet representatives in the Federal Republic. The message essentially was as follows: We are serious about economic reform; we will be heavily involved in domestic revitalization for a long time; we cannot be a serious threat to you if we are so heavily involved in domestic change; and it is in your interest to participate in our reform process.

The remaining political party, the Greens, were of limited interest to the Soviets, primarily because they were only a marginal party. Although they had contacts with the Greens, the Soviets did not focus much attention on them. They did, however, invite two leading members of the Greens (Jutta Ditfurth and Jurgen Meier) to the celebrations of the 70th anniversary of the October Revolution in Moscow. Also, other leading Green politicians (e.g., Petra Kelly) had the opportunity to talk with Soviet Foreign Minister Eduard Shevardnadze during his visit to Bonn in January 1988.

There may be one important lesson the Soviets (or at least some Soviets) learned from the experiences of the Greens and of the peace movement. The Greens were the most prominent political force in the Federal Republic arguing that the deployment of the Pershings in West Germany would dramatically increase the prospects for confrontation or war. Instead the deployment led to disarmament, and the chief foreign policy spokesman for the Greens publicly admitted that the party had acted on incorrect assumptions.

At least some Soviets understood that the Soviet military threat was a political factor in the West that worsened the security situation for the Soviet Union. For example, in a meeting bringing together the SPD with a member of the Soviet General Staff and a leading civilian proponent of reasonable sufficiency, an open disagreement on the threat perception issue surfaced. The General Staff official argued that the Soviet Union needed to rely on substantial conventional forces, especially tanks and artillery, to defend itself, whereas the civilian strategist argued that such forces were viewed as threatening in the West. He argued that regardless of whether or not the Soviet Union considered these weapons to be defensive, the West did not. Because the West did not, it would seek to overarm in response, so the Soviet Union had to alter threat perceptions by a more effective disarmament policy.

In addition to West German government and party officials, the Soviets paid a great deal of attention to German journalists as well. There were virtually no Soviet specialists among the West German journalists, who for the most part were more interested in the domestic changes in the Soviet Union. The image conveyed by the West German press and by interviews with West German journalists was that the Soviet Union was in the throes of serious change. This focus tended to reinforce the problems of conveying the continuing challenges represented by Soviet foreign and security policy.

Illustrative of the Soviet efforts to more effectively influence journalists was the marketing of the most important Soviet asset, Gorbachev himself. For example, after the signing of the INF agreement the Soviet embassy invited journalists in Bonn to a Worldnet-like occasion. The journalists had the opportunity to watch a televised speech by Gorbachev about the Washington summit and the INF treaty.

Finally, in various meetings with West German security elites, Soviet representatives indicated that they could accept the legitimacy of NATO, an American military presence in Europe, and the forward defense of West Germany, but all by means of much smaller forces and limits on modernization.

The Soviets went out of their way to avoid giving the impression that they wanted to divide NATO or to separate the United States from Western Europe. For example, the Soviet embassy declared its willingness to participate in a conference together with military representatives from the American and French embassies. The Soviets also went out of their way to suggest that they were serious about changing their military doctrine. For example, in March 1988 members of the General Staff met with Bundeswehr officials, and during the course of this meeting the Soviets pointed out that they were elaborating the military-technical dimensions of their new security concept.

Gorbachev's 1989 Visit to Bonn

The state visit of Soviet President Mikhail Gorbachev to Bonn in the summer of 1989 was the most important event in Soviet-German relations during the 1988-1989 period. What mattered most was not the treaties and agreements that were signed during the visit; rather it was the way Gorbachev presented himself to the West Germans and their response to that image.

Agreements Signed During the Visit

The "Joint Declaration" which was signed by Chancellor Kohl and President Gorbachev on June 13, 1989, was widely regarded as the most important agreement announced during Gorbachev's visit. The whole text of this "Joint Declaration" was printed in most national German newspapers.

Gorbachev put his signature on a declaration containing many items the West had always encouraged the Soviet Union to recognize, including the dignity of the individual, the right of all people to determine their own faith, the pre-eminence of international law before national policy, human rights, cultural exchanges, reunification of families, and respect for minorities.[1] A central point in the "Joint Declaration" also dealt with the creation of a peaceful future in Europe, with the "common European house" as the final goal. Some important elements for Peace and Cooperation in Europe were listed: the right of every state to determine its own political and social system, to carry on the process of arms control and disarmament, to establish a constant dialogue at the highest political level, to promote exchanges (especially of young people), comprehensive economic cooperation including new forms (e.g., communication between the European Community and Comecon), cooperation in the field of environmental policy, and encouragement of the cultural diversity of Europe.

Security policy was also prominent in the declaration. Both states condemned any attempt to attain military superiority, and they agreed that war should no longer be an instrument of policy. Security policy and the structure of the armed forces should seek only to reduce the risk of war and to attain peace with fewer weapons, a thesis frequently propounded by Chancellor Kohl.

Also important was the fact that the Soviet Union agreed with the FRG that the existing military asymmetries had to be removed and that the military arsenals should be reduced to a lower level. Both countries agreed that neither side should have the ability to launch a surprise attack and to take the offensive to gain territory. Both sides also called for a 50 percent reduction in the U.S. and Soviet strategic nuclear arsenals.

After the signing of the joint declaration, eleven treaties and agreements between the FRG and the Soviet Union were signed at the ministerial level. One of the most important was the "Treaty on the Promotion and the Mutual Protection of Investments." This treaty was of great importance for economic cooperation between the two sides because it could help stimulate investments by German companies in the Soviet Union. Also important was the "Agreement on Greater Cooperation in the Education and Training of Economic Experts and Managers." Other agreements were signed in the fields of scientific cooperation and youth exchange.

It was recognized in the FRG that the Soviet Union signed all those treaties and agreements using the official name of West Germany--"Federal Republic of Germany"--in the Russian and German versions of the texts. In former years they had always used what could be translated as "German Federal Republic".

Gorbachev's Meetings with West German Officials

The beginning of a state visit is always dominated by atmospheric considerations. During the welcoming ceremony for Gorbachev it was already obvious that the relationship between Chancellor Kohl and him had improved significantly. The personal meetings and state dinners that followed were all described as very harmonious.

In addition to meeting with such government officials as Kohl and Foreign Minister Genscher, Gorbachev also met with politicians from nearly all the major parties in the FRG. He met with SPD Chairman Hans-Jochen Vogel, representatives of the Greens, German Communist Party leader Herbert Mies (something that was not widely noted in the FRG), Bundestag President Rita Süssmuth, and others.

Gorbachev also met with business representatives, including a major speech before the "Ostausschuss der Deutschen Wirtschaft" (the previously mentioned institution coordinating German trade with the East). This was the longest speech of Gorbachev's visit, demonstrating the importance placed on economic cooperation.

Gorbachev's overall message during his visit included the following 12 points, although obviously some were stressed more than others during his various appearances:

First, he reminisced about the history of this century and especially the horror of the Second World War (e.g., in his speech at the state dinner which President Von Weizsäcker gave for him at the Augustusburg Castle near Bonn).

Second, he emphasized the joint traditions and connections between the FRG and the Soviet Union (e.g., in his press conference).[2]

Third, he repeatedly called the FRG a great European state (e.g., in his speech at the state dinner which Chancellor Kohl gave for him in the "Redoute" in Bonn-Bad Godesberg).[3]

Fourth, he spoke about a new chapter in the relationship between the two states (e.g., again in his speech in the "Redoute").[4]

Fifth, he made clear that his goal was not to come fundamentally to new agreements between the FRG and the Soviet Union, but rather to give the existing treaties and agreements more substance and make them more concrete (e.g., again in his speech in the "Redoute").[5]

Sixth, he pointed out that there could be a glorious future if cooperation between the two states were intensified. Because of this chance the two peoples supported closer cooperation--according to Gorbachev--and the politicians had to accept this wish (e.g., in his press conference on Thursday, June 15, 1989,[6] in his speech at the Augustusburg Castle,[7] or in a speech at the University of Stuttgart on Wednesday June 14, 1989).[8]

Seventh, cooperation in the economic field should have priority, since this would inevitably lead to better political relations. He said this explicitly in a speech he delivered after a dinner which Prime Minister Lothar Späth from Baden-Württemberg gave for him in Stuttgart. Here Gorbachev said that if the two countries depended on each other in the economic field, foreign policy would become more stable.[9] He made a similar statement in his remarks before the "Ostausschuss der Deutschen Wirtschaft."[10]

Eighth, he confessed his own mistakes, especially in the field of economics, but he emphasized that the Soviet Union was beginning to try new methods to overcome old mistakes. This would occur mainly through perestroika and new thinking, which he called irreversible. On the other hand, he criticized the Kohl government for what he regarded as discriminatory measures against stronger trade connections. He encouraged German business leaders to invest in the Soviet Union and in trade connections with them. ("All who do not wait will gain fantastic profits".) He astutely mentioned the great economic problems West Germany had with its shipyards and the fact that thousands of longshoremen were unemployed, while the Soviet Union had a great need for modernization of its merchant marine fleet. He also urged stronger cooperation in the high-technology fields of aerospace and nuclear power; both industries which were more popular with German businessmen than the German public. Gorbachev also pointed out that if West Germany were not willing to cooperate in these areas, rivals were already waiting (e.g., Japan, Scandinavia).[11]

Ninth, Gorbachev emphasized the importance of arms control and disarmament. He called the 1989 NATO summit and the Bush initiative an answer to the latest initiative from the Soviet Union and the Warsaw Pact.[12] He termed the Western proposals "responses to the needs of our time," yet he pointed to some old-fashioned thinking "between the lines"-- something that according to him nearly disappeared when top officials from capitalist and socialist countries meet. In this connection he praised the position of the Federal Government, which he regarded as helpful for the decision-making process within NATO that led to the adoption of these proposals. The proposals as a whole were close to "our own proposals and unilateral measures."[13]

Tenth, Gorbachev often spoke during his visit to the FRG about the "Common European House." When asked about the future role of the United States and Canada in such a European house, Gorbachev said in his June 15 press conference that he did not expect the United States to reduce its interests in Europe and that the building of that house requires participation of the United States and Canada. But at the same time he made clear that the final goal should be to remove all foreign troops from every European country.[14]

Eleventh, despite the hopes of some "reunification" enthusiasts, Gorbachev did not come up with new ideas or initiatives on "the German question" and, as a first step, the dismantling of the Berlin Wall. During a subsequent press conference Gorbachev denied a ZDF television news report that, during the private dinner with the Kohls, he had mentioned the possibility that within a foreseeable time the Berlin Wall could fall.[15] During the press conference he said that the Berlin Wall had been built by the regime in East Berlin as the result of a specific situation and that it could only be pulled down if the government of the GDR decided that this situation no longer existed. Yet he added that nothing under the sun is eternal.[16]

And twelfth, he underscored that global problems are becoming more and more important, especially the environment and such Third World crisis areas as the Middle East.[17]

Gorbachev's visit was clearly a watershead event for Soviet-German relations and for the broader Soviet-Western relationship as well. The goals of that visit were in line with the vision articulated in the Strasbourg synthesis identified earlier. By the fall of 1989, a new agenda was shaping up to deal with the combined pressures of the Revolution of 1989 and of German unification.

Conclusions

The Soviets developed a number of important themes in their approach toward Western Europe during the 1985-1989 period. Above all, they promoted the idea that there was a "new" look in Soviet policy. Soviet officials were more realistic and willing to accept the "realities" of modern society as they understood it. The Soviets claimed to accept the legitimacy of a number of Western institutions which used to be anathema to them, such as NATO and the EEC.

While the Soviets have not liked any of these institutions, they existed, and they finally recognized that these institutions had to be dealt with. For example, with respect to NATO, high ranking Soviet officials, including Gorbachev himself, frequently stated during 1987 and 1988 that they were not trying to drive wedges in the Alliance and that they accepted the legitimacy of some form of American presence in Europe.

Furthermore, the Soviets emphasized to West Germans that the nature of Soviet society was changing. The current image became one of a society which had been stultified by the old but which had been unleashed by new thinking. Over the past thirty years the West German elite had perceived the vitality of Soviet society to be in steady decline. The Soviets were explicitly trying to reverse this trend by using the "new thinking" and glasnost campaigns to highlight innovation in Soviet society.

In addition, Soviet spokesmen in the Federal Republic used the favorable image of Gorbachev himself to promote the belief that fundamental reconciliation in East-West relations was possible. West German elites perceived Gorbachev as promising a potentially serious reduction in the pressures to maintain the current defense effort. The dilemma became: how to take advantage of the opportunities proffered by the Gorbachev administration while still making a serious effort to counter a continuing Soviet military threat. West German policymakers already believed that no increase in the West German defense effort would be at all possible because of Gorbachev's success in changing the threat perceptions of the West German public. They feared that as the image of the Soviet threat receded further, the sacrifices required to maintain a large manpower pool through conscription would seem increasingly difficult to justify.

Above all, Soviet spokesmen underscored that there was a growing and more realistic possibility of East-West reconciliation if Soviet initiatives were met with correspondingly serious proposals by the West. Simply put, the message was as follows: "We are now reasonable; work with us and we can put the old confrontations behind us and live in a more peaceful and interdependent world."

In short, Soviet public diplomacy was significantly aided by the new dynamism of Soviet domestic and foreign policy, as well as by the new realism in Soviet assessments of developments in the West. The Soviet Union also promoted its image as a society in crisis, which therefore could no longer pose a serious threat to West Germany.

Notes

1. See e.g., the commentary in the **Frankfurter Allgemeine Zeitung**, 14 June 1989, p. 1.
2. See **Presse und Informationsamt der Bundesreigierung**, Ostinformationen, 16 June 1989, p. 10.
3. See **Bulletin**, no. 61, 15 June 1989, p. 541.
4. **Ibid.**
5. **Ibid.**
6. See **Presse und Informationsamt der Bundesregierung**, Ostinformationen, 16 June 1989, p. 1.
7. See **Bulletin**, no. 61, p. 547.
8. See **Presse und Informationsamt der Bundesregierung**, Ostinformationen, 15 June 1989, p. 4.
9. **Ibid**, p. 2.
10. See **Presse und Informationsamt der Bundesregierung**, Ostinformationen, 14 June 1989, p. 11-19.
11. **Ibid**, especially pp. 17-18.
12. See **Bulletin**, no. 61, p. 540.
13. **Ibid.**
14. See **Presse und Informationsamt der Bundesregierung**, Ostinformationen, 16 June 1989, pp. 7-8.
15. The Associated Press Wire with the title "ZDF: Gorbatschow stellt Mauer und Stacheldraht in Frage" is printed in, **Presse und Informationsamt der Bundesregierung**, Ostinformationen, 15 June 1989, p. 6 (translated from the German by Armin Leon).
16. See **Presse und Informationsamt der Bundesregierung**, Ostinformationen, 16 June 1989, p. 7.
17. See **Bulletin**, no. 61, p. 548.

7

Soviet Assessments of the German Unification Process, 1989-1990

This chapter identifies and assesses the dynamic and evolving positions taken by various Soviet analysts and policymakers in the debate about German unification. To achieve the goal of accurately portraying Soviet perspectives on the German unity issue in such a fluid period of modern history, this chapter is organized into two sections. The first section presents the basic positions articulated by senior Soviet foreign policymakers, notably Shevardnadze in the period from the Fall of 1989 until December of 1990. The basic phases and underlying objectives articulated by senior officials are the main emphases in the first section.

In the second section the main themes within the Russian press from November 1989 through December 1990 are outlined. By presenting brief summaries of the major themes on a month-by-month basis, the sense of dynamism in trying to shape and defend a Russian position in this fluid period is underscored.

The monthly summaries developed here have been drawn from the Soviet press translated in the Foreign Broadcast Information Service. Three major daily newspapers are examined here--*Izvestiya, Pravda*, and *Krasnaya zvezda*. It is little surprise that *Krasnaya zvezda* advocated a very conservative approach to the various German issues; more noteworthy was the difference in attitude between *Pravda* and *Izvestiya*. *Pravda* consistently adhered to a much more conservative analysis of what was developing and what the Soviet Union ought to do; *Izvestiya* displayed greater evidence of "new thinking."

Pro-reform publications, which are covered in FBIS as well, include: *Moscow News* and *Komsomolskaya pravda*; *Sovetskaya Rossiya* was representative of the other end of the spectrum. Thus, since the themes treated each month may cut across the various publications, the way in which they are treated can vary dramatically.

Obviously the issue of Germany's future and German unification came to a head in November 1989 with the fall of the Berlin Wall. For the several months prior to that time, most Soviet analyses of Germany in the daily press looked at the state of bilateral relations (both between the USSR and FRG and between the FRG and GDR). The latter, of course, included the mounting problem of East German emigration.

The structure of the second section of this chapter is to identify one or two key themes for each of the months from November 1989 until December 1990. While not specifically mentioned in these month-by-month summaries, there were, of course, numerous official contacts between the USSR and the FRG and GDR. The press coverage of these contacts was always at least adequate, and frequently received more attention than what would normally be accorded even official visits.

Evolving Soviet Perspectives on German Unification, October 1989-December 1990

The views of senior Soviet decisionmakers operated in four different political universes in the very fluid and dynamic period from October 1989 until December 1990. The four periods saw dynamic shifts from one set of assumptions to another as concepts sought to catch up with reality.

The first period preceded the fall of the Berlin Wall. The challenge was to promote reform within the GDR, to keep two Germanies but to promote reform in the USSR through integration within the new Europe.

The second period encompassed the first quarter of 1990 through the elections in the GDR. The perception was that the elections would slow down the process of change and allow the Soviet leadership to prepare the ground for the emergence of the new Germany. The new European security system had to be built prior to the emergence of a unified Germany.

The third period ran from the post-election situation through the July meeting between Kohl and Gorbachev. Here the Soviet leadership tried to influence the terms of the emergence of the new Germany as a means for shaping the new European-Soviet bargain. Rather than the new European security system preceding the new Germany, the sequence was reversed. The task was to try to have as much influence as possible in shaping the new European system through the increasingly inevitable bargain to create the new Germany.

The fourth period ran from July through December 1990. In this period the task was to formalize the agreement reached in July. But formalization was considered essential to ensure future stability within Europe and to anchor the Soviet role in the new Europe.

Running throughout these four periods were three basic underlying objectives of the Shevardnadze-Gorbachev leadership. First, the new Germany and the new European security systems were interlinked. The Soviet leadership hoped that the unification process could be slowed down in order to create the new European security system in advance of the formation of the new Germany. In a significant article published in *Izvestiya* in January 19, 1990, Shevardnadze put it this way: the process of intra-German reconciliation is a "...process (which) cannot be separated in some way from the general course of dealings between the East and West of Europe. The more dynamic the process of rapprochement among European states in general and the formation of the structures of cooperation and good-neighborliness between them, the better the preconditions will develop for similar changes in FRG-GDR relations."[1]

Second, the Soviet leadership linked change in their German policy with change in the USSR itself. Initially, they hoped to see change in the GDR to be linked with change in the Soviet Union and within the Soviet bloc. They hoped for a more gradual process of change. As Shevardnadze put it, "Our foreign policy is pulling this country into the civilized world acting as a guarantee of the reformation of socialism."[2]

Third, the Soviet leadership constantly spoke of the need to be vigilant in dealing with the structures for the new Germany. They needed to ensure that Soviet interests were clearly taken into account in the process of change. In part, this was due to the need to fend off domestic critics. The Soviet leadership dyad of Gorbachev and Shevardnadze was heading off attacks from the right against accepting German reunification without prior change in the European situation. The most vocal critical was Y. Ligachev. He argued at a Party meeting in February 1990 that "It would be unbelievably short-sighted and a mistake if we didn't see a Germany with huge economic and military potential looming on the international horizon. I think it is time to recognize the new danger and to speak about it as loud as possible to our own people and party."[3]

Preceding the Fall of the Berlin Wall: Reform within the Blocs

The main theme during this period is a simple one: peoples have the right to self-determination but not at the expense of the existing borders and "postwar realities" in Europe. This theme was put most forcefully by Shevardnadze in a speech to the United Nations in September 1989. "Every nation is free to choose the ways and means of its own development--but to do so in a responsible manner. It must not lock itself in the dark rooms of national selfishness or ignore the interests of other peoples and the entire community of nations."[4] After asserting the legitimacy of self-determination, Shevardnadze was quick to circumscribe the claim of the Germans to this right. "Fascism, which started the war, is the extreme and ugliest form of nationalism and chauvinism. German nazism marched under the standards of revanchism. Now that the forces of revanchism are again becoming active and are seeking to revise and destroy the postwar realities in Europe, it is our duty to warn those who, willingly or unwillingly, encourage those forces."[5]

Gorbachev underscored the broad interpretation which the Soviet leadership now provided to self-determination in a trip to Finland at the end of October. In Helsinki, the Soviet leader recognized the legitimacy of Finnish neutrality. He then went on to indicate that the Soviets would not be troubled if Finland chose to become a member of the European Community. This was the first recognition by a Soviet leader of the possible right of European neutrals to join the EC.

Concomitant with Gorbachev's visit to Finland, Shevardnadze was attending a notable meeting of the Warsaw Pact in which he was de facto authorizing its future dissolution. The only point upon which the member state representatives agreed was the importance of keeping Germany divided. The Soviet foreign minister was visiting Warsaw a month after the Solidarity government had come to power. During the Warsaw Pact meeting he promised, de facto, not to use military force in the future to prevent change in Eastern Europe. Shevardnadze argued that the military aspect of the Warsaw Pact should be deemphasized in favor of a more "political" defense agreement, and that problems of security within the Pact would be resolved "through political measures" in the future.

Speaking on the second day of his visit to newly democratic Poland, Shevardnadze said the change in the Pact's character would have to be gradual, however. "We should not forget about defense," he cautioned.[6]

The culmination of Soviet leadership actions in this period was Gorbachev's visit to Berlin for the fortieth anniversary of the GDR. During his visit Gorbachev made it clear that he did not support the regime of Honecker, but wanted to see reform instead. But he hoped for reform socialism within the Soviet bloc, and not the end of the Soviet sphere of influence. Somehow self-determination, reform and socialism were to work toward the same end--maintenance of Soviet influence in Eastern Europe. Such was Gorbachev's utopian vision in late 1989.

Notably in the meeting between the East German and Soviet heads of state, there was a clear clash of views. And by letting this difference of positions to become known publicly, Gorbachev was seeking to undercut the East German leader. According to the official East German news agency ADN, during three hours of talks, Honecker told Gorbachev that East Germany will adhere to "the basic values" of socialism. "The hopes of bourgeois politicians and ideologues who are aiming for reforms heading to bourgeois democracy and on to capitalism are built on sand," Honecker was quoted as saying. "The Socialist Unity Party will consistently follow the proven course for the good of the people, in the unity of economic and social policies, continuity and renewal," he said. ADN reported that the meeting took place in an atmosphere of "traditional friendship." A day earlier, Gorbachev had urged Warsaw Pact ally East Germany to work with "all forces in society." Gennady Gerasimov, spokesman for the Soviet Foreign Ministry, said that during their meeting, Gorbachev repeated to Honecker a Russian saying that "he who is late is punished." Asked whether that referred to the East German government's repeated rejection of reforms, Gerasimov said: "No, we were talking about our experiences. But journalists do interpret things."[7]

Preceding the March Elections in the GDR

Late 1989 and early 1990 marked a period of extreme confusion in European diplomacy as leaders in the East and the West tried to sort out their objectives in dealing with the new situation in Eastern Europe, and especially with regard to the GDR. For the Soviets, the underlying approach was to accept the abstract right of the Germans to become unified but to try to slow down the process of change. By retarding the unification process, the Soviets hoped to build new European security structures within which Germany could then be embedded.

First, the Soviet leadership tried to intimidate the West German leadership from embracing the East too quickly. During Genscher's visit to Moscow in December, Shevardnadze forcefully lectured the West German foreign minister on the importance of not taking advantage of the weaknesses of the East German state to promote West German domination. His private tone was even tougher than his public presentation of policy. But publicly, the Soviet leadership railed against the "revanchist" tone of the Kohl speech on reunification presented at the end of November.

Shevardnadze cautioned that long-term European interest must be taken into account. What some were doing in the FRG with regard to the GDR was "fraught with dangerous consequences." He added that Kohl's ten point program was "bordering on outright diktat."[8]

Second, the Soviet leadership sought allies within Western and Eastern Europe to leverage West German policy. Gorbachev met with French President Mitterrand in order to underscore their joint displeasure with too ambitious and too rapid a process of incorporation of the GDR within the FRG. Soviet leaders also met with the Polish leadership to underscore their concern with the West Germans upsetting the post-war boundaries and political arrangements made at the end of World War II.

Third, Shevardnadze paid an historic visit in December to the European Community and to NATO. During this visit, he outlined his vision for change in the structures of Europe. There needed to be an historic shift away from the blocs toward an all-European system. Confrontation was a thing of the past; now the challenge was to build the system for tomorrow.

The Foreign Minister was attending the EC to sign a ten year agreement between the Soviet Union and the EC. He used the occasion to note the opportunities for change in Europe. Shevardnadze declared that the agreement constituted another step in the political and economic changes sweeping across Eastern Europe "at this historic moment when the Cold War is over. This is a result of a gigantic effort made by the peoples of Europe to overcome political and military confrontation, to overcome the economic division of our continent," he said.[9]

Throughout this period, the foreign minister underscored the need to build the new European structures prior to German unification. But unlike the conservative critics of the Gorbachev administration, Shevardnadze was already laying out by the end of December conditions for accepting German unification. Among the concrete questions he posed were the following:

> Where are the guarantees that a united Germany will not, in the long term, threaten peace and security in Europe?
> Will a united Germany be willing to accept borders and reject any territorial claims?
> What place will a united Germany have in Europe's military-political alliances?
> What will be a united Germany's military role and its economic role?
> What will be the attitude of a united Germany toward allied troops on its soil?
> How will a united Germany be connected with the Helsinki process?
> Will a united Germany take the interests of the other European states into account?[10]

Fourth, the Soviet leadership sought to use the new leadership of the GDR as a lobbying group to protect Soviet interests. They expected an SPD victory in March and hoped to work with the West and East German SPD to shape a new Germany. At the heart of Soviet demands was that the new Germany would be part of a new European security system and would not be part of the Western bloc. Most often the Soviets spoke of the new Germany as being neutral or following a French model with respect to the Western Alliance. But, above all, the insistence was that a new Germany could not be a motor force for further Western development.

In January 1991, then GDR leader Modrow proposed a step-by-step process of unification. The Soviets underscored the significance for them of such a process. Shevardnadze underscored that this proposal showed that "the GDR understands that the problem of German unity does not affect the Germans alone." He added that "It is not the actual idea of German unity that encounters suspicion...but the revival associated with this idea of the sinister phantoms of the past and notions of the possibility of a growth of militarism." He argued that the German unification process must be synchronized with the all-European process, it must be gradual, existing borders must be preserved, both states must be militarily neutral and the military potential of both states must be dramatically reduced.[11]

The step-by-step process was also important to Gorbachev and his willingness to accept German unification. As Michael Dobbs noted concerning the Modrow-Gorbachev meeting on 30 January 1990:

> Soviet President Mikhail Gorbachev appeared today to soften the Kremlin's long-standing opposition to German reunification in talks with East German Prime Minister Hans Modrow, while emphasizing that the issue should be solved jointly by East and West. At a news conference here following a day of talks with Soviet leaders, Modrow spoke of a "stage-by-stage" union of East and West Germany, describing reunification as a real possibility. He said he had discussed the idea with Gorbachev and the Soviet leader had not ruled it out.
>
> Earlier, before the start of the talks in the Kremlin, East German reporters pressed Gorbachev for his attitude toward reunification, which had become a dominant political issue in East Germany, where the Communist Party today dropped its opposition to it. The official Soviet news agency *Tass* quoted Gorbachev as saying that the question "was not unexpected," and adding: "No one casts any doubt upon it. Time itself is having an impact on the process and lends dynamism to it. It is essential to act responsibly and not seek the solution to this important issue on the streets."[12]

During a visit to the Soviet Union by Oskar Lafontaine (the SPD candidate for Chancellor) in February, Gorbachev conveyed his expectation that the SPD would win the election in March in the GDR. He expressed strong support for the SPD's position in favor of creating a new European security structure within which to embed the new Germany. Both leaders rejected the notion that the new Germany should be a member of NATO.

In early March when Modrow visited Gorbachev prior to the GDR elections, the Soviet leader made his feelings clear about the future security role for Germany. "We cannot give our agreement to this (NATO membership). It is absolutely excluded," Gorbachev said in a television interview after talks with East German Prime Minister Hans Modrow.[13]

From March to July 1990

The unexpected victory of the CDU in the March GDR elections quickly transformed the agenda. Events were pressing for German reunification under the aegis of the Federal Republic. The Soviet leadership now accepted unification, but sought to use the process to shape their new relationship with Europe. That is, whereas before the Soviet leaders hoped to see new European security structures constructed prior to unification, they now sought to shape new structures through the bargains forging a unified Germany. They hoped to do this in part through the two-plus-four talks, in part with dealings with the Americans, and in part in dealings directly with the West German leaders.

In this period, the Soviet leadership tried out a wide variety of proposals as components of the bargain to shape the new Germany. They continued the "crazy Eddie" tradition of Gorbachev in which they were willing to propose almost anything that the other side would accept.

First, the Soviets proposed a wide variety of structures within which German security could be solved. Among these are the following: membership in the Warsaw Pact, dual membership in the two alliances, a French model of participation in NATO, neutrality, demilitarization, a dramatic reduction of armed forces in each state and then merging them into a new model army of defensive defense, a model which could be adopted by others.

Second, an insistence that whatever the structural arrangements, the GDR should be treated as a special territorial reserve within Europe. If part of NATO, it could not become territory on which NATO forces could operate.

Third, any changes in German security policy should be linked with other East-West negotiations which were going on, notably the conventional arms control process. It was indispensable that overall Western force reductions must be correlated with West German reductions.

Fourth, West Germany must adhere to agreements made in the past about non possession of weapons of mass destruction. Most significantly, any new German state must adhere strictly to the nuclear non-proliferation treaty.

Fifth, the new Germany must honor the former economic obligations of the GDR. In other words, any contracts signed by the GDR in the past must remain valid for a new German state.

In addition to specific demands, expectations were shaped on the Soviet side in the process of dealing with German unification which became part of the package of accepting unification. Above all, Soviet leaders expressed their expectation that Germany would protect Soviet interests within the European construction process.

On the issue of German membership in NATO, the Soviet leaders rejected this right up to the Gorbachev meeting with Kohl in July 1990. But prior to that meeting a shift was notable in the Soviet treatment of the NATO membership issue. The Soviet leaders insisted that if the new Germany became a member of NATO, this organization must be reformed. NATO reform and German unification were treated as inextricably intertwined from the Soviet point of view.

In May, Shevardnadze clearly laid out the Soviet leadership point of view. Above all, there was a need to internationalize the all-European development process and to create totally new structures on an all-European basis. "It would be naive to suppose that in the new circumstances, the old political and organization instruments will suffice." He then added, "Why are all-European security structures needed? Because the bloc system was designed for a scenario of direct, face-to-face confrontation between the sides' armed forces--and confrontation at ever higher qualitative level of means of mutual destruction.... The blocs sprang up as a consequence of the cold war. They cannot remain the same when the cold war has become a thing of the past." He then identified the key political institutions of the all-European process as the following: the Council of Europe, the Committee of Foreign Ministers, and the institutionalization of the CSCE.[14]

The European construction process as outlined was tied to the German political settlement. "We do not think that this question ought to be approached exclusively from today's positions, the positions of current realities. The situation here will not remain static. Therefore, the final settlement formula ought to be geared more toward the future than toward the present, let alone the past." He then laid down some concrete requirements from the Soviet point of view. "The determining factors when we decide on our position will be: first, the dynamics of change in NATO's concepts and strategic doctrines and the degree of this bloc's transformation into a political-military rather than a military-political alliance. Second, the pace and depth of the all-European structures, and, naturally, the Bundeswehr's military parameters. Third, the speed and scale of the creation of all-European structures and institutions, primarily in the security sphere."[15]

From July to December 1990

In the quote above, Shevardnadze referred to "when we decide on our position." In the July meeting between Kohl and Gorbachev, the decision was finally taken. The prelude to the July meetings was a June meeting between Shevardnadze and Genscher in Munster in which some issues were resolved. But the visit of Kohl to the Caucasus was the setting within which the final obstacles were overcome. The Soviet leader did not take his usual entourage of German experts and basically made agreements directly with Kohl. As the final details were negotiated, Kohl talked directly with advisors in Bonn prior to ensure as sound a German position as possible in his negotiations with Gorbachev.

By the time of the July meetings, NATO reform was underway with the July NATO declaration. The Soviet leadership insisted that this direct connection between NATO reform and German reunification was central to an acquiescence in German membership within NATO. As Shevardnadze put it, "The choice in favor of NATO posed a serious problem to us at a time when NATO stuck to its old positions. The forthcoming transformation of the bloc enabled us to take a different view of the changing NATO's role and place in Europe."[16]

Critical to the Gorbachev-Kohl deal in the Caucasus were three key elements. First, the Germans accepted an overall ceiling on their military forces of 370,000. Gorbachev asked originally for a level of under 300,000 but accepted the higher level. Second, the West Germans accepted the creation of special conditions for the territory of the GDR (not to have weapons of mass destruction, peacetime deployment of NATO forces, etc.). Third, the Germans would pay for the removal of Soviet forces from the former territory of the GDR.

In the minds of the Soviet leaders, the deal made with Kohl was closely connected with a general bargain with the West in which the Soviet Union would no longer be isolated, but rather become part of global development. As Serge Schmemann wrote in late July 1990,

> The agreements reached last week between Mr. Gorbachev and Chancellor Helmut Kohl of West Germany were not simply a Soviet-German deal, but the culmination of a long round of summit meetings and conferences involving all the Western nations in which Moscow searched for assurances of Western contacts. In the end, as Mr. Gorbachev repeatedly stressed at his news conference, what swayed the balance was not only Germany's assurances on the size of its future army or the upkeep of Soviet troops, but also the pledges from the West that it would not abandon Mr. Gorbachev. These included NATO's pledge to end the posture of confrontation, the promises from the European Community and from the industrialized nations to consider aid for Moscow.[17]

In August, the Soviets engaged in difficult negotiations with West German officials over the financial terms whereby Soviet forces would leave German territory. The negotiator on the Soviet side was the representative of the Minister of Foreign Affairs and he rode roughshod over the Soviet military officials involved in the negotiation. Finally, a general exchange between German deutschmarks and a withdrawal schedule was agreed upon by the two sides. But there was concern on the West German side that a number of problems remained, and that the Soviets might come back later to demand a higher level of compensation.

In September, the final terms for a Soviet-German treaty were agreed to and this treaty was considered vital by the Soviets. The treaty would be ratified by the end of the year. In September, Shevardnadze underscored the importance of the treaty as signifying "a new stage" in German-Soviet relations. Among the key points underscored by the Soviets in the treaty were the following: it rules out the first use of armed forces against each another and also rules out providing military aid or other assistance to an aggressor attacking the other party; it grants respect for the rights and interests of each side; it underscores the requirement to have only defense sufficiency; to resolve controversial matters through bilateral consultation; to further develop the Helsinki process and to push for a new level of cooperation in the spheres of economy, culture and information exchanges.[18]

Above all, the Soviet leadership emphasized the important role the new Germany could play in the transformation of Europe and that their expectation of transformation was part of the bargain to create the new

Germany. This expectation shaped Soviet objectives throughout the 1990 decision making process. In June, Shevardnadze argued that "A united Germany will not fit the landscape of a new Europe if everything in Europe remains as it was before. In that case, German unity would simply amount to a boost of power on the side of one of the two groups which opposes the other."[19] By July he argued that "A united Germany, with its ramified links with the West and the East of Europe, can become a pillar of a common European home. All European nations, not least of all Germans themselves, stand to gain from this."[20]

Monthly Summaries of Evolving Soviet Views on the German Unification Issue, November 1989-December 1990

November 1989

Even as early as November 1989, the Soviets were using the image of the FRG "swallowing up" the GDR;[21] this was an idea some Soviet commentators would persist in using for months to come. During the month of November, there was a great deal of coverage of GDR developments (mainly the political changes and the border opening), particularly by the key correspondents such as Lapskii (*Izvestiya*) and Podklyuchnikov (*Pravda*).[22] Other important themes as well included an overwhelming rejection of the idea of German unification, some fears and concerns about German territorial claims (namely with regard to Poland),[23] and a strong negative reaction to Kohl's 10-point plan.

On the broad question of Soviet reaction to German unification, the assessments ranged from Yakovlev's balanced approach that the Germans would decide this issue, with no interference from the Soviet Union, to a flat rejection of the idea, including by such well-known figures as Nikolai Portugalov.[24] Portugalov stated: "I do not believe in reunification. I proceed from the fact that socialism is not negotiable for most GDR citizens. As far as national legitimation is concerned: Of course, there is no GDR nationality. There are Germans on both sides."[25] During this time, the Soviets were also careful to give extensive coverage to the position of the GDR government on the matter of unification.[26] In this connection, Bovkun, Lapskii, and Podklyuchnikov--all prominent correspondents on Germany--noted the GDR government's rejection of

Kohl's 10-point plan.[27] Other Soviet commentaries on Kohl's plan criticized it for not being serious and accused him of trying to dictate to the GDR.[28]

December 1989

There was a great deal of Soviet coverage of German issues during the month. The main themes that emerged were: (1) that unification was not on the agenda, although there were volumes said and written about it, and (2) a considerable amount of attention paid to the internal dynamics of the GDR, especially by *Izvestiya*'s correspondent Lapskii.

On the first theme, Perfilev rejected the idea of unification and cautioned about the threat of revanchism.[29] For his part, Afanasevskii argued that talk of unification was premature, and noted that the USSR and France were in agreement on this point.[30] Plekhanov believed that the unification issue should be up to the German people to decide and he supported Germany being demilitarized or neutral.[31] Finally, Yurii Solton took issue with the position his colleague, Glazunov, had taken on the issue; the former argued that Moscow had always realized the German question existed and that reunification "is no illusion."[32] Thus, it was evident that already a variety of viewpoints had begun to emerge on how to handle the German issue.

On the second theme, Lapskii covered such topics as the future of socialism in the GDR;[33] coverage and analysis of the SED, its congress and future prospects;[34] and one piece on neo-Nazism in Germany.[35] There were also many other analyses, especially of the SED and the political changes the GDR was experiencing, including by *TASS*, *Sovetskaya Rossiya*, and *Pravda*.[36]

January 1990

This month the subject matter on Germany ran the gambit, with no particularly heavy emphasis on any one issue, and not the same extent of coverage in previous or subsequent months. In the area of bilateral relations, Modrow, Genscher, and Kohl were all given the opportunity to discuss the importance of their respective country's relations with the Soviet Union.[37] Discussions about GDR politics frequently also contained criticisms that the FRG was interfering in this arena.[38] On the topic of unification, the tone became less negative. For example, Bovkun reasoned that the process was entering a "calmer phase," and simultaneously noted West German support for perestroika.[39] For his part, Grigorev wrote that Kohl was now emphasizing a European framework for unification as well as wanting to expand Soviet-German economic cooperation.[40] These two analyses show quite clearly the linkage the Soviets drew between accepting unification and expecting economic benefits in return.

One of the clearest indicators of the shift in Soviet thinking could also be seen during Modrow's visit to Moscow. While Gorbachev continued to reject unification, arguing instead for moving toward a confederation of the two states, he stated that no one doubted that unification would eventually happen, but stressed the need for an analytical approach and responsible actions.[41]

Nonetheless, Soviet analysts and policymakers remained cautious.[42] For example, *TASS* criticized Kohl's intransigence on the border issue, and a *Krasnaya zvezda* article urged a cautious approach to the unification issue.[43]

February 1990

The main motif for the month was an acceptance of unification only if the new Germany would not become a security threat to its neighbors. Related to this was the question of a united Germany's membership in NATO, which was resolutely rejected. There were three particularly noteworthy articles which addressed the security dimension in February.

First, there was a lengthy article in which Valentin Falin rejected a previous report by Portugalov who supported the French model for German membership in NATO. Falin argued that neutrality must be understood more broadly and that the idea of an entire united Germany belonging to NATO is "absurd."[44]

Second, in a rather surprising move, a session of the Soviet Foreign Ministry collegium issued a statement on its discussions of the German question. This statement rejected all options for German membership in NATO and averred that no other Soviet institution had the right to decide Soviet security policy.[45]

The third noteworthy item was a discussion by Sergei Karaganov, an expert on Europe and member of the USSR's Institute of Europe. Karaganov's central point was that, whether the USSR liked it or not, unification would take place. He recognized that while the Soviet Union had some cause for concern, there was no "significant danger," that neutrality was hard to achieve, and that it would be best to link Germany to as many organizations as possible. However, he continued, a united Germany's membership in NATO, was "completely unpalatable." Finally, Karaganov cautioned that unification was potentially unstable, and he outlined possible future problems, such as polarization in Germany, and manifestations of revanchism.[46]

March 1990

Articles devoted to the debate about German membership in NATO made up roughly one-third of all the articles on unification this month, and the remaining two-thirds generally at least mentioned the security angle. Notably, there was a difference between Gorbachev's and Yeltsin's position; Gorbachev categorically rejected the possibility of Germany belonging to NATO, while Yeltsin argued that if Germany was united before the Warsaw Pact and NATO dissolved, then Germany should decide the membership question for itself.[47]

Not surprisingly, there were many articles which flatly rejected Germany remaining in NATO, frequently arguing that such a move would upset the overall balance of forces in Europe.[48] Several military perspectives on this issue were offered in this vein. Marshal Akhromeev made several statements on the subject, his main points being that he rejected a united Germany's membership in *either* NATO or the Warsaw Pact; its options would include being neutral or belonging to another security organization.[49] Colonel I. Vladimirov wrote in *Krasnaya zvezda* that a united Germany within NATO would upset the military balance in Europe, that the "inability" of the Western European Union to control the arming of the Bundeswehr demonstrated that Germany cannot be controlled, and that a peace treaty would be necessary.[50]

Several articles by civilian specialists further illustrate the divide in Soviet thinking on this issue. For example, D. Proektor argued that Germany did not pose a military threat and he advocated the French option for German membership in NATO.[51] For his part, Aleksandr Bovin made the case that a neutral Germany would not strengthen stability in Europe, that the inclusion of the GDR's territory in NATO would not really affect Soviet security, and suggested that perhaps some Soviet troops should be kept on current GDR territory, even after its inclusion in NATO.[52] Finally, Vyacheslav Dashichev flatly stated that

Germany could be a member of NATO; if the German government and people wanted this, no one would oppose it.[53]

On more general treatments of unification, many Soviets continued to raise the border issue, and they also expressed concern about the rapid pace of unification (namely, that the FRG was pushing too far too fast).[54] Also, the need for a peace treaty was frequently noted, as was mentioned above.[55] Finally, many of the more general articles on unification included assessments of other countries' reactions to unification.[56]

April 1990

The question of German membership in NATO attracted a substantial amount of the attention, although coverage of German issues generally was lighter than in other months. The main security theme was that it was necessary to ensure Soviet security and that if a united Germany were allowed in NATO, this would upset the balance (this was not a new position, it was developed over the previous month or so).[57]

An article by Bovkun is worthy of note: he concentrated mainly on the military aspects of unification, cautioning that if a united Germany became neutral, this then raised the problem of U.S. and Soviet troops having to withdraw. Bovkun wanted to see both his country and Germany take a more balanced approach: "We must stop suspecting all Germans of revanchism, and they must stop being afraid that perestroika in the USSR will grind to a halt and go into reverse."[58]

Also, the outspoken Dashichev outlined his ideas for options whereby Germany could remain in NATO. His stance ultimately led the USSR Ministry of Foreign Affairs to deny that he represented any official Soviet view on the matter.[59]

Finally, Falin made the argument that a divided Europe presupposed a divided Germany, while a united Germany within a divided Europe would pose a threat to everyone. Hence, a peace treaty was necessary.[60]

May 1990

There was heavy coverage of Germany this month. Virtually every article on unification mentioned the "military-political status" issue, with many supporting the idea of dual membership in the blocs, and many also continuing to mention the issue of a peace treaty. Numerous analyses emphasized that the old security system could not adapt to this change (of a united Germany); therefore, there was a need for a new European security system. Finally, Soviets analysts frequently noted their concern about the rapid pace of unification.

To address some of these issues in greater detail, it should first be noted that Foreign Minister Shevardnadze gave an interview in which he indicated that the USSR would like to see a united Germany become non-aligned, and in many commentaries one begins to see a move away from insistence on Germany adopting a neutral status. Shevardnadze also raised the possibility of Germany belonging to both NATO and the Warsaw Pact, an idea which many others then began to support.[61]

In contrast, Major General Batenin rejected the ideas of German neutrality, non-alignment, and dual membership in the two existing blocs. His reasoning was that the first two options would not enhance European security, and the latter was not useful since the Warsaw Pact did not have a viable future. Instead, he proposed political membership in NATO for all the united Germany, with the FRG retaining military status as well, but this military status would not apply to GDR territory.[62] Batenin's position certainly did not reflect the position of other military leaders, such as chief of the General Staff Moiseev, who argued for a demilitarized and neutral Germany.[63]

Once again, Dashichev became involved in the debate, apparently trying to bridge the gap between himself and the Soviet leadership. In an article in *Komsomolskaya pravda* on 15 May 1990, he noted Soviet concerns about unification as well as his support for the Gorbachev-Shevardnadze foreign policy line. However, the USSR's German policy was not following this line, and he believed that it was unrealistic to expect Germany to be outside NATO, which would mean NATO's elimination.[64]

On the issue of the peace treaty, although Dashichev and others rejected the idea, others such as Valentin Falin and *TASS*'s Aleksandr Antsiferov supported Gorbachev's call for such a treaty.[65] On another continuing theme, *Pravda* correspondent Evgenii Grigorev discussed the fast pace of the unification process, declaring that the West Germans were speeding it up because they were unsure of continuity in Soviet foreign policy.[66]

Finally during the month, the draft treaty for Germany's economic union was completed. Most of the articles and broadcasts focusing on this dimension included assessments of the GDR's uncertainty about the effects of this union and general problems associated with economic unification.[67]

June 1990

In a month of light coverage on Germany, there were very few articles that did not deal with unification issues, and many of the latter continued to focus on the question of Germany's future military-political status. Perhaps the most significant shift can be seen in a statement by President Gorbachev, where he took the position that once NATO would change its doctrine and structures and would become a purely political organization, German membership in NATO could be accepted.[68]

Two articles showed the continuing range of opinion on the issue of NATO membership for a united Germany. On the one hand, a *New Times* article argued that although the GDR was being swallowed up by the FRG, German membership in NATO had become inevitable and that this did not pose a new threat to the USSR.[69] On the other hand, Pogodin argued that the Western assumption that Germany would be a member of NATO was equivalent to a policy of Western diktat.[70]

July 1990

July marked a very important month in the unification process with the Kohl-Gorbachev meetings (held in Stavropol, Arkhyz, and Zheleznovodsk), where they came to agreement on the key impediments to unification. Unification issues, especially the matter of NATO membership, were the main focus of the attention. Following these meetings and the resolution of the main problems, a new theme began to emerge as well in Soviet analyses: that Germany should act as the bridge between East and West.[71]

There was obviously a substantial amount of coverage surrounding the German-Soviet high-level meetings, not only factual accounting of the proceedings, but also analyses of the negotiations.[72] Increasingly, Soviet analysts shifted to a position of accepting a united Germany in NATO. This was due, in part, they claimed to the results of the NATO Council meeting in London, which indicated a shift in NATO's approach. Although prior to this meeting there was certainly continued opposition to that idea.[73]

Other items of note included the fact that Soviet analysts frequently liked to attribute the possibility of unification to Soviet policy, namely to perestroika. In other words, they argued that without perestroika, unification would never have been possible.[74] Nor were economic issues ignored (although they were certainly overshadowed by the security dimension). For instance, A. Kondakov explored the likely problems and impact that the economic union would have on the USSR.[75] Finally, many in the military particularly began to discuss the question of Soviet troops in the GDR, how long it would take to withdraw them, the problems with the costs of supporting these troops, and the need for the German government to compensate the Soviet Union for this expense.[76]

August 1990

Not surprisingly, almost all articles on Germany in this month were connected to unification. Dashichev continued to pursue a unique posture. During this month, he outlined why unification benefitted the Soviet Union in an interview in the newspaper *Der Morgen*.[77] For his part, *Izvestiya*'s correspondent Bovkun discussed the political effects of unification, namely on the German political parties.[78] As in preceding months, the Federal Republic's Foreign Minister Genscher continued to receive substantial coverage in the Soviet media, including interviews on the topics of unification and on Soviet-German relations.[79]

The theme of Soviet-German relations was explored by other commentators as well in the context of reports commemorating the twentieth anniversary of the signing of the Moscow Treaty between the FRG and USSR. One such article argued that there was no need to fear Soviet-German relations either now or in the future, a reference to concerns being expressed in some of the Western countries on the possible negative consequences of a close alliance between these two countries (with obvious memories of such collaboration between Stalin and Hitler).[80]

Picking up on some of these ideas, the editor of *Literaturnaya Rossiya*, Aleksandr Fomenko, explored the development of a Moscow-Berlin dyad, with references to historical parallels, and he saw a similarity in the two countries' geopolitical situations. He reasoned that the Germans could serve as an intermediary between East and West Europe, while the USSR would perform this same function between Europe and Asia. Fomenko also saw a new divide emerging--one between North and

South--and drew an interesting distinction between German unification and Soviet disintegration:

> While the FRG and GDR are uniting into Germany, the USSR--to the sound of shouts about the need for a "new Union treaty"--is gradually being broken apart by separatists of all possible stripes. With the now obvious collapse of Soviet-communist ideology, it is becoming more, and more difficult, to maintain the military-political association of the "republics" that were created at one time to replace the unified Russian state in order to destroy its memory once and for all.[81]

On the economic dimension, the main focus of attention was placed on the horrendous state of the GDR's economy, including a recognition of the impediments to West German investment in the GDR.[82] Finally, the problems of Soviet troops stationed in the GDR were addressed, such as East German opposition to their presence (including accusations that they have ruined the environment), the impact of troop withdrawals, and Soviet soldiers protests against being sent back to the USSR, the latter being reported in a German newspaper.[83]

September 1990

Now that the main issues surrounding unification had been resolved, attention in the Soviet media was fairly evenly split between continuing coverage of unification and expanded coverage of bilateral relations. On the topic of unification, articles and commentaries frequently noted continuing concerns associated with the process, such as the pace and cost of unification, a belief that Soviet interests had not been well-represented in the negotiations, and a recognition of considerable concern among the Soviet public at large about unification (especially about NATO membership). In terms of this latter concern, most of the writings tried to assuage it, in part reasoning that NATO was changing and that the threat to the Soviet Union was not what it used to be, in part emphasizing the important economic benefits to be derived from cooperation with Germany.[84]

In response to a question about why the Soviet Union withdrew its proposal for German neutrality, Aleksandr Zholkver explained the shift in the Soviet position in the following way:

> I would not say that we withdrew it. It is just that in present conditions it did not meet with support. There were various reasons for this. Paris and London considered that German neutrality could spoil its close economic links with France and Great Britain. Washington considered that German neutrality would complicate U.S. relations with Western Europe. Among the Germans themselves, many expressed the fear that a Germany that is not a member of any alliance could become a factor of instability in Europe.[85]

Other issues were discussed as well. There was also some discussion of the progress toward reaching an agreement with Germany on the withdrawal of Soviet troops.[86] The Soviets placed heavy emphasis on the initialing of the Treaty on Good-Neighborliness, Partnership, and Cooperation Between the Soviet Union and the FRG. In one interview, Gorbachev indicated that a grand treaty between the two countries was ready to be initialled and that they were making progress in coming to an agreement on German support for the cost of Soviet troops stationed in the eastern part of Germany.[87] Finally, Foreign Minister Shevardnadze discussed the importance of the unification treaty, the fact that Germany did not pose a threat to the USSR, and the value and potential of Soviet-German bilateral relations.[88]

October 1990

The most common theme this month was unification, although there were also quite a few reports of military issues. Before turning to unification coverage, Colonel V. Markushin published a notable article in *Krasnaya zvezda* which discussed the errors of Soviet analysis in predicting and understanding changes in Europe, including in Germany. Of particular interest was his assessment of the integration process in Europe:

> The rebirth of a united Germany is taking place in the context of the economic, currency, and political unification of Western Europe. Integration is the most powerful factor for security, just as disintegration and the prevalence of centrifugal tendencies always involves the undermining of security and destabilization.

> But integration could entail an excessive inclination to close in, and to transform the European economy into a kind of "European fortress," to use Helmut Kohl's words. This is fraught with the danger of losing the rapprochement between East and West that has been achieved. There is an awareness of this danger, it seems, among sober-minded politicians. In any case, many firm statements are being uttered on the desire to extend the European edifice to include all the new annexes from the East.[89]

In terms of unification, Marshal Akhromeev's position was that unification was bound to happen sometime and that this was quite natural. He did, however, also argue that there was no need for NATO to exist.[90] Among other official statements, Shevardnadze averred that unification increased stability and helped in the formation of a new Europe.[91]

A particularly good article by a key specialist on Germany, Nikolai Portugalov, merits a brief review as well.[92] In it he stressed that he trusted a united Germany and suggested that Germany should become a member of the UN Security Council. He also noted that the West Europeans thought (and some even hoped) that the USSR would impede unification; but, he argued, Germany could be the key savior for the USSR, namely to help it develop a market economy and save it from complete disintegration. On Germany's role in Europe and in shaping the USSR's future, Portugalov stated:

> As of now Germany will gain a world political dimension because of its bridging function between East and West Europe as well as because of its contribution to the development of complete market structures in the East. At the same time, this is the safest way to prevent disintegration of the Soviet Union into 15 nuclear powers.... Only Germany will be able and want to make this contribution, not alone but in a leading position. Other powers, which also could do this, do not yet want to face this task--at least not at the required scope.[93]

But at the same time, Portugalov also discussed the need to keep Germany in check:

> West European integration also--not to speak of NATO, which is becoming obsolete--would be slightly too narrow a corset for the united Germany. Comparable with a complete insurance would be Germany's integration in world responsibility--for instance by the decision of the UN plenum to raise it to the rank of permanent member in the Security Council. In the meantime, it seems anachronistic to see the possession of nuclear powers (sic) as the only criterion of a big power.[94]

On the military agenda, an agreement was reached on the withdrawal of Soviet troops, including the level of German compensation (a total of twelve billion marks, with seven million of this designated for the construction of housing for the returning Soviet personnel), but there were continuing tensions between the Soviet troops and the local population.

November 1990

While the official signing of the Soviet-German treaty received considerable attention for several days, beyond this reporting and general blandishments about this signalling a new phase in their relations, the attention paid to Germany in the Soviet media diminished considerably. While the treaty was initialled in September by Shevardnadze and Genscher, the formal signing of the document took place on 9 November 1990 between Gorbachev and Kohl in Germany. With this trip, Gorbachev was the first head of state to visit the united Germany.[95]

Nonetheless, there were several items worth noting in the coverage this month. First, there was a lengthy article by Presidential adviser Vadim Zagladin in which he noted the history of the Soviet attitude toward unification and made the case that perestroika began this process. He also argued that unification was seen to be inevitable, but that the West was hoping for the USSR to stop this process. Perhaps most revealingly, Zagladin explains the logic behind the changed Soviet position on German membership in NATO:

> We proceeded from the premise that Germany's unity was inevitable, that we should not interfere with it and that it was impossible to prevent its joining NATO, if it itself wished to do so. This meant that the practical task before our policy was

> limited to one thing: to ensure the creation of such conditions and to bring about such changes on the European political scene that would meet as far as possible the interests of our country's security."[96]

As indicated by Zagladin, as well as by many other Soviet commentators during the many months in which the unification agenda was being worked out, a constant theme was that unification would not have been possible without Gorbachev and his perestroika and new thinking. Soviet analysts constantly portrayed the FRG as the West's leading supporter of perestroika. The notion that Germany could be the USSR's economic savior was a central tenet as well.

Dashichev offered his assessment of Gorbachev's trip to Germany and the new bilateral treaty, and argued that in bilateral relations, the USSR and the new Germany must look to the future rather than concentrating on the past. Dashichev further noted that a divided Germany was the reason the USSR had not been "reintegrated" in Europe.[97]

Toward the end of November, a new theme began to emerge as well, namely humanitarian assistance. Germany was seen as the leader of the relief effort, although other countries' contributions were (briefly) recognized.[98]

December 1990

For the month of December, Germany's humanitarian aid to the Soviet Union and the ever-present theme of military issues accounted for most of the coverage. Unification and the treaty with Germany made up the remainder of the media accounts. With regard to humanitarian aid, Grigorev assessed German readiness to render this assistance, while others analyzed the problems of transporting and delivering the goods.[99]

In terms of military issues, a protocol was signed on the agreement for Germany to help provide housing for the troops returning to the USSR and military officers discussed the progress in withdrawing troops from Germany.[100] Some of these commentaries, particularly by the military, also insisted that reports indicating poor (and even violent) relations between the troops and the local population were either unfounded or exaggerated.[101]

Finally, on the subject of unification, *Moscow News* published a public opinion poll conducted in the USSR assessing Soviet citizens' reaction to unification. They were virtually split on whether they viewed this development with satisfaction or anxiety, and they were also split on whether USSR has lost what it gained in WWII.[102] Displaying a more moderate approach to the subject, now that unification was a fait accompli, Manki Ponomarev reasoned in *Krasnaya zvezda* that Germany belonging to NATO did not damage Soviet security.[103]

In short, there were dramatic changes in the Soviet position on the German question throughout the 1989-1990 period. But the Soviet leaders hoped that the bargain about the new Germany would provide them an important opening to the European integration process. It is to this linkage to which we now turn.

Notes

1. Shevardnadze, **Izvestiya**, 19 January 1990 in FBIS-SOV-90-013, p. 13.
2. Shevardnadze quoted in Sidorova, **New Times** (1, 1990) translated in FBIS, SOV-90-011, p.9.
3. As quoted in **The Washington Post**, 7 February 1990.
4. Printed in **Pravda** on 27 September 1989 in FBIS-SOV-89-186, p.8.
5. **Ibid.**, p. 9.
6. As quoted in **The Washington Post**, 26 October 1990.
7. As quoted by the **Associated Press**, 7 October 1990.
8. As quoted in **TASS**, 5 December 1989 in FBIS-SOV-89-233, p.48.
9. As quoted in **The Washington Post**, 19 December 1990.
10. As cited in **Pravda**, 20 December 1989 in FBIS-SOV-243, pp. 27-29.
11. As cited in **TASS**, 2 February 1990 in FBIS-SOV-90-024, pp. 33-34.
12. **The Washington Post**, 31 January 1990.
13. **Reuters News Wire**, 7 March 1990.
14. As presented in **Izvestiya**, 30 May 1990 in FBIS-SOV-90-104, p.1.
15. **Ibid.**
16. As cited in **TASS**, 17 July 1990 in FBIS-SOV-90-138, p. 3.
17. **The New York Times**, 22 July 1990.
18. As cited in **TASS**, 13 September 1990 in FBIS-SOV-90, p. 179.
19. As quoted in **Pravda**, 23 June 1990 in FBIS-SOV-90-122.

20. As quoted in **TASS**, 1 July 1990 in FBIS-SOV-90-127, p. 2.

21. See, for example, Ye. Grishin, "FRG: What Did the Parliamentary Debate Reveal?" **Izvestiya**, 10 November 1989, p. 4 in FBIS-SOV-89-217, p. 37.

22. Articles by Lapskii are included in: "GDR: Seeing the Mistakes that Have Been Made," **Izvestiya**, 31 October 1989, p. 4 in FBIS-SOV-89-210, p. 41; "GDR: Dramatic Days," **Izvestiya**, 10 November 1989, p. 4 and "Seeking a Way Out of the Crisis," **Izvestiya**, 11 November 1989, p. 4, both in FBIS-SOV-89-217, pp. 25-26 and 28; "GDR: Changes Every Day," **Izvestiya**, 14 November 1989, p. 4 in FBIS-SOV-89-218, pp. 33-35; and "Policy Statement," **Izvestiya**, 20 November 1989, p. 3 in FBIS-SOV-89-223, pp. 19-20. Podklyuchnikov articles include "Extraordinary Congress to Convene," **Pravda**, 15 November 1989, p. 6 in FBIS-SOV-89-219, pp. 26-27; "SED: Preparing for Congress," **Pravda**, 17 November 1989, p. 7 in FBIS-SOV-89-222, pp. 22-23; and "Pen Portrait of GDR Premier Hans Modrow," **Pravda**, 20 November 1989, p. 6 in FBIS-SOV-89-224, p. 35. Other views range from those of Gerasimov and Kondrashov on the GDR changes (on BBC television broadcast, 13 November 1989 in FBIS-SOV-89-219, pp. 27-28 and **TASS**, 15 November 1989 in FBIS-SOV-89-220, pp. 35-36, respectively) to **Sovetskaya Rossiya**'s assessment of the new GDR government: I. Osinskiy, "Will Quintet Play? On Multiparty System Under Conditions of Perestroika in GDR," **Sovetskaya Rossiya**, 18 November 1989, p. 5 in FBIS-SOV-89-224, pp. 37-38.

23. This, of course, raises the theme of German revanchism. For treatments of this issue, see, for example, M. Tretyakov, "Alarm Signals," **Pravda**, 2 November 1989, p. 5 in FBIS-SOV-89-212, pp. 36-37 and G. Charodeev, "What Mr. Teltschik Does not Like," **Izvestiya**, 12 November 1989, p.4 in FBIS-SOV-89-217, p.5.

24. In **Kyodo**, 15 November 1989 in FBIS-SOV-89-219, p. 24.

25. "Portugalov: Germans on Both Sides," **Bild**, 15 November 1989, p. 2 in FBIS-SOV-89-219, pp. 24-25.

26. For example, Krenz's statements include those carried on Moscow television, in **TASS**, and **Trud**, published in FBIS-SOV-89-222, p. 20; FBIS-SOV-89-224, p. 36; and FBIS-SOV-89-228, p. 42.

27. Bovkun and Lapskii, "Treaty-Based Community or Swallowing of GDR?" **Izvestiya**, 30 November 1989, p. 4 and Podklyuchnikov, "Plans for Engulfment Again?" **Pravda**, 30 November 1989, p. 5, both in FBIS-SOV-89-229, pp. 15-16 and 31, respectively.

28. See, for example, Nikolai Shishlin broadcast, published in FBIS-SOV-89-228, pp. 54-55; Yurii Gremitskikh statement, published in FBIS-SOV-89-229, p. 31.

29. Interview with Paris Domestic Service, published in FBIS-SOV-89-230, pp. 43-44.

30. Nikolai Afanasevskii, "Germany's Reunification: A Premature Problem," **Le Figaro**, 13 December 1989, in FBIS-SOV-89-242, p. 22.

31. Sergei Plekhanov on Top Priority television show, 22 December 1989, published in FBIS-SOV-89-248, pp. 3-4.

32. Yurii Solton, Moscow World Service broadcast, 11 December 1989, published in FBIS-SOV-89-238, p. 39.

33. V. Lapskii, "GDR: Appeal to Refrain from Violence," **Izvestiya**, 6 December 1989, p. 4 in FBIS-SOV-89-233, p. 41

34. V. Lapskii, "GDR: 8 December--Extraordinary SED Congress," **Izvestiya**, 8 December 1989, p. 4 in FBIS-SOV-89-235, pp. 24-25; Lapskii, "GDR: Questions Mounting," **Izvestiya**, 12 December 1989, p. 4 in FBIS-SOV-89-237, p. 31; Lapskii, "GDR: What Path the Reform Will Take," **Izvestiya**, 14 December 1989, p. 8 in FBIS-SOV-89-239, pp. 21-22; and Lapskii, "GDR: Extraordinary Congress Ends," **Izvestiya**, 18 December 1989, p. 11 in FBIS-SOV-89-243, pp. 16-17.

35. V. Lapskii, "Against the Threat From the Right," **Izvestiya**, 13 December 1989, p. 3 in FBIS-SOV-89-239, pp. 22-23.

36. See, for example, **TASS**'s Vadim Chudov, "Morale Low Amid Turmoil in GDR," **TASS**, 5 December 1989 in FBIS-SOV-89-232, pp. 36-37; Yu. Shapkov, "We Are the People Too," **Sovetskaya Rossiya**, 10 December 1989, p. 5 in FBIS-SOV-89-237, pp. 32-33 and Shapkov, "Renewal Begins," **Sovetskaya Rossiya**, 12 December 1989, p. 3 in FBIS-SOV-89-238, pp. 39-40; and S. Baygarov, S. Zyubanov and M. Podklyuchnikov, "At SED Extraordinary Congress," **Pravda**, 17 December 1989, p. 8 in FBIS-SOV-89-242, pp. 23-26.

37. For Modrow statements, see "GDR People's Chamber Session: Government Statement by H. Modrow," **Sovetskaya Rossiya**, 12 January 1990, p. 5 in FBIS-SOV-90-011, pp. 39-40 and **TASS**, 30 January 1990, in FBIS-SOV-90-021, p. 17. Genscher's views were published in: E. Grigorev, "Chance for the European Home," **Pravda**, 2 January 1990, p. 7 in FBIS-SOV-90-002, p. 29; "Prospects for Cooperation," **Pravda**, 16 January 1990, p. 5 in FBIS-SOV-90-011, p. 54, and in E. Grishin, "H.D. Genscher: 1990 Must Become Year of Disarmament," **Izvestiya**, 19 January 1990, p. 4 in FBIS-SOV-90-015, pp. 1-2, while Kohl was in E.

Germany, E. Grigorev, "H. Kohl's News Conference," **Pravda**, 12 January 1990, pp. 1 and 7 in FBIS-SOV-90-011, pp. 52-53.

38. See, for example, E. Grigorev, "Kreuth in Leipzig?" **Pravda**, 6 January 1990, p. 7 in FBIS-SOV-90-006, pp. 53-54; TASS' Albert Balebanov broadcast, 11 January 1990 in FBIS-SOV-009, p. 38, and V. Lapskii, "Election Campaign with FRG Involvement," **Izvestiya**, 18 January 1990, p. 4 in FBIS-SOV-017, p. 9.

39. E. Bovkun, "FRG: Nostalgia for the Future," **Izvestiya**, 6 January 1990, p. 5 in FBIS-SOV-90-008, pp. 54-55.

40. Grigorev, **Pravda**, 12 January 1990, in FBIS-SOV-90-011, pp. 52-53.

41. As reported by East Berlin ADN International, 30 January 1990, in FBIS-SOV-90-020, p. 21 and various reports on Modrow's visit published in FBIS-SOV-90-021, pp. 16-18.

42. Albert Balebanov, **TASS** broadcast, 3 January 1990, in FBIS-SOV-90-003, pp. 29-29.

43. Col. V. Markushin, "Special Circumspection Needed," **Krasnaya zvezda**, 11 January 1990, p. 3 in FBIS-SOV-90-009, p. 7.

44. Interview with Falin in **Der Spiegel**, 19 February 1990, pp. 168-172 in FBIS-SOV-90-036, pp. 31-36.

45. Reported by **TASS**, 24 February 1990 in FBIS-SOV-90-038, p. 1.

46. Sergei Karaganov on Top Priority television program, 23 February 1990 in FBIS-SOV-90-038, pp. 7-10.

47. Gorbachev interview by Gabriele Krone-Schmalz and Stefan Kuehnert, **Frankfurter Allgemeine**, 8 March 1990, p. 4 in FBIS-SOV-90-047, pp. 27-28.

48. See, for example, Aleksandr Tolpegin, "Not Only a German Issue," **Za rubezhom**, no. 7, 9-15 February, 1990, p. 1 in FBIS-SOV-90-046, pp. 3-5; and Yurii Solton commentary on Moscow International Service, 19 March 1990 in FBIS-SOV-90-058, p. 52.

49. See, for example, Marshal Akhromeev, "No Unified Germany in NATO," **Le Monde**, 30 March 1990, p. 4 in FBIS-SOV-90-062, p. 4.

50. Col. I. Vladimirov, "United Germany and NATO," **Krasnaya zvezda**, 15 March 1990, p. 3 in FBIS-SOV-90-052, pp. 6-7.

51. D. Proektor, "'For' and 'Against' a United Germany," **Sovetskaya Rossiya**, 28 February 1990, p. 5 in FBIS-SOV-90-043, pp. 9-11.

52. Aleksandr Bovin, Moscow Television Service, 3 March 1990, in FBIS-SOV-90-045, pp. 4-5.

53. As reported in Hamburg DPA, 17 March 1990, in FBIS-SOV-90-053, p. 39.

54. Illustrations of this point of view are found in: Vitalii Korionov, "Observer's Reflections on the German Question," **Pravda**, 2 March 1990, p. 5 in FBIS-SOV-90-042, pp. 33-35; "Statement by the All-Union Council of War and Labor Veterans," **Krasnaya zvezda**, 3 March 1990, p. 5 in FBIS-SOV-90-044, pp. 11-12; and E. Bovkun, "Bonn: Unscheduled Train," **Izvestiya**, 12 March 1990, p. 5 in FBIS-SOV-90-050, pp. 38-40.

55. See also Valentin Falin statement reported by **TASS**, 12 March 1990, in FBIS-SOV-90-048, p. 4.

56. See, for example, the report by various correspondents, "The German Question--Where and How It is Posed," **Komsomolskaya pravda**, 17 March 1990, p. 3 in FBIS-SOV-90-064, pp. 21-23.

57. See, for example, Tomas Kolesnichenko, "But If You Take a Common Sense View...," **Pravda**, 4 April 1990, p. 5 in FBIS-SOV-90-067, p. 1, and Gremitskikh press briefing, 13 April 1990, in FBIS-SOV-90-072, p. 3.

58. E. Bovkun, "Germany Between East and West," **Izvestiya**, 2 April 1990, p. 3 in FBIS-SOV-90-063, pp. 32-33.

59. As reported by Cologne Deutschlandfunk Network, 31 March 1990 in FBIS-SOV-90-063, p. 34.

60. Falin comments on Moscow Television Service, 3 April 1990 in FBIS-SOV-90-066, p. 11.

61. See, for example, USSR's People's Deputy Dzasokhov comments on Vremya, 3 May 1990 in FBIS-SOV-90-087, p. 3.

62. Batenin, "Preferred Variety: All of Germany in NATO," **Berliner Zeitung**, 4 May 1990 in FBIS-SOV-90-090, pp. 2-4.

63. As reported in East Berlin ADN International Service, 18 May 1990 in FBIS-SOV-90-099, p. 61.

64. In FBIS-SOV-90-097, pp. 5-7.

65. Aleksandr Antsiferov, as reported by **TASS**, 11 May 1990, in FBIS-SOV-90-093, pp. 14-15 and Valentin Falin commentary to East Berlin Deutschlandsender Network, 18 May 1990 in FBIS-SOV-90-098, pp. 30-31.

66. Grigorev, "On Haste and Speed," **Pravda**, 18 May 1990, p. 6 in FBIS-SOV-90-098, p. 13.

67. See, for example, Viktor Levin commentary on Moscow Domestic Service, 14 May 1990, in FBIS-SOV-90-095, p. 13 and May Podklyuch-

nikov, "Contract of Sale," **Pravda**, 21 May 1990, pp. 1 and 6, in FBIS-SOV-90-103, pp. 8-9.

68. Peter Vasilev report on 12 June 1990, in FBIS-SOV-90-115, pp. 2-3.

69. Dmitrii Pogorzhelskii, "The German Puzzle," **New Times**, no. 22, 29 May-4 June 1990, pp. 16-17 in FBIS-SOV-90-115, pp. 3-4.

70. Aleksandr Pogodin commentary on Moscow World Service, 17 June 1990 in FBIS-SOV-90-117, p. 3.

71. See, for example, Col. General Nikolai Chervov, "United Germany Should Not be NATO Member," **Svenska Dagbladet**, 1 July 1990, in FBIS-SOV-90-129, p. 5.

72. See, for example, Grigorev's assessments in "What Will the Chancellor Bring With Him?" **Pravda**, 14 July 1990, p. 5 in FBIS-SOV-90-136, pp. 34-35 and "USSR-FRG: Post-Summit," **Pravda**, 19 July 1990, p. 6 in FBIS-SOV-90-140, pp. 31-32. Viktor Levin's assessment on Moscow Domestic Service, 15 July 1990, in FBIS-SOV-90-136, p. 36. And S. Guk's assessment in "USSR-FRG Dialogue: Who Conceded More to Whom?" **Izvestiya**, 19 July 1990, p. 1 in FBIS-SOV-90-140, p. 32.

73. For those who say NATO membership should be accepted, see, for example, Aleksandr Bovin, "Signal From London," **Izvestiya**, 10 July 1990, pp. 1 and 4 in FBIS-SOV-90-132, pp. 7-10. For opposition to the idea, see Valentin Falin's statement carried by Hamburg DPA, 3 July 1990, in FBIS-SOV-90-129, pp. 5-6. Portugalov shows a softening of his position even before the NATO meeting, where he allows that a compromise on NATO membership might be possible and that the USSR believes, in principle, in the idea of a nation's right to self-determination on the question of alliance memberships. See his comments on Moscow Domestic Service with Viktor Levin, 5 July 1990, in FBIS-SOV-90-130, pp. 2-4.

74. See, for example, Aleksandr Antsiferov, "Helmut Kohl's Visit," **TASS**, 13 July 1990 in FBIS-SOV-90-138, p. 9.

75. A. Kondakov, "FRG Plus GDR: A New Superpower?" **Ekonomika i zhizn'**, no. 27, July 1990, p. 19 in FBIS-SOV-90-140, pp. 10-12.

76. See, for example, General Vladimir Lobov's comments as reported by Oleg Moskovskii in **TASS**, 19 July 1990 in FBIS-SOV-90-140, p. 28; Major General Vasilii Kazachenko's interview in **Neues Deutschland**, 16 July 1990, p. 4 in FBIS-SOV-90-140, pp. 28-29; and A. Krainii, "Crazy Marks Are What Our Troops Need to Leave Germany, and Absolutely Insane Marks to Stay," **Komsomolskaya pravda**, 22 July 1990, p. 2 in FBIS-SOV-90-143, pp. 26-29.

77. As reported by East Berlin ADN International, 13 August 1990, in FBIS-SOV-90-157, p. 3.

78. E. Bovkun, "Farewell to Prussian Socialism," **Izvestiya**, 30 August 1990, p. 5 in FBIS-SOV-90-170, pp. 14-15.

79. For the former, see Genscher interview by V. Zapevalova, "United Germany Will Have Nothing in Common with the Germany of Tragic Recollections," **Literaturnaya gazeta**, no. 31, 1 August 1990, p. 14 in FBIS-SOV-90-150, pp. 4-7 and interview with Aleksandr Zholkver on Moscow Television Service, 25 August 1990, in FBIS-SOV-90-166, pp. 44-45. On the latter, see his interview with E. Grigorev, "A New Quality of Relations," **Pravda**, 15 August 1990, p. 4 in FBIS-SOV-90-159, p. 30.

80. For this point, see **TASS**'s Vladimir Rodin commentary on 10 August 1990, in FBIS-SOV-90-156, pp. 41-42. Gorbachev and Kohl's official messages to each other are published in **Izvestiya**, 13 August 1990, p. 3 in FBIS-SOV-90-158, pp. 23-24.

81. Aleksandr Fomenko, "A Moscow-Berlin Axis?" **Literaturnaya Rossiya**, no. 34, 24 August 1990, p. 19 in FBIS-SOV-90-215, pp. 27-29, at p. 27.

82. M. Podklyuchnikov, "Decision Adopted, Problems Remain," **Pravda**, 26 August 1990, p. 7 in FBIS-SOV-90-168, pp. 28-29 and E. Bovkun, "Contradictory Assessments," **Izvestiya**, 17 August 1990, p. 5 in FBIS-SOV-90-169, pp. 7-8.

83. See, respectively: Lt. Colonel I. Kosenko, "What Should be Done with the Russians?" **Krasnaya zvezda**, 12 August 1990, p. 3 in FBIS-SOV-90-158, p. 21; A. Soloshenko, "Expenditures Will be Recouped, But...," **Trud**, 17 August 1990, p. 3 in FBIS-SOV-90-168, p. 30; and report in **Volksstimme**, carried by Paris AFP, 31 August 1990, in FBIS-SOV-90-170, p. 14.

84. See, for example, **TASS** correspondent Vladimir Serov's comments, 6 September 1990, in FBIS-SOV-90-174, p. 5; E. Grigorev, "Based on Trust," **Pravda**, 8 September 1990, p. 4 in FBIS-SOV-90-176, pp. 3-4; and K. Aleksandrov, "Where Are You Looking, Germany?" **Rabochaya tribuna**, 31 August 1990, p. 3 in FBIS-SOV-90-176, pp. 6-7.

85. Aleksandr Zholkver on Moscow Domestic Service, 21 September 1990, in FBIS-SOV-90-185, p. 8.

86. See, for example, **TASS** correspondents Konstantin Voitsekhovich and Aleksandr Kanishchev's comments on 12 September 1990, in FBIS-SOV-90-178, p. 4.

87. Gorbachev interview by Sergei Lomakin on Vremya, 12 September 1990, in FBIS-SOV-90-178, pp. 45-46.

88. Text of Eduard Shevardnadze's speech to the USSR Supreme Soviet Committee for Foreign Affairs, by **TASS**, 20 September 1990, in FBIS-SOV-90-184, pp. 20-23.

89. Col. V. Markushin, "Germany. Europe. Security," **Krasnaya zvezda**, 28 September 1990, p. 3 in FBIS-SOV-90-194, pp. 6-7, at p. 7.

90. Sergei Akhromeev, "Unity was Bound to Come," **Die Welt**, 3 October 1990, p. 8 in FBIS-SOV-90-192, p. 5 and Akhromeev interview in "Germany, the New Europe, and Perestroika," **Neues Deutschland**, 4 October 1990, p. 8 in FBIS-SOV-90-198, pp. 30-33.

91. Remarks by Shevardnadze to Andrei Ptashnikov on Moscow Domestic Service, 3 October 1990, in FBIS-SOV-90-193, p. 1.

92. Interviews with Portugalov in Peter Keller, "Justified Claim to Role of a Great Power," **Der Standard**, 6 October 1990, p. 4 and in "The Thorny Path to Becoming a World Power," **Der Spiegel**, 8 October 1990, pp. 184-190, both in FBIS-SOV-90-196, pp. 38-40.

93. **Ibid.**, p. 39.

94. **Ibid.**, p. 40.

95. As expected, all the main commentators on Germany filed reports on this meeting, such as E. Bovkun, "Investments in the Future," **Izvestiya**, 9 November 1990, p. 1 in FBIS-SOV-90-218, pp. 18-19; and several by E. Grigorev and V. Drobkov, "View from Petersberg Hill," **Pravda**, 9 November 1990, pp. 1 and 5 in FBIS-SOV-90-218, pp. 19-20; "It Is Up to Us," **Pravda**, 11 November 1990, p. 6 in FBIS-SOV-90-219, pp. 31-32; "The Germans and the United States," **Pravda**, 14 November 1990, pp. 1 and 5 in FBIS-SOV-90-221, pp. 29-30.

96. Vadim Zagladin, "The Soviet View of German Reunification," **Ian Press Release**, 16 October 1990, pp. 2-10 in FBIS-SOV-90-216, pp. 16-19, at p. 18.

97. Vyacheslav Dashichev's interview in "Now Our Path toward Europe is Clear," **Horizont**, no. 37, 15 November 1990, pp. 16-17 in FBIS-SOV-90-228, pp. 27-29.

98. For a variety of Soviet coverage of Horst Telschik's visit to Moscow to set up a humanitarian assistance program, see FBIS-SOV-90-230, pp. 35-37.

99. E. Grigorev, "They Are Ready to Help Us," **Pravda**, 27 November 1990, p. 5 in FBIS-SOV-90-235, pp. 20-21 and interview with Deputy Foreign minister Ernest Obminskii, "We Need Transparency in Distributing

Relief Goods," **Welt am Sonntag**, 2 December 1990, p. 30 in FBIS-SOV-90-234, pp. 27-29.

100. Mikhail Voronenkov, **TASS** report, 6 December 1990 in FBIS-SOV-90-236, p. 31.

101. See, for example, **Ibid.** and Lt. Colonel Yu. Alyaev, "These Are Happy People...," **Krasnaya zvezda**, 7 December 1990, p. 4 in FBIS-SOV-90-238, pp. 28-29. For one report of violence between the Germans and Soviets, see V. Zapevalov's article in **Literaturnaya gazeta**, no. 46, 1990.

102. Yurii Levada, "Social Barometer," **Moscow News**, no. 46, 25 November-2 December 1990, p. 4 in FBIS-SOV-90-238-S, p. 9.

103. Manki Ponomarev, "Such Similar Letters," **Krasnaya zvezda**, 18 December 1990, p. 3 in FBIS-SOV-90-245-S, pp. 3-4.

8

The Soviets and the New Federal Republic of Germany: Dealing with the New Europe

In the first part of this chapter, the themes presented in the specialized journals and press will be identified. Articles published in the foreign policy journals (*Mirovaia Ekonomika i Mezhdunarodnaya Otnosheiniia* and *SShA*) are the special focus of attention. The period covered is from mid-1989 to the end of 1990. Articles published within a journal on a given date were, of course, written before that date. The rule of thumb is two months before publication but there are clear deviations from this standard rule. But this section ignores making judgments about when an article was published, and the emphasis is upon themes presented throughout this period, regardless of publication date.

In the second part of this chapter, some general conclusions are presented concerning the Soviet approach to the new Europe emergent from the debate about German unification. The main thrust of the domestic tendencies and their foreign policy consequences are identified and discussed.

Broad Themes on German Unification

In general, the range of opinion on themes presented in the specialized foreign policy fall into three categories: reformist, centrist, and conservative. The differences in these positions revolved largely around how threatening German unification was to Soviet or Russian interests.

The *reformist* position focused upon how German unification was part of the general European construction process. Emphasis was placed on how Soviet acceptance of a united Germany within the Westernization process would be part of the modernization process of the Soviet Union itself.

The *centrist* position focused upon how German unification had to be inextricably intertwined with a new Europeanization process, neither Western nor Eastern. The Soviet Union must not be marginalized in the process of adapting to German unification.

The *conservative* position focused upon establishing very stringent safeguards against a resurgent Germany. The need to protect the Russian nation against German revanchism was underscored. The specialized foreign policy press largely saw a debate between the reformist and centrist positions. The conservative position was largely left unstated in this press but was evident in the military press, especially *Krasnaya zvezda* and in the political presentations of conservative Russian politicians, such as Yegor Ligachev.

The *reformist* position consisted of a number of key planks for the advocacy of reform in the USSR itself.[1] First, the damage to Russian interests which resulted from the "old" policy of confrontation was emphasized. The Soviet Union's old power position was eroding and a new foreign policy had to be crafted to deal with the erosion of the Soviet position within Europe.

A second plank of the reform position was the need for reform in the USSR to stabilize the European situation. The disintegration of the USSR would pose serious problems for European stability.

The third key element of the reformist position was an emphasis upon the continued viability of West European institutions, especially the European Community, in dealing with the future of European construction. The emphasis was placed upon the Soviet Union not only dealing with these institutions but trying to participate in the institutional life of the European construction process.

The fourth key element was an acceptance of NATO as an integral component of the European construction process. Several analyses underscored that NATO was not a threat to the Soviet Union as long as the Western democratization process continued.

The reformists emphasized the central role of Germany to the European construction process. By accepting German unification, the Soviet Union would be able to enlist Germany as an ally in Russian participation in the European construction process. By rejecting it, the Russians would only continue to isolate themselves from the Europeanization process.

One variant of the reformist vision was economic. A particularly clear presentation of this orientation was presented by Smol'nikov. This analyst argued that keeping Germany in NATO was preferable to neutral autonomy. Germany needed to be within the Western institutional framework to continue to develop in a multinational way conducive to a partnership with the USSR.

Smol'nikov underscored the significance of economic ties for the future of the Soviet Union. "For the Soviet Union and Germany...the prospect is opening up for creating an economic space from the Rhine to the Urals. In this space, many future forms of economic relations can be developed, including free economic zones, joint enterprises, and banks. A close interweaving of Soviet and German economic potentials could not only substantially transform the economic make-up of the Old Continent, but would also, in our view, be an important contribution to European security."[2] Smol'nikov went on to underscore the importance of Germany playing a central role within the European Community in order for the Soviet-German economic relationship to be part of the new Europeanization process. It is important "that the processes of unifying Germany not lead to a slowing down of the economic-political unification of the European Community. Only the full-blooded participation of Germany in formulating today's economic and political structure of the Community will reliably contribute to ensuring European stability and security."[3]

A second variant of the reform position was presented by Baranovskii. This analyst underscored that there are three new elements in the East-West dynamic: the crisis situation in the USSR, Eastern Europe's new reorientation, and the emergence of a new Germany. Central to dealing with all of these processes--and notably with their conjunction--are the European Community, NATO, the Council of Europe and CSCE. In other words, existing Western institutions are central to the resolution of the new East-West dynamics and should not be undercut by Soviet diplomacy or aspirations for a new synthesis.

For Baranovskii, the crisis of development in the Soviet Union poses a fundamental challenge to European stability. If the Soviet Union cannot reform and carry out extensive modernization, a new East-West divide will open up with Eastern Europe in the West and the Soviet Union isolated and stewing in its own backwardness. Europeanization is critical for the further development of the USSR.

The *centrist position* emphasized the importance of changing the European and East-West security and economic structures as the price for German unification. It was reasoned that the new Germany ought to be a motor force for creating a new synthesis in East-West relations and not the cornerstone for the Westernization of the East.

The centrist position rested upon an advocacy for a cautious and gradual approach to the German unification issue. Gradualism was necessary in order to ensure that the Germans and the West would build a security structure meeting Soviet concerns. As Pavlov put it, "Speaking of the need for a step-by-step approach, the Soviet side does not intend to somehow impede the construction of German unity, but, on the other hand, it does not see reasonable arguments in favor of it being artificially spurred on by someone."[4]

The centrist position advocated placing the united Germany within a non-bloc situation. That is, the united Germany should be neutral or the bloc-to-bloc confrontation must be altered with new structures to be created to deal with the new Germany. From this point of view, the centrist position about unification rested upon a long legacy of Soviet efforts to jettison West Germany out of NATO.

In other words, dealing with German unification became the policy problem leading the question of the future of European security structures. As Pavlov articulated this process of development, "Whereas before there was the opinion that overcoming the East-West divide might result in overcoming Germany's division, now the order has been reversed."[5]

For the centrists, NATO membership for the new Germany was unacceptable. Pavlov underscored why this was so in the following words: the membership of a unified Germany in NATO would lead "to an unacceptable disruption of the military-strategic balance between the Warsaw Pact and NATO and thereby to an undermining of the very foundations of stability and security in Europe."[6]

For centrists, the Westernization of the East through a unified Germany was unacceptable. As Maximychev and Menshikov put it, "A unified Germany must not become just an 'extended FRG'."[7] They added that "The Soviet Union advocates synchronizing the formation of a unified Germany with a positive evolution of the European process and the shaping of a fundamentally new system of European security to replace the bloc system. German unification should neither lead to less security for any country nor upset the balance of interests at any country's expense."[8]

For centrists, it was important to build new European security structures to encase the new Germany. For example, Major General Vladimirov and Colonel Posokhov argued that a European security alliance should be created through the reshaping of NATO and the Warsaw Pact. Any European country would be allowed in and it would operate under general European institutions and the UN. They underscored the need for such a structure because "political, economic and financial European integration will not be able to succeed if it is not accompanied by the appropriate military-political integration."[9]

The conservative position was underrepresented in the specialized foreign policy literature. This is not surprising given that the major foreign policy journals were primarily populated with reformers and centrists. Nonetheless, the conservative position can be identified not only by inference but with regard to a number of specific comments made by conservative policymakers and analysts.

The *conservative position* was not specifically a rejection of the changes induced by the Revolution of 1989 (although reactionary voices could be heard to this effect). Rather, it was an advocacy of trying to protect Soviet interests directly through the negotiation of the terms of German unification. Whereas the centrists argued for a creative synthesis of East and West through the creation of new security structures, the conservatives were more intent on protecting the integrity of the Soviet empire (within the USSR) and the Russian nation. In other words, above all the conservatives argued for protecting the integrity of Russia from the assaults for German and Western influence within Russia.

In addition, the conservatives advocated a policy of little or no negotiation with the West Germans until they accepted a new security solution for Germany. For conservatives, the objective would be a virtual demilitarization of Germany, not simply armed neutrality.

One conservative group--the All-Union Council of Veterans of War, Labor and the Armed Forces--issued a statement in late February 1990, which underscored the concern for the impact of Westernization upon the East. Events were going too fast and would undermine the all-European peace process. West Germany was conducting "undisguised interference" in East Germany's internal affairs. The West Germans were still pursuing "revanchism" and were unwilling to guarantee the postwar borders of Eastern Europe. German military industry must be converted to civilian use. Neo-nazi and "revanchist" organizations must be disbanded so that Germany would not be a threat. East Germany must continue to have its own existence within a German confederation. The organization then called for the Supreme Soviet to protect Soviet interests and, notably, to pressure the FRG to stop interfering in the internal affairs of East Germany.[10]

An important theme of Soviet conservatives was the impact of the unification process on Western influence in the East. The way the Gorbachev administration handled the German unification issue only led to excessive Western influence in the process. This criticism became even more strident in the wake of Shevardnadze's resignation in early 1991 as foreign minister.

But even in the early phase in dealing with German unification the conservatives were harping on the excessive Western influence theme. Notably in an article published in *Literaturnaya Rossiya* (a conservative journal) two days before the March 1990 East German elections, Alexsandrov (a pseudonym for a high-ranking Kremlin official) argued that the four powers should dictate terms to West Germany in the unification process and not comply with West German demands for "swallowing up" East Germany. The political and military leaders of the Soviet Union have (with the other powers) the right to "exercise supreme power in Germany."

The article goes on to warn of the danger of "Pan-Germanism," which is associated with the FRG desire to change the postwar borders. The right of the German people to self-determination should be subordinated to the rights of Germany's neighbors for security. The Western allies--notably the United States--are especially criticized for ignoring Soviet interests and failing to cooperate to ensure that adequate safeguards against German revanchism are provided. The article goes on to argue that only a nonaligned Germany would be acceptable to the Soviet leadership.[11]

Even after the deal had been cut for German unity, Russian conservatives continued to be critical of the Gorbachev administration. For example, in a series of letters to the editor of *Rabochaya Tribuna*, Soviet citizens expressed "the lack of faith in the assurances coming from Bonn that the reunited Germany will eschew the idea of revenge." One of the letters noted that "The most real guarantee that the sad history of world wars will not be repeated would be the withdrawal of the reunified Germany from NATO and the assignment of a neutral status to it." Another letter stated that "My soul will not rest in peace...until the Germans of the future Germany reject the army and destroy the entire military industry, and Germany issues a law that metes out punishment for progagandizing war, revenge, and changing of borders."[12]

The most visible representative of the Russian conservative position during the year of unification was clearly Yegor Ligachev. Throughout the year, he sought to confront Gorbachev on various issues from the standpoint of representing a more conservative position. This included the major foreign policy subject of the year--the German issue. Notably in an important Central Committee debate in early February 1990, Ligachev directly confronted Gorbachev in front of the CPSU on the German issue. He argued that "It would be unbelievably short-sided and a mistake if we did not see a Germany with huge economic and military potential looming on the international horizon. It is time to recognize the new danger and to speak about it as loud as possible to our own people and party."[13]

In short, the variant positions on German unification were linked to distinctive views of the future European security order and the fate of the Soviet Union. Clearly, the Soviets were shifting from the luxury of framing a geopolitical foreign policy stance with little interference from domestic affairs to a spirited struggle over the future of Soviet foreign policy dictated by domestic concerns. As Shevardnadze put it just two months before his resignation, "If negative and destructive trends remain in this country (the Soviet Union), if the division of economic, financial and other state structures goes on, no international agreements will ensure our reliable security and peaceful life. Foreign policy is the continuation of domestic policy, and we should always bear this in mind."[14]

The Future

This book has identified and assessed the evolving Soviet approach to the Federal Republic of Germany throughout the Gorbachev period, from 1985 until the end of 1990. Soviet policy toward the FRG has been a microcosm of the general Soviet policy toward Western Europe and Soviet assessments of changes in policy toward the FRG mirror broader changes in their policy toward Western Europe.

In general terms, since the early 1970s, Soviet policy has gone through three phases of development. The first phase continued into the beginning of the Gorbachev administration as it inherited the classic approach refined by the Brezhnev administration. In this approach, the Soviets gambled to win a bet: to expand their influence within Western Europe while undercutting Western Alliance institutions in exchange for the risk of greater West European influence over Eastern Europe. This bet rested on the ability to contain change in the East while promoting disintegration of the Western bloc. But for this bet to be won, the Soviet Union would need to contain a dynamic course of development.

By the time the Gorbachev administration came to power, it was clear that the Soviets were losing this bet. Notably, the Soviet model was disintegrating due to domestic pressures which were reinforced by an inability to crack the Western coalition. The Brezhnevites had succeeded in combining two failures: Soviet economic and political decline with encirclement by the foreign enemies of the Soviet Union.

Gorbachev acted to try to reverse the negative course of history in the second phase of Soviet policy. He placed his own bet for historical development. No longer did the Soviet leadership try to work simply within the confines of the mediated relationship of Eastern and Western Europe. Europeanization and Westernization were moving too briskly for conservative management of a mediated intra-European relationship. It was necessary to announce a new synthesis of East and West within which "socialism" in the East would be informed by and influence the development of "capitalism" in the West. What I have termed the Strasbourg synthesis was the basic gamble made by Gorbachev.

The fall of the Berlin wall made it clear that the Soviet leadership had lost this bet as well, at least for the time being. Perhaps over the long haul Westernization and capitalism will fail in Eastern Europe and may never take root in the USSR, and the pressures for a new synthesis could then return. But the dramatic events of the fall of 1989 meant the end of the viability of the Strasbourg synthesis. Ergo, the need to develop a third phase in their approach, but the new phase would prove difficult.

Throughout 1990, not only did the Gorbachev administration have to deal with the German unification process and the explosion of political change in Eastern Europe, but it had to deal with the explosions of tensions within the USSR as well. Suddenly the Russian leadership was faced with the twin pressures of Westernization moving East (to the GDR and to Eastern Europe) and the pressures to create a new Russian and/or Soviet development model as well. This book closes with the signing of the Soviet-German treaty of December 1990, but this treaty and the process which led to its conclusion are clearly not the beginning of the end, but the end of the beginning.

One of the most important tensions for the future of European security policy will come from the different understandings the Soviets and Germans will take to the unification process. For the West Germans, the unification process was the culmination of a forty year process of change within Europe--it was the beginning of the end. But for the Soviets, the unification process was increasingly part of the struggle for the future of the Soviet Union--it was the end of the beginning.

Already within the effort to deal with German unification several different instincts or approaches emerged within the Russian elite and these differences presaged the struggles to come in the 1990s over the future of the USSR. Namely, the German unification dynamic saw further fragmentation of the Soviet elite concerning the future of their European policy.

For Russian *reactionaries*, Germany should not be united and Gorbachev "lost" Germany. The empire should be preserved at home and the handling of the German issue only weakened the internal hold of the Russians over the Soviet empire.

For Russian *conservatives*, German unification could be accepted but not in the manner in which the Soviet government handled the process. The Soviet side allowed too many concessions but even now the Soviet Union might be able to recover its influence in shaping the new European order through its alliance with Germany if the requisite approach were adopted. The goal in this approach would be primarily negative--to use German fear of Soviet military power as a means of ensuring German acquiescence in a more equitable (from the Soviet point of view) definition of legitimate Soviet interests within Eastern Europe.

For Russian *centrists*, the German unification process had a sense of inevitability about it. The process could not be resisted but only coped with. Especially for Gorbachev, dealing with German unification was closely connected with maintaining a viable central Russian or Soviet state. Gorbachev underscored his responsibility as head of state to protect the Russians from negative effects flowing from German unification. The German unification process must not undercut the integrity of the Russian state or the Soviet empire. Accepting German unification was part of a process of ensuring the West's help, tolerance for, or acquiescence in the continued existence of a central state within the USSR.

For Soviet *reformers*, the German unification process was part of the broader Europeanization effort which the Soviets must join in order for reform and modernization to occur. For Shevardnadze, it was a visit to Brussels (to the EC and to NATO) in December 1989, which symbolized how he would deal with the German unification process.

But by the summer of 1990, the Gorbachev administration had accepted German unity within a Western context. At this point, the focus shifted to trying to define the new Europe within which Germany would operate. The Gorbachev administration seemed to insist on a number of conditions for the new Germany which it hoped would provide some Soviet levers for influence within the new Europe.

First, Gorbachev and Shevardnadze insisted on the reorganization of NATO. The NATO declaration of July 1990 about restructuring was hailed by the Soviet leaders as the beginning of a process of reform which must continue if the new Germany would not pose a threat in the future to the Soviet Union.

Second, the Soviet leadership insisted on the Germans paying a cost for the agreement. Politically, the Soviets wanted and obtained limitations on German forces. By so doing the Soviets could leverage the process of conventional arms control within Europe. Economically, the Soviets insisted on being paid to remain in Germany militarily during the transitional period. Developmentally, the Soviets demanded and received some economic aid for accepting unification.

Third, although these were short-term requirements, the Soviet leadership hoped to put in motion a long-term trend--the emergence of Germany as a lobby within Europe for the Soviet Union. With the emergence of the new Germany, its role would be augmented in both the EC and the Alliance. If German attitudes could be shaped to be supportive of long-term Soviet objectives, then unification would be worth the cost. This was the new bet being made by the Soviet leadership by the end of 1990. But Soviet leaders did not agree on the terms of the bet or the hoped for outcomes. For Russian *conservatives*, a more aggressive and explicit attitude would be required to ensure this, especially with regard to security policy. For Soviet *reformers*, security policy would be downplayed to gain German aid in the Soviet Europeanization process. For Gorbachev, an ally would be needed to bolster his handling of politics in the USSR and he clearly believed that by making concessions to Kohl on unification, the Germans would become de facto supporters in Gorbachev's effort to maintain central control in the USSR.

A number of key items emerged on the Soviet foreign policy agenda concomitant to accepting German unification, and clearly Soviet leaders hoped the trends would reinforce one another. Above all, the Soviet leadership sought to enlist the Germans as allies in reshaping the European order.

From the economic standpoint, the Soviets encouraged the European Community to broaden its membership and to include Eastern Europe and the Soviet Union. Clearly, at least some Soviet leaders, notably the reformers, hope that the deepening process--the explicit integration of Western Europe--will be undercut by broadening pressures.

From the security standpoint, trends within the German debate against collective defense and for collective security were clearly encouraged by the Soviets. By highlighting the CSCE process, by encouraging the dissolution of the Warsaw Pact and by signing the CFE treaty, the Soviets were trying--in part--to invalidate the need for a NATO reform which would revitalize collective defense in the West. Rather, they encouraged the process of transforming NATO into a collective security system by making it a more "political" rather than a "military" alliance. Clearly Soviet leaders were seeking complicity from key German elites in this process of transformation of Western security institutions.

But the basic ambiguity on the Soviet side about Western involvement in the future Soviet development model remained and was not eliminated by accepting the German unification process. The *reformers* hoped for Western participation in the stability of the Soviet Union--economically, politically and culturally. For the *conservatives* this is exactly what was to be avoided. To their way of thinking, the integrity of the Russian nation must be preserved against excessive Western interference and influence.

Was the acceptance of German unification a bargain for the Europeanization of the Soviet Union or for the protection of the Soviet empire against external interference? This critical question for the future of the USSR was only raised anew by the developments of 1989 and 1990. It will remain for the domestic struggle of the 1990s within the USSR to shape a new synthesis of domestic and foreign policy to deal with the West in the future.

Notes

1. In addition to articles cited below, the main articles articulating the reformist position are the following: Yu. Borkov and B. Orlov, "Shto nam stoit obshcheevropeiskii dom postroit'," **MEMO**, no. 1, 1990, pp. 49-58; Yu. P. Davydov, "K novomy evropeiskomy poriadky," **SShA**, no. 3, 1990, pp. 42-46 (this issue of SShA contains several articles on the new European situtation); Roundtable, "Edinaya Germaniya i ee sosedi," **MEMO**, no. 8, 1990, pp. 68-74; and Igor Maximychev, "German Unification," **International Affairs**, no. 10, 1990, pp. 36-42.

2. S. Smol'nikov, "Novaya logika evropeiskogo razvitiy," **MEMO**, no. 6, 1990, p. 28.

3. **Ibid.**, pp. 28-29.

4. N. Pavlov, "Germanskii vopros i 'obshcheevropeiskii dom'," **MEMO**, no. 6, 1990, p. 17.

5. **Ibid.**, p. 6.

6. **Ibid.**, p. 9.

7. Igor Maximychev and Pyotr Menshikov, "One German Fatherland?" **International Affairs**, no. 7, 1990, p. 37.

8. **Ibid.**, p. 38.

9. Major General Alexander Vladimirov and Col. Sergei Posokhov, "A European Security Alliance," **International Affairs**, no. 10, 1990, p. 81.

10. **Veteran**, no. 9, February 26-March 4 1990 in JPRS-UMA-90-11, pp. 55-56.

11. **Literaturnaya Rossiya**, no. 11, 1990, pp. 16-17 as analyzed in Alexander Rahr, "Conservative Opposition to German Unification," **Report on the USSR**, 11 May 1990, pp. 15-17.

12. Aleksandrov, 31 August 1990 in FBIS-SOV-90-176, p. 7.

13. Don Oberdorfter, "Domestic Needs Outweigh Foreign Issues in Gorbachev's Platform," **The Washington Post**, 7 February 1990, p. 55.

14. **TASS**, 20 September 1990 in FBIS-SOV-90-184, p. 20.

Index